AF292015

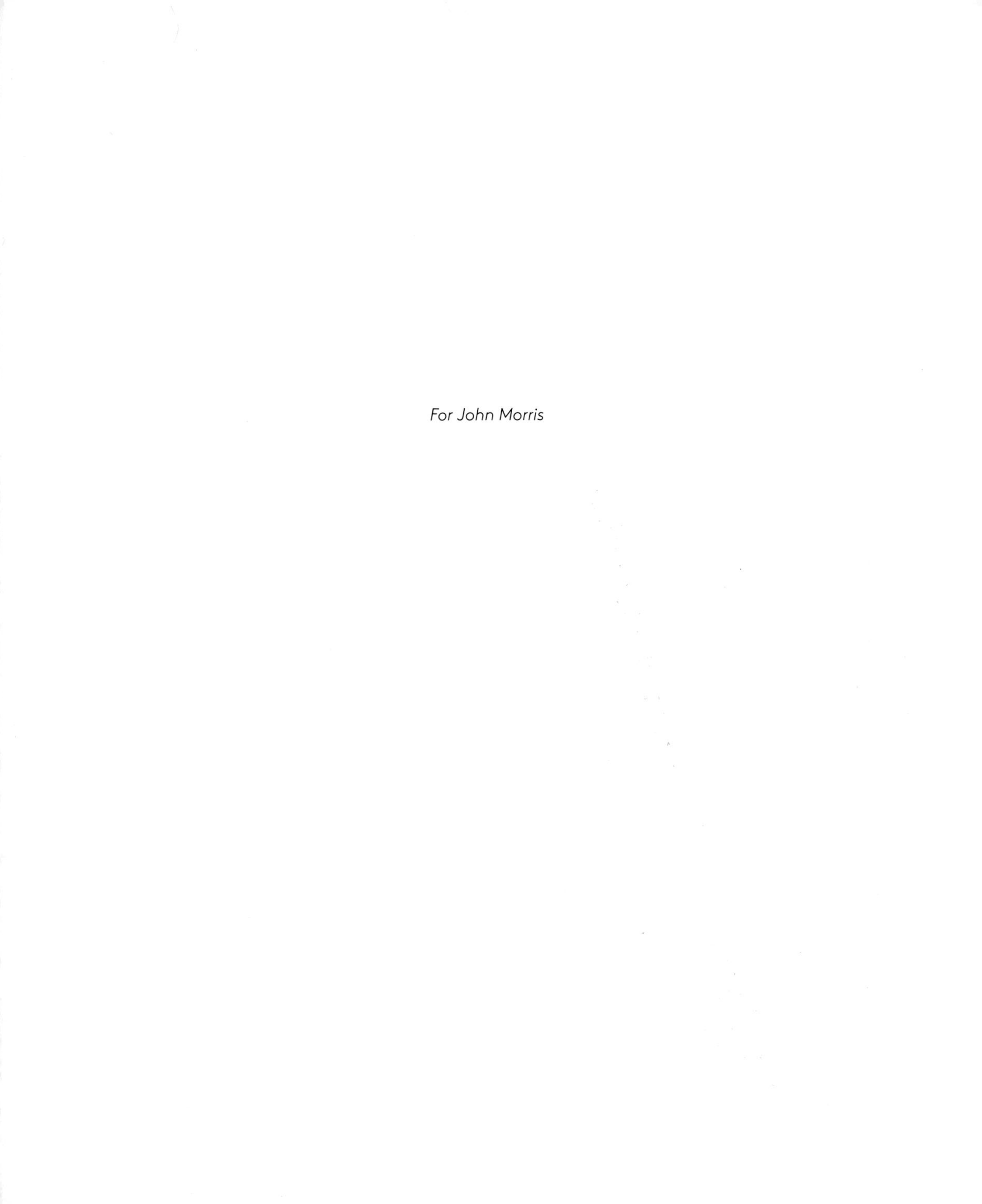

For John Morris

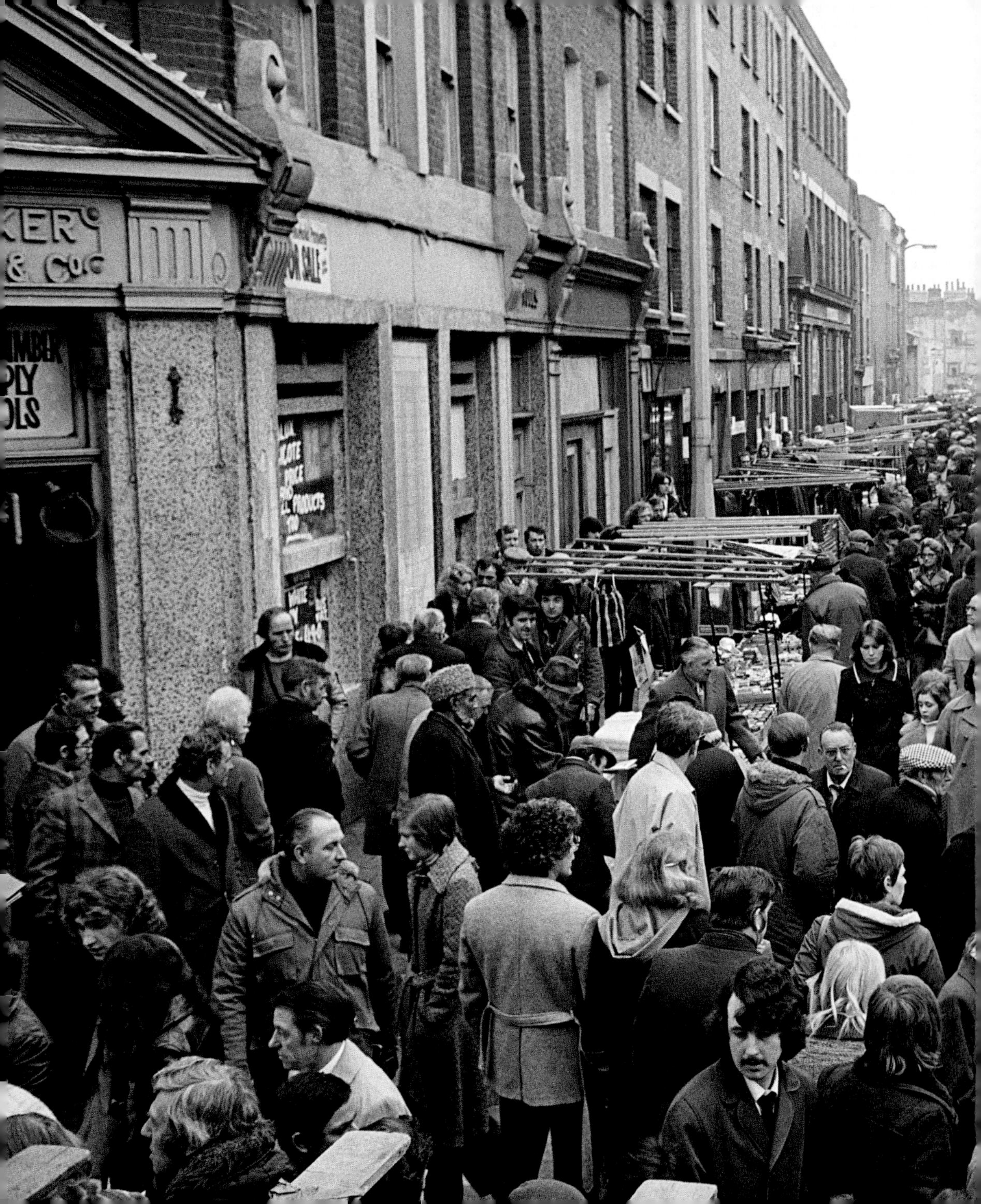

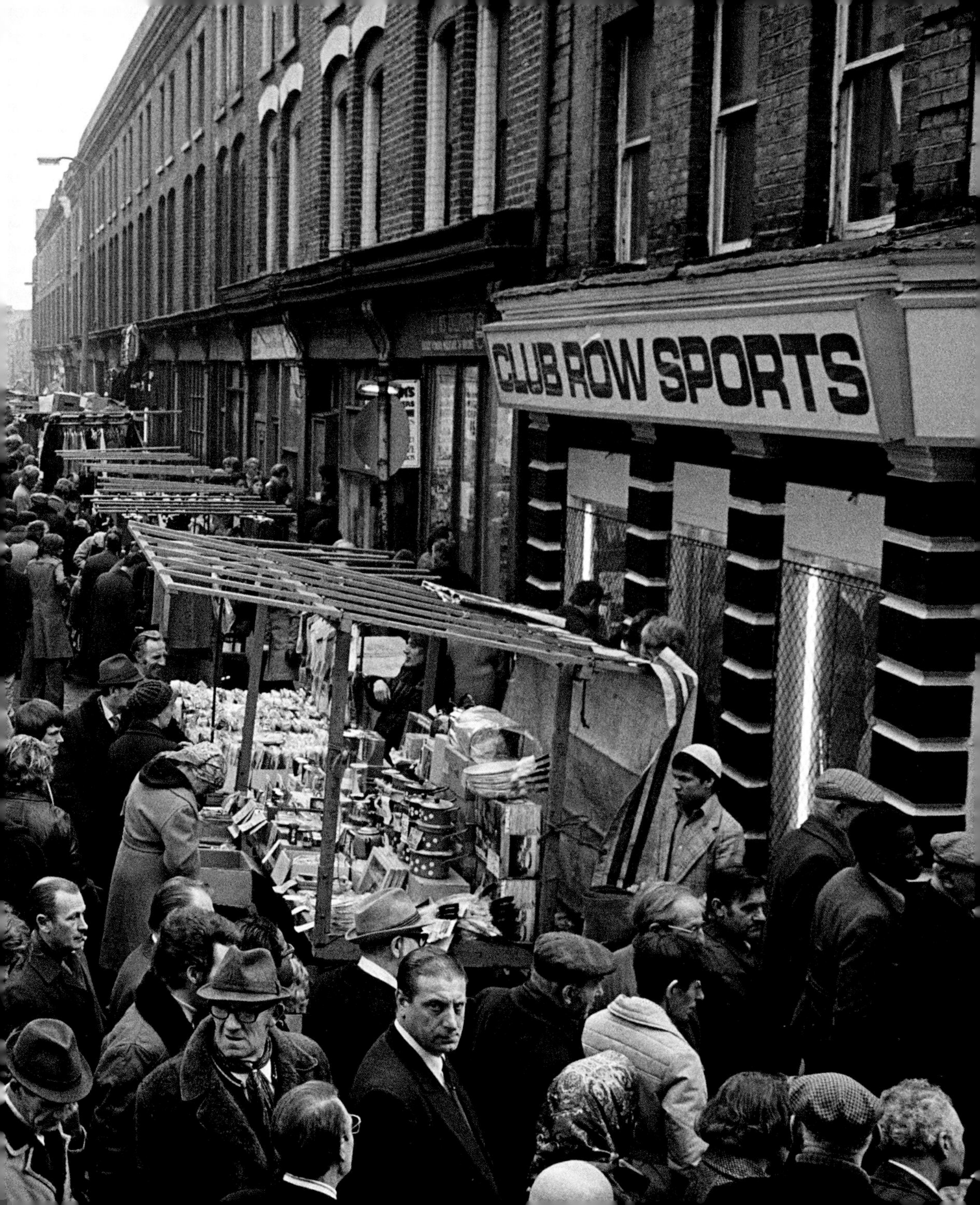

CLUB ROW SPORTS

(Previous) Cheshire Street, London E2, 1976

PAUL TREVOR

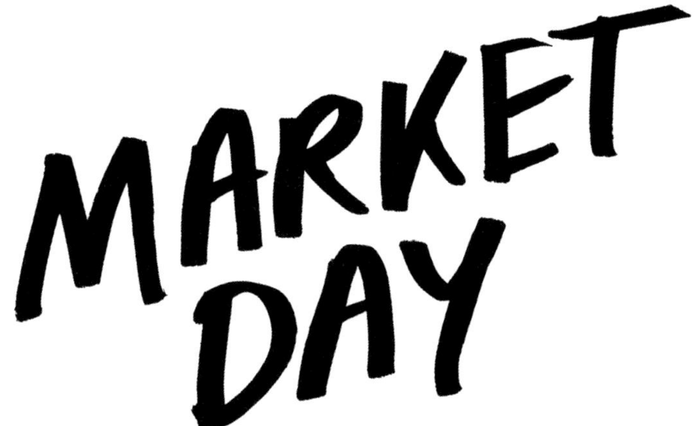

MARKET DAY

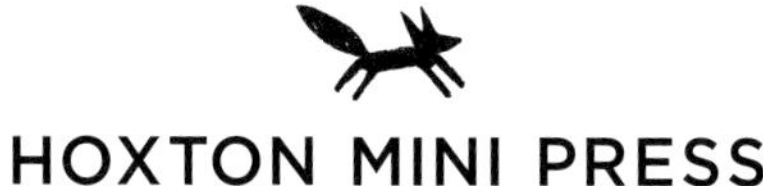

HOXTON MINI PRESS

*I was drawn to the Sunday market by the people,
by the contrast between the energy they created
and the run-down state of the place, and by the
spontaneous and highly visual 'street theatre'
on display. Like theatre, the show was repeated
every week, but the performance was never the
same. You never knew what to expect, which
is probably why I persisted with it for so long!*

Paul Trevor

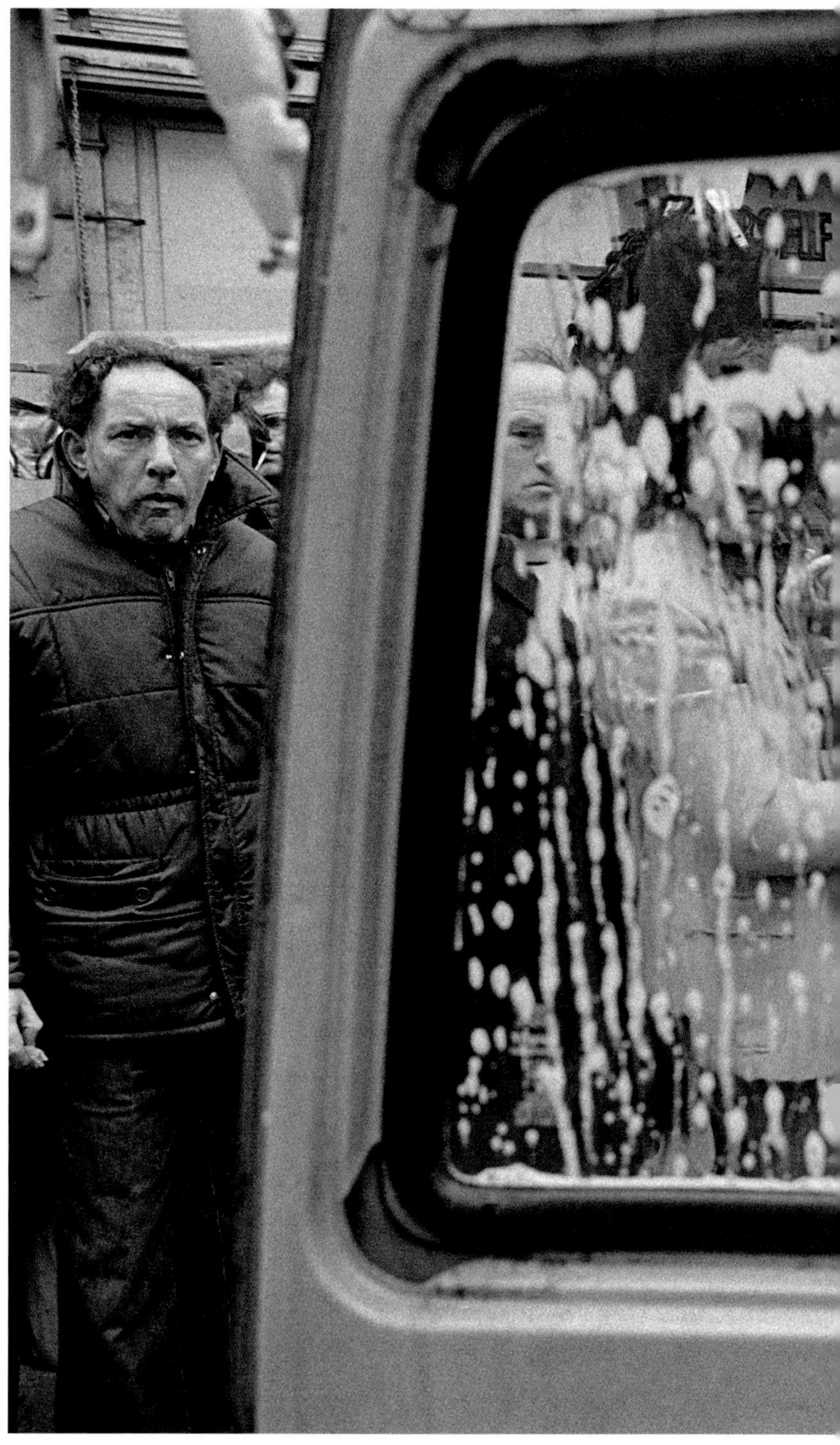

Sclater Street, London E1, 1980

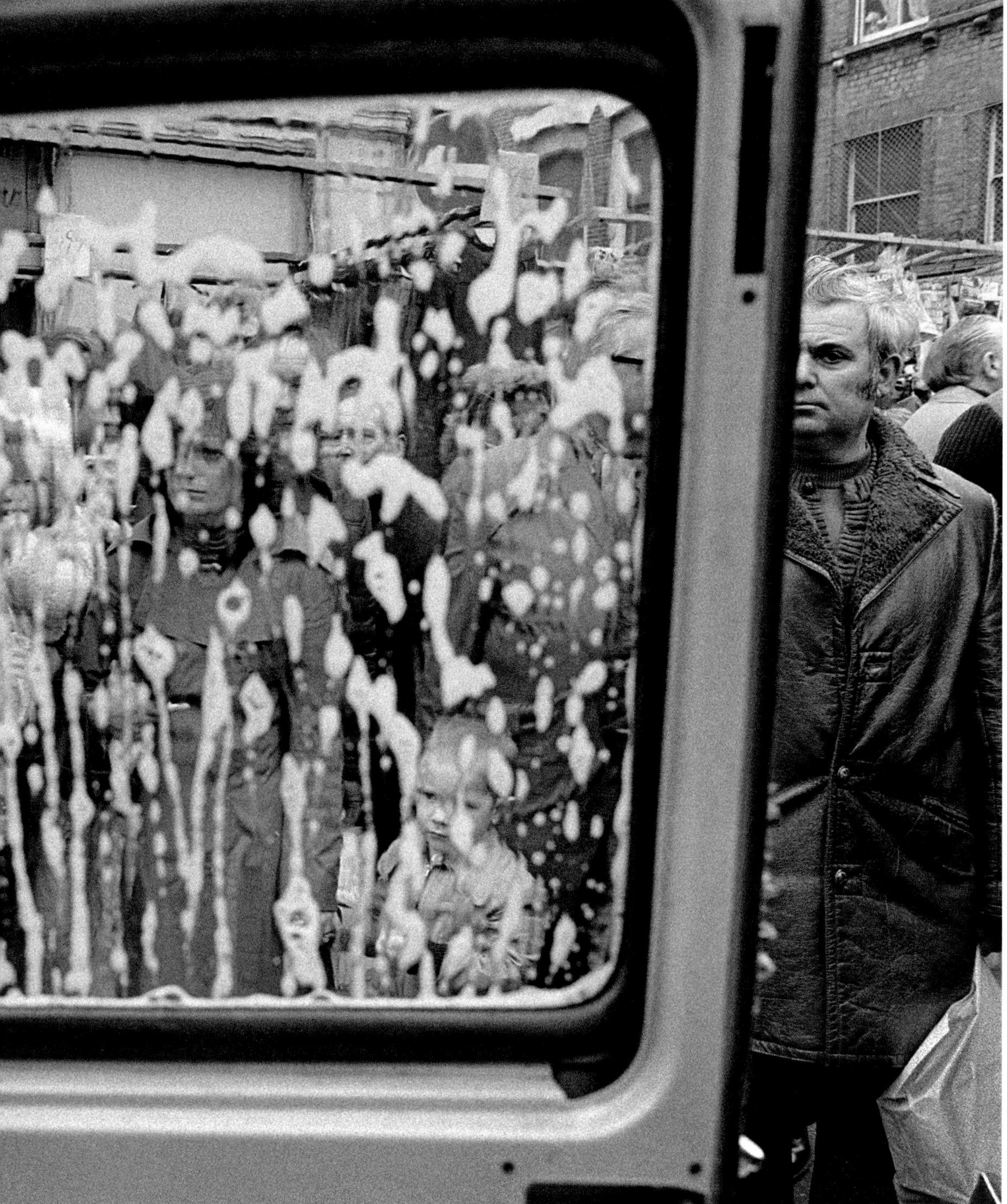

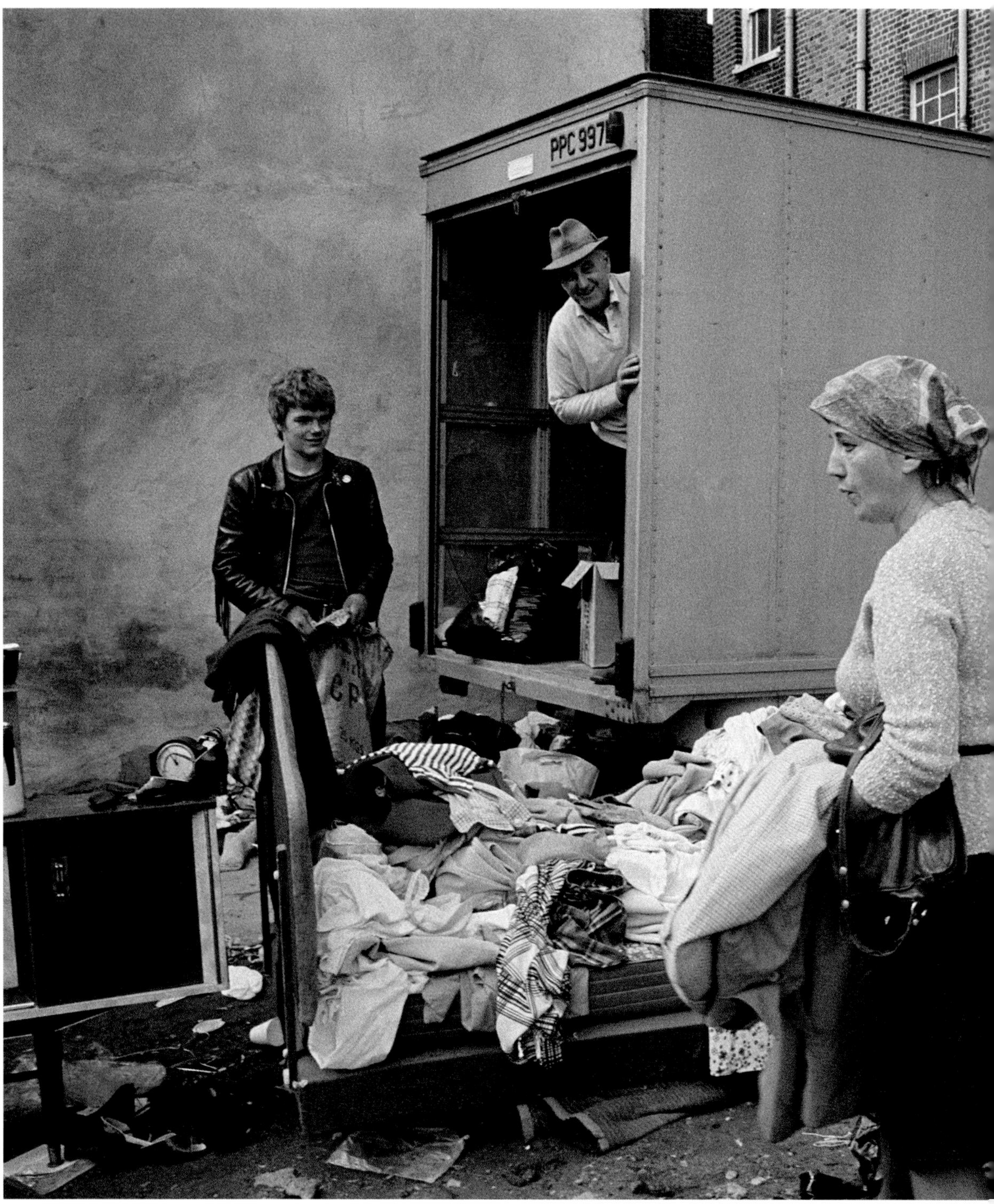

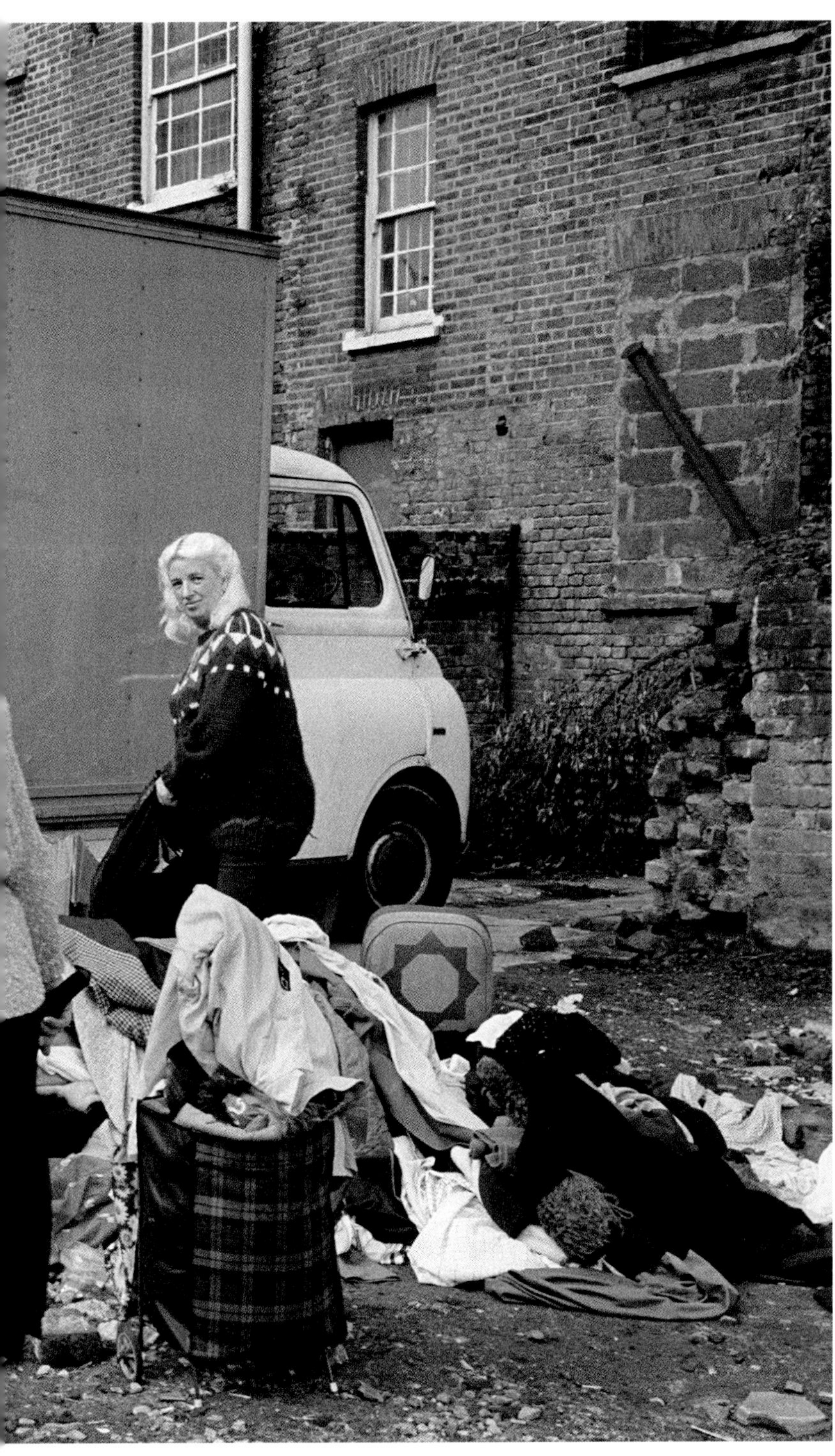

Grimsby Street, London E2, 1982

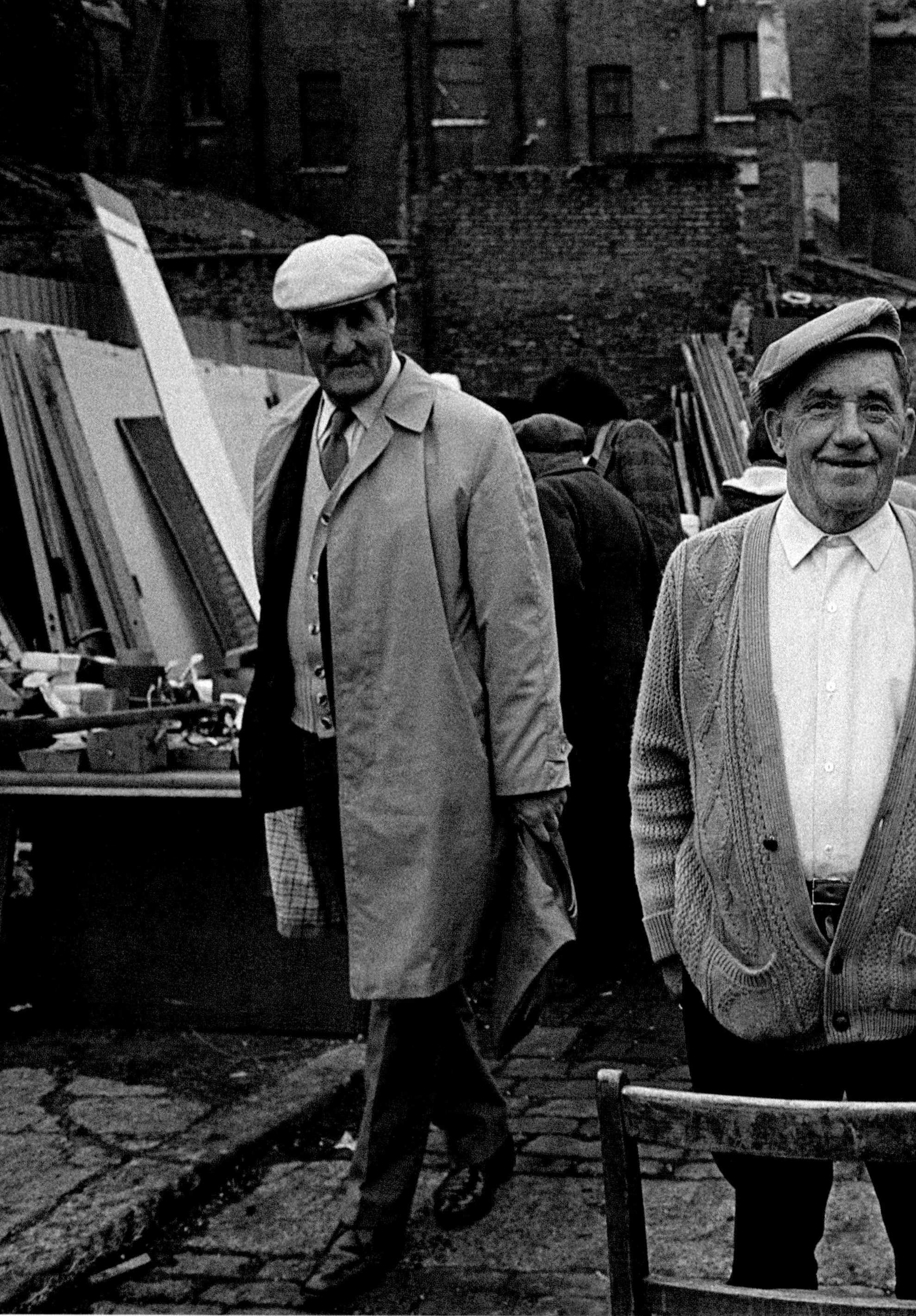

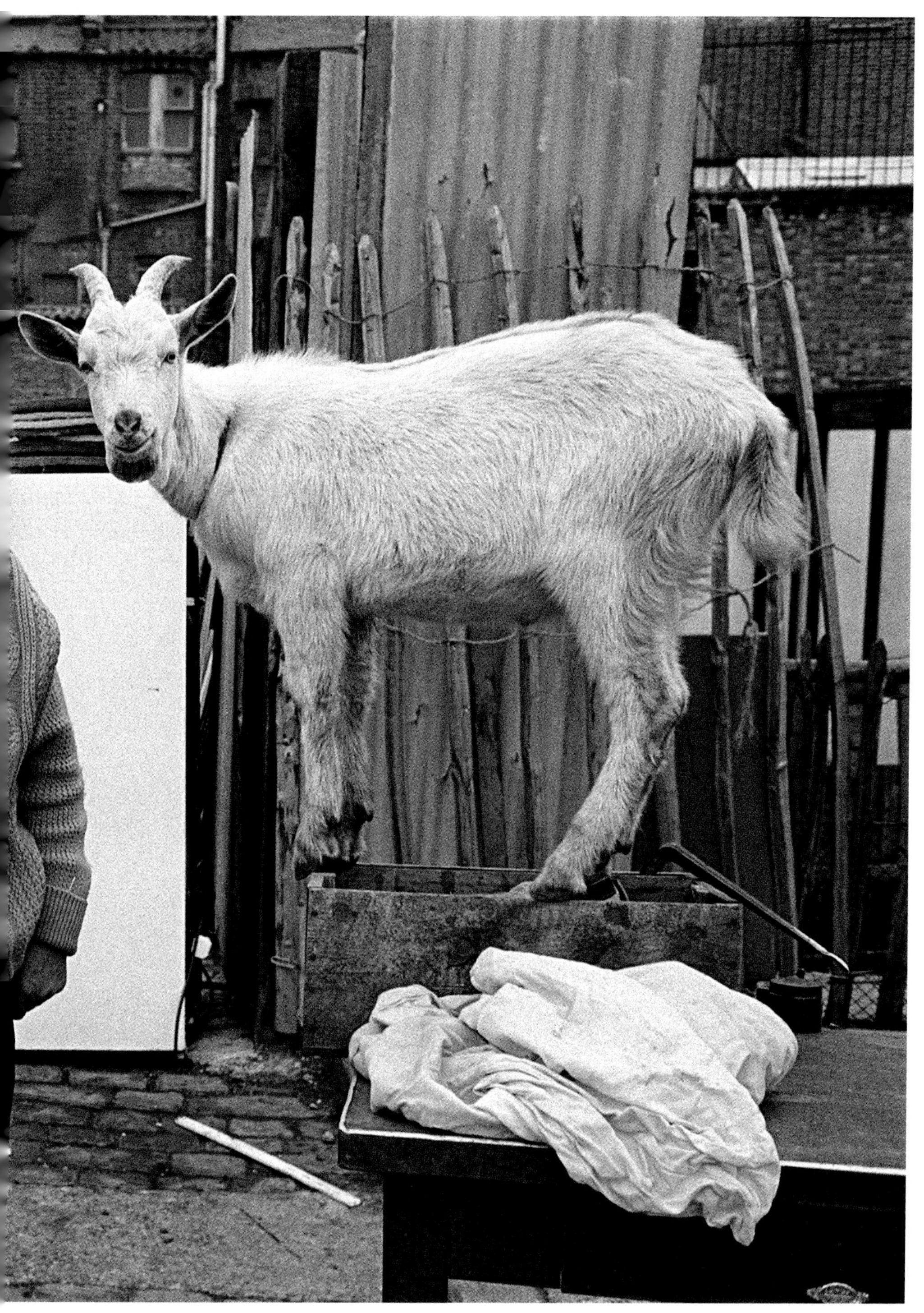

Granby Street,
London E2, 1975

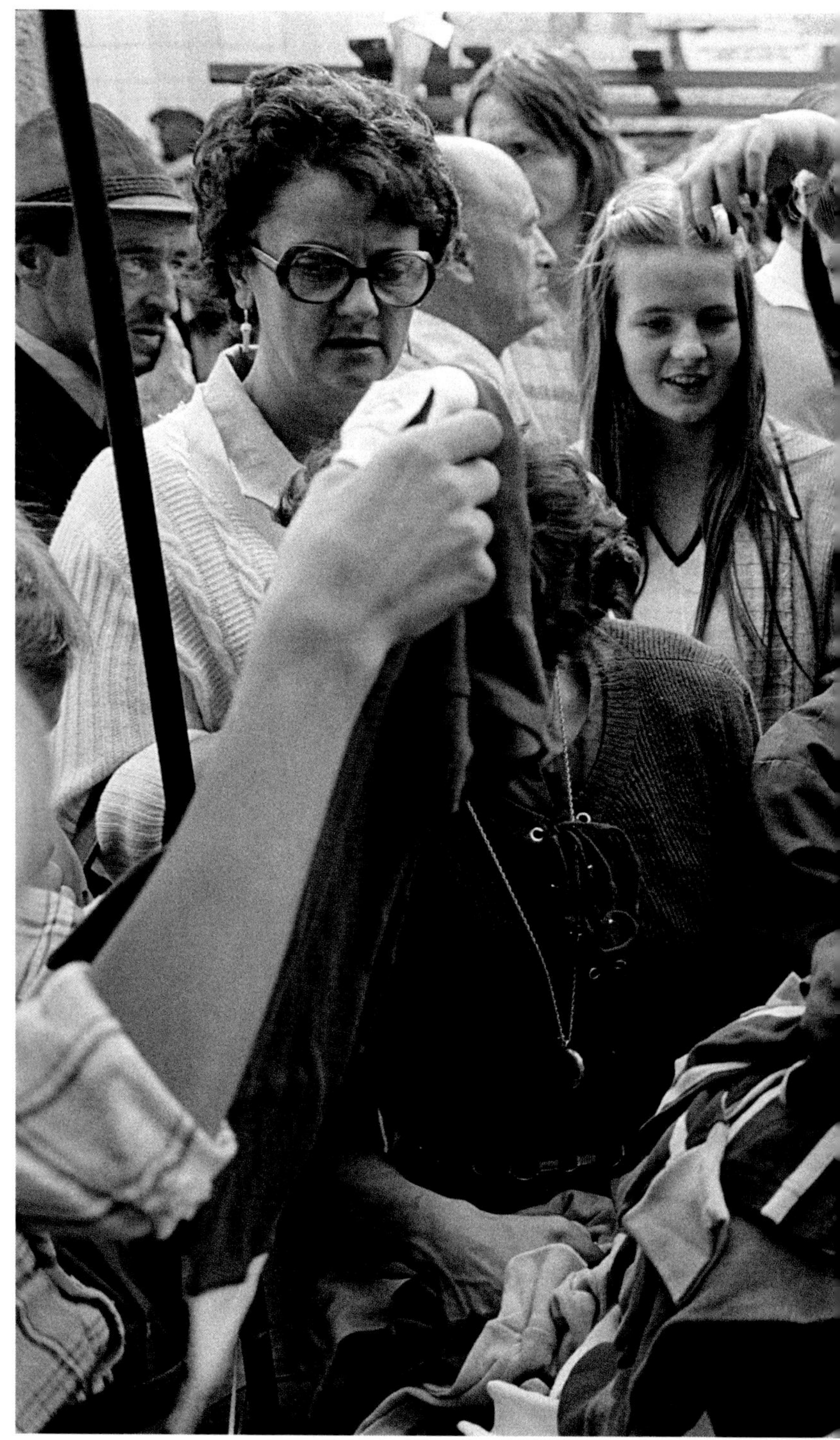

Cheshire Street, London E2, 1975

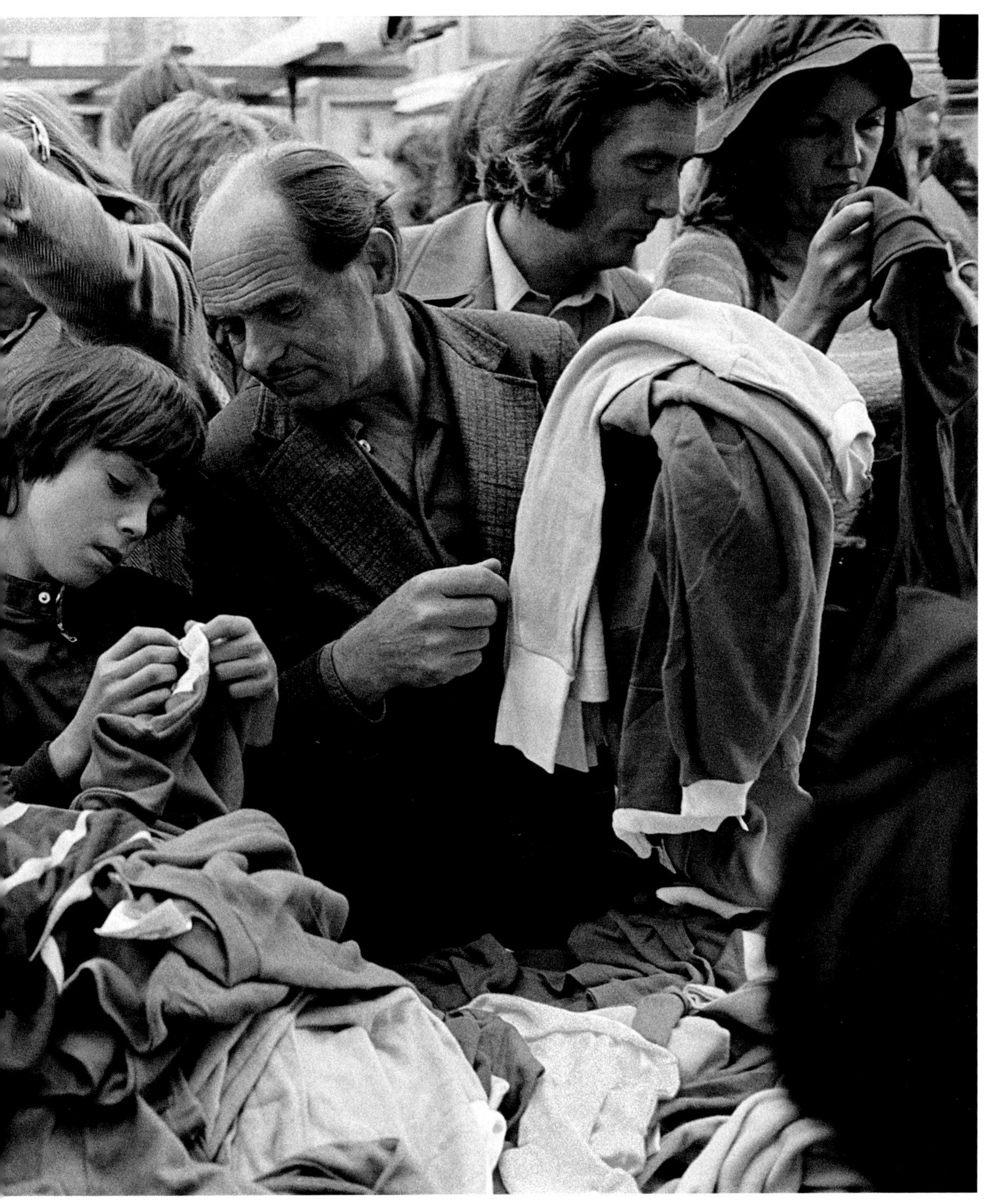

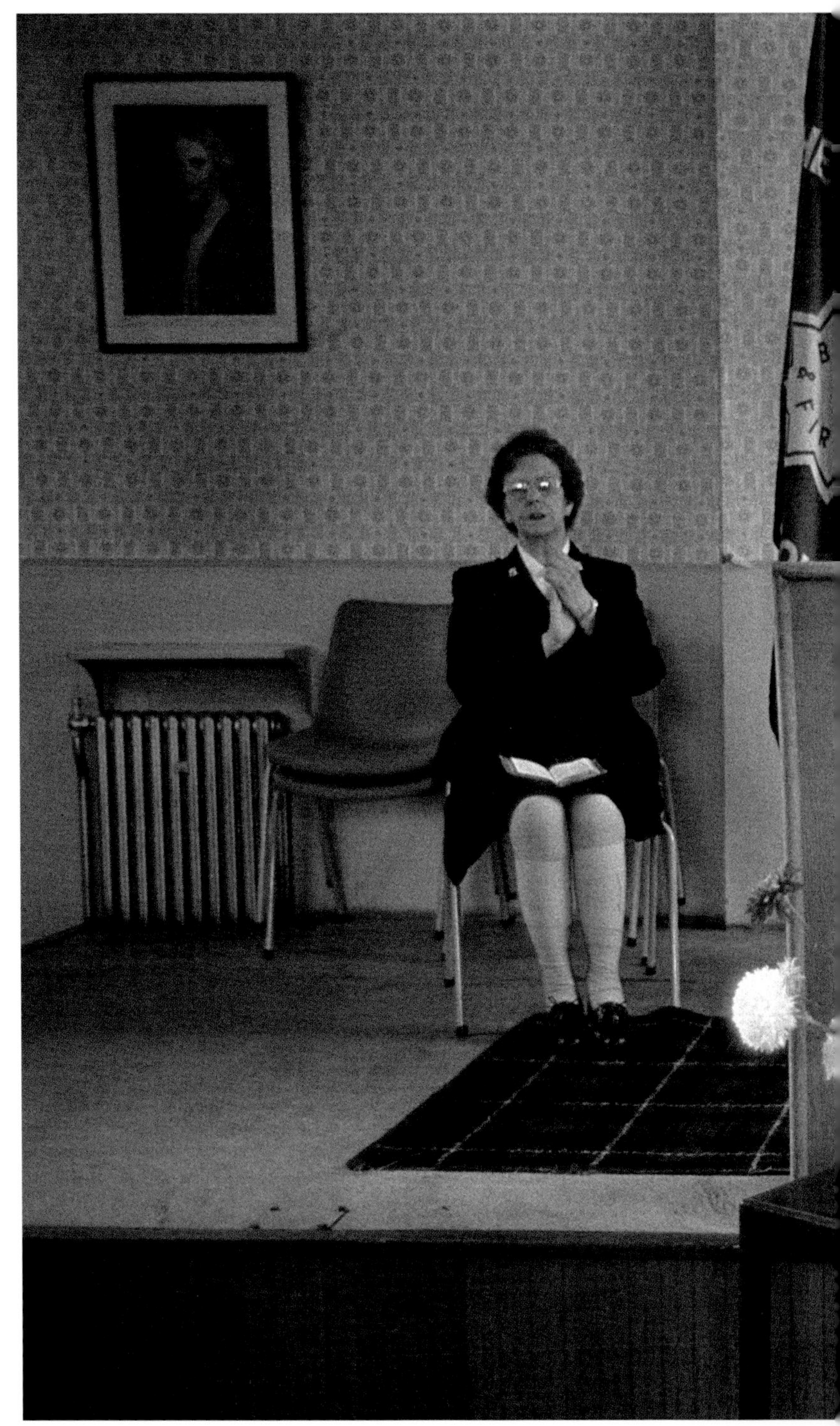

Salvation Army Hostel for women,
Hopetown Street, London E1, 1975

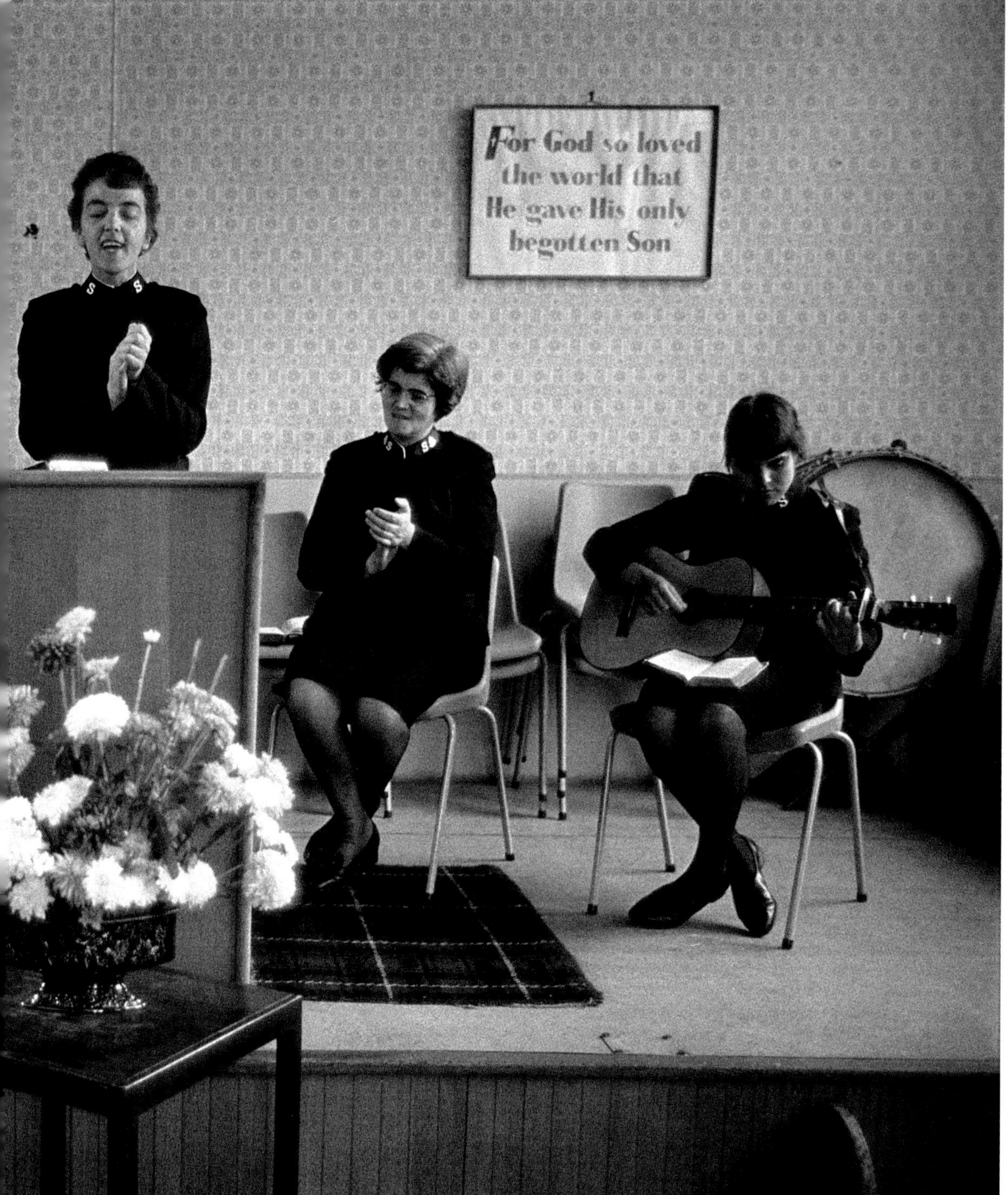
For God so loved
the world that
He gave His only
begotten Son

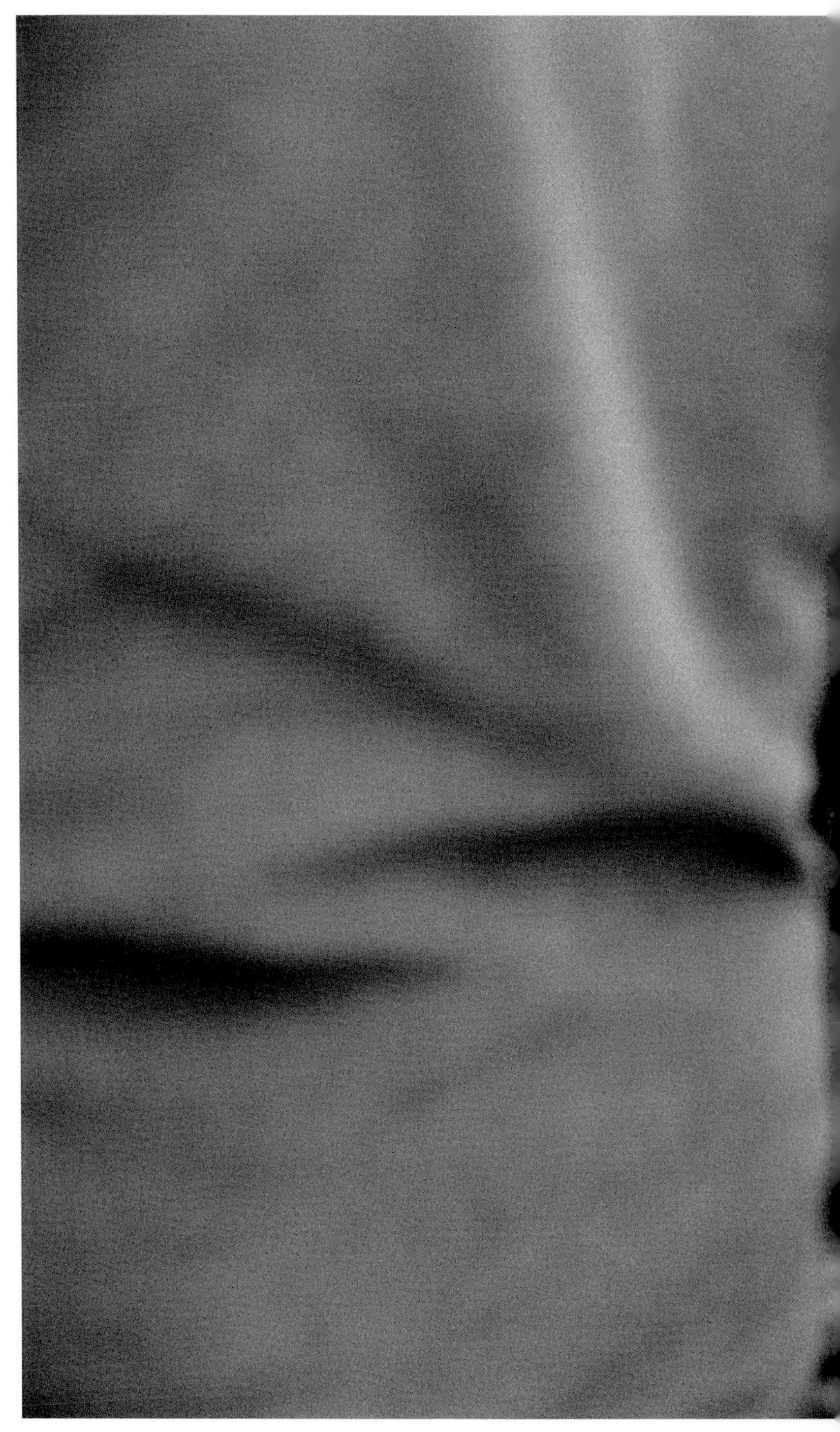

Cheshire Street, London E2, 1977

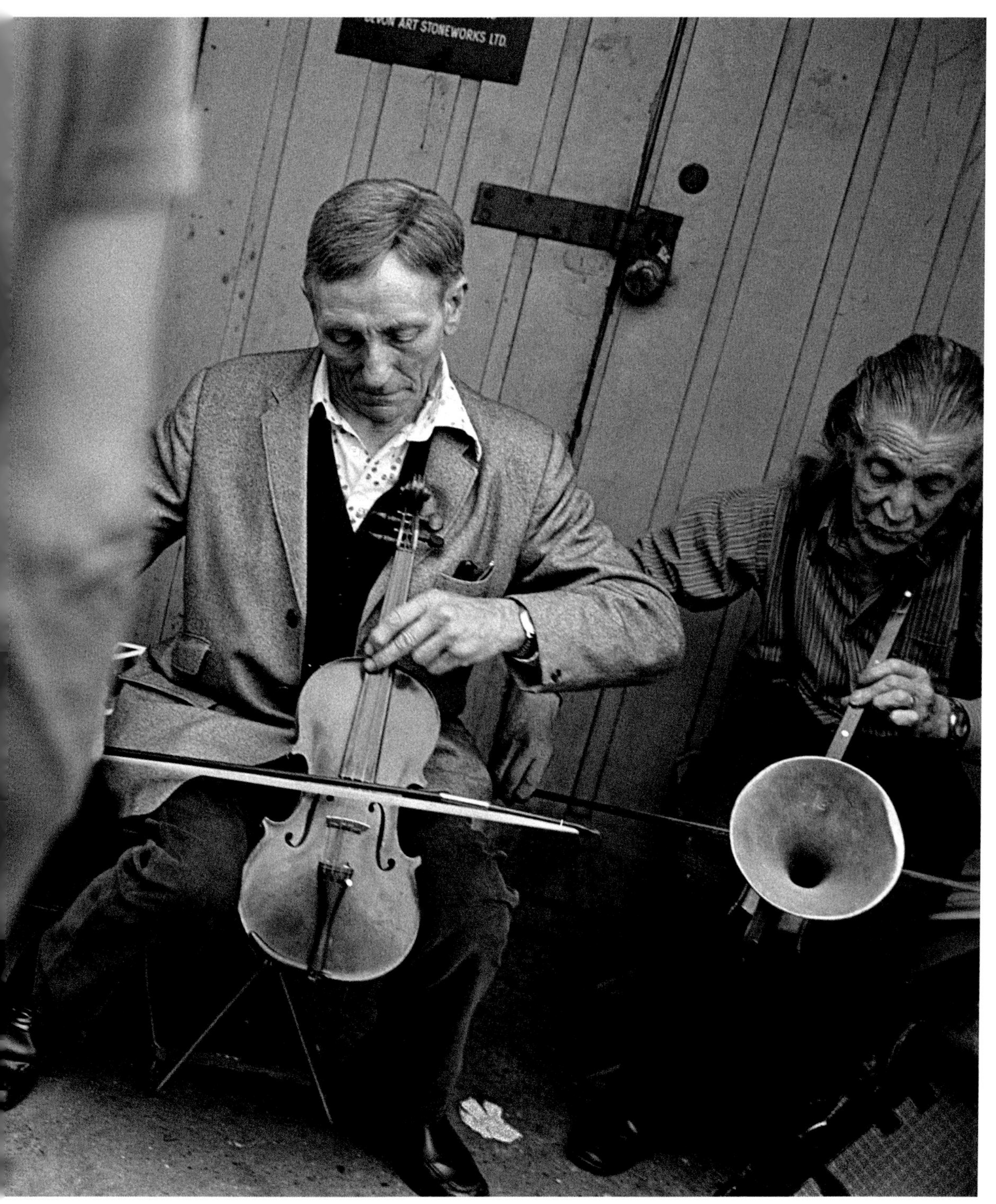
ART STONEWORKS LTD.

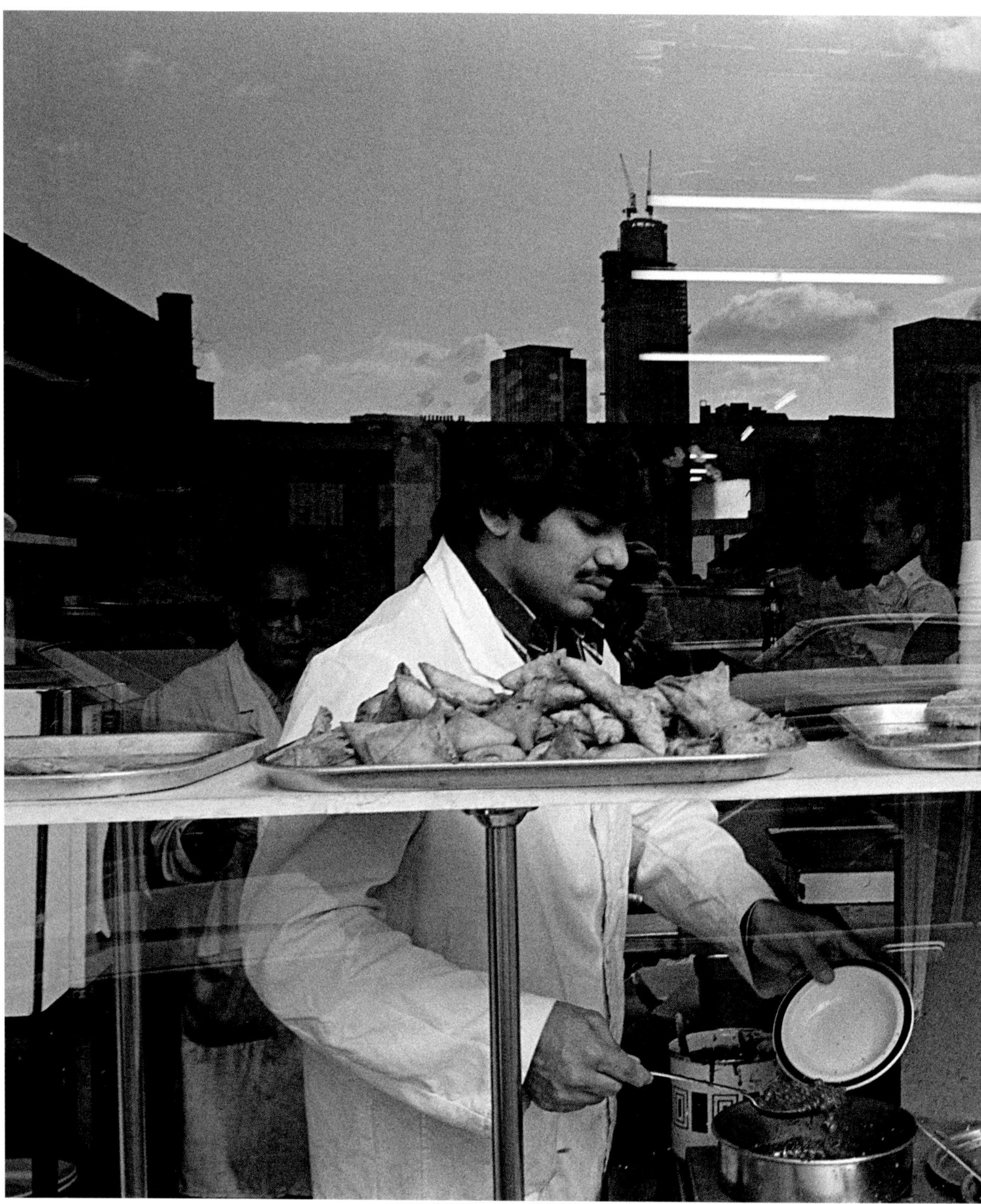

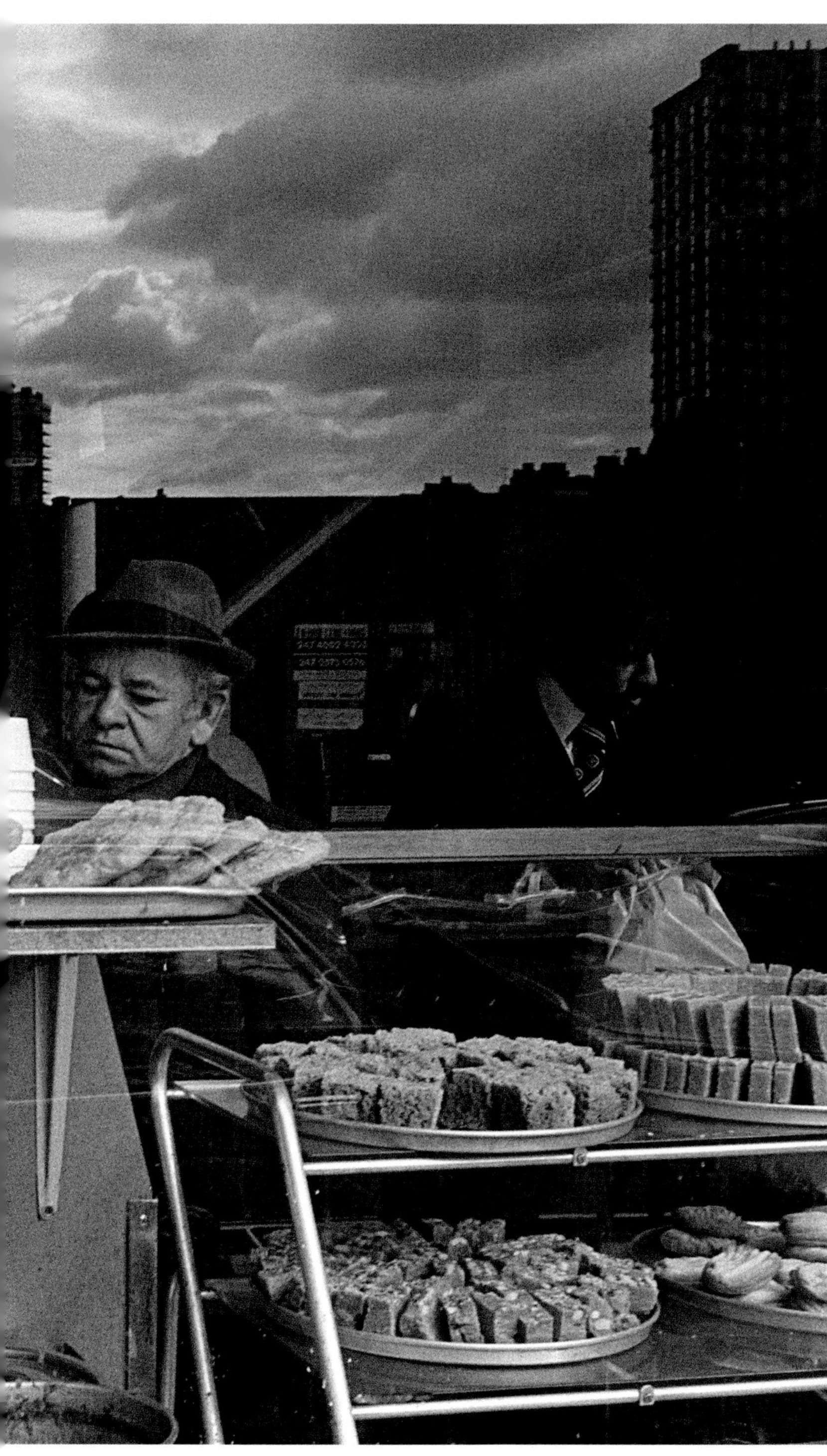

Brick Lane, London E1, 1977

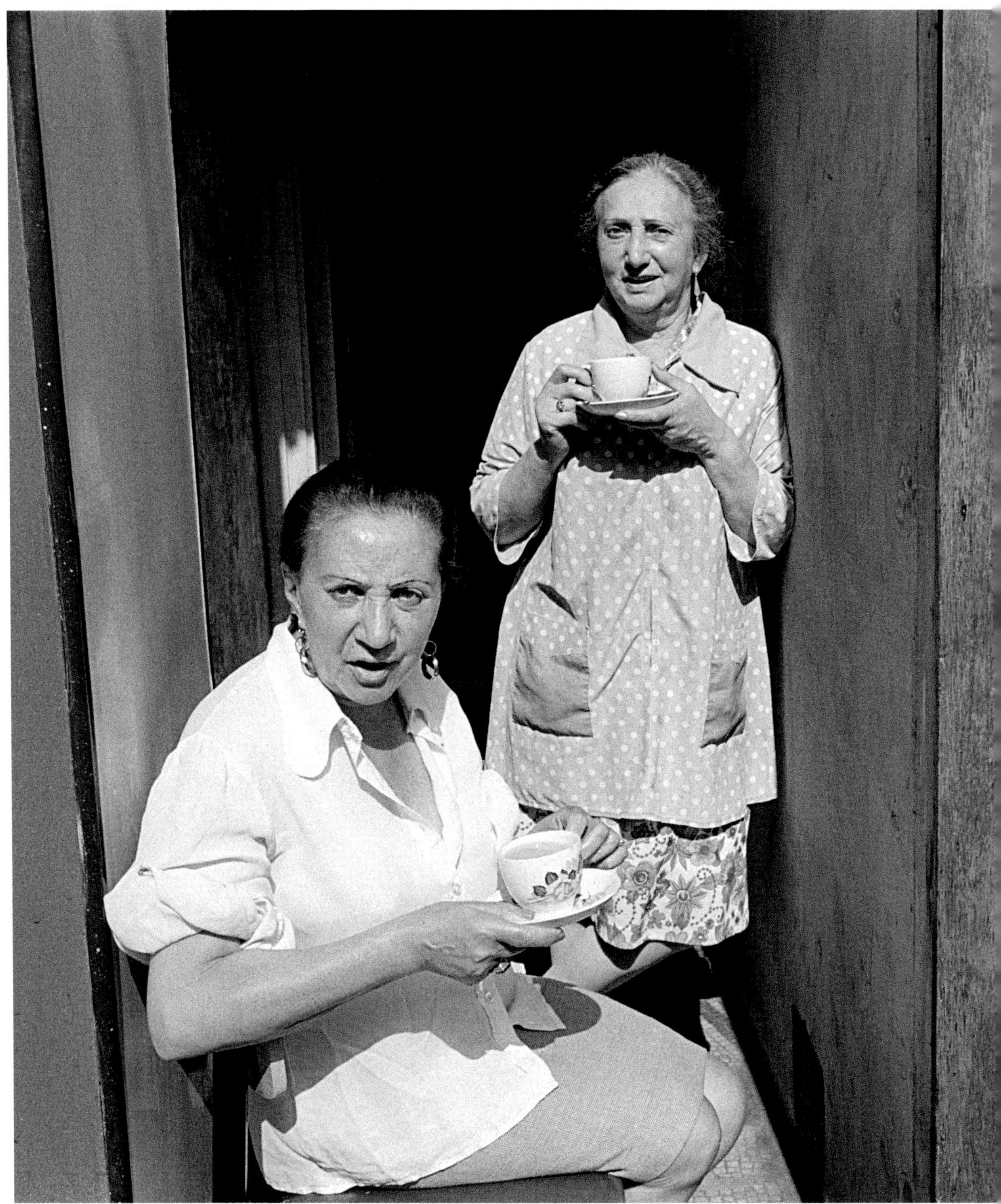

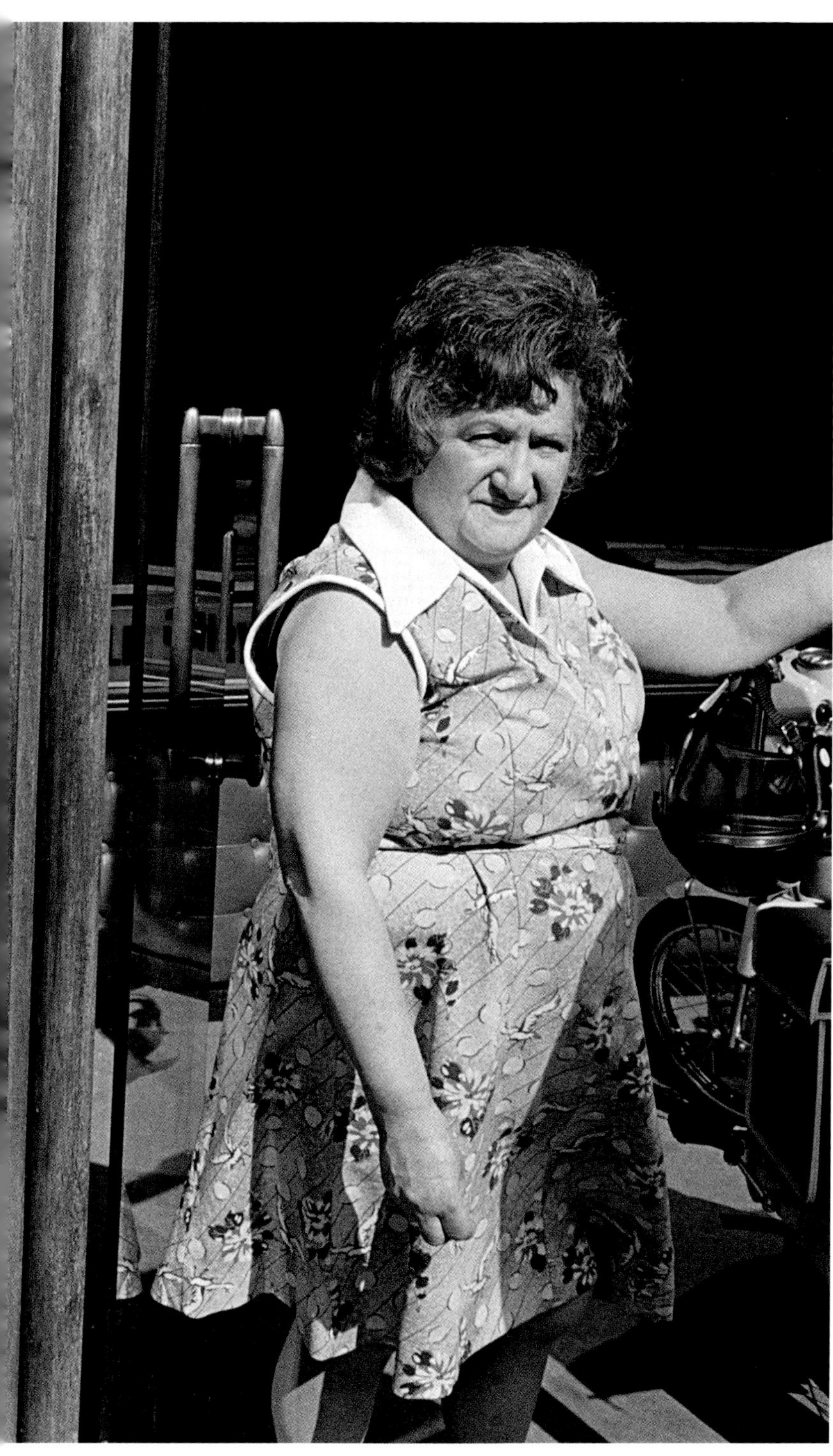

Brick Lane, London E1, 1978

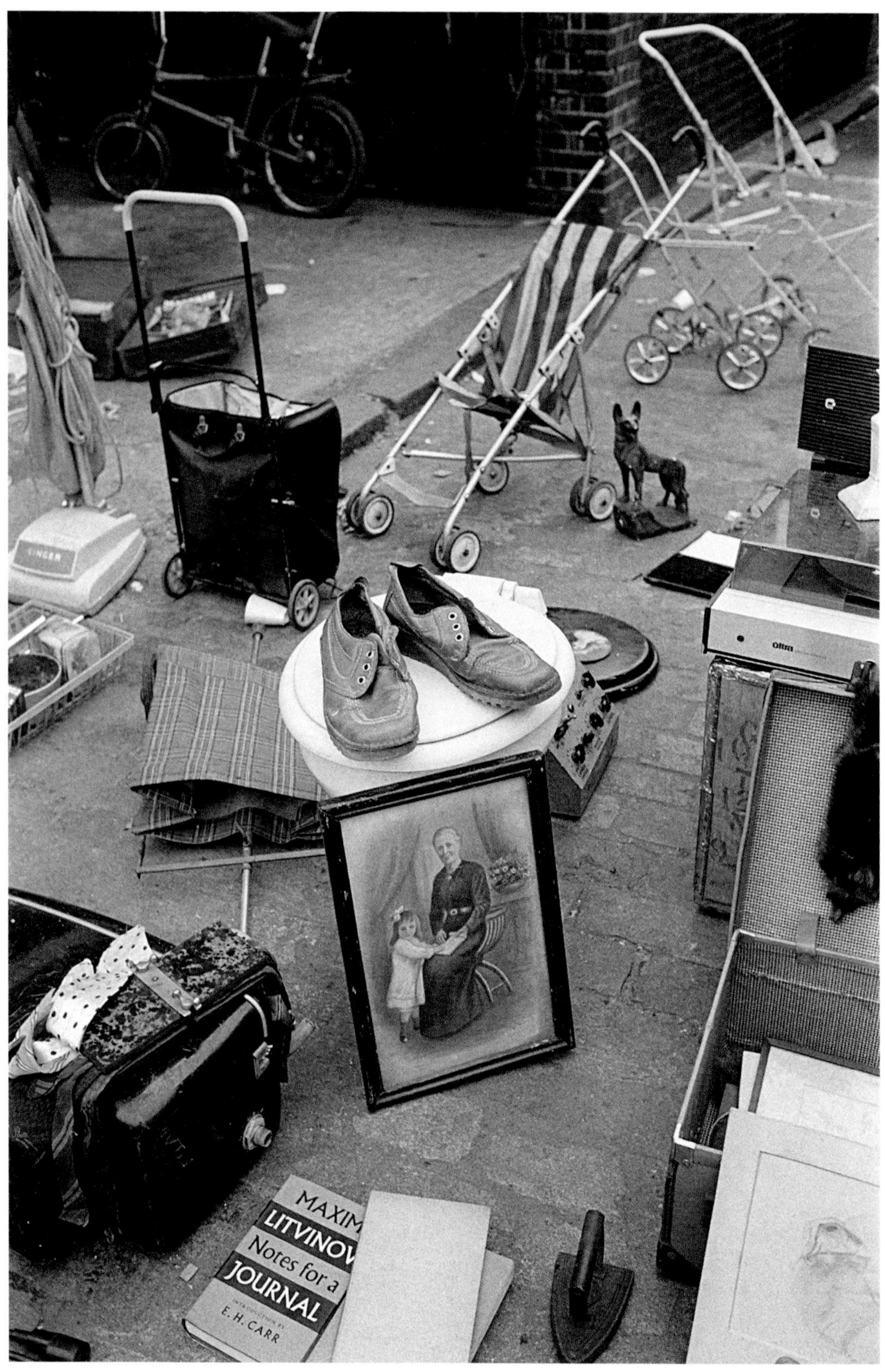

Hare Marsh, London E2, 1981

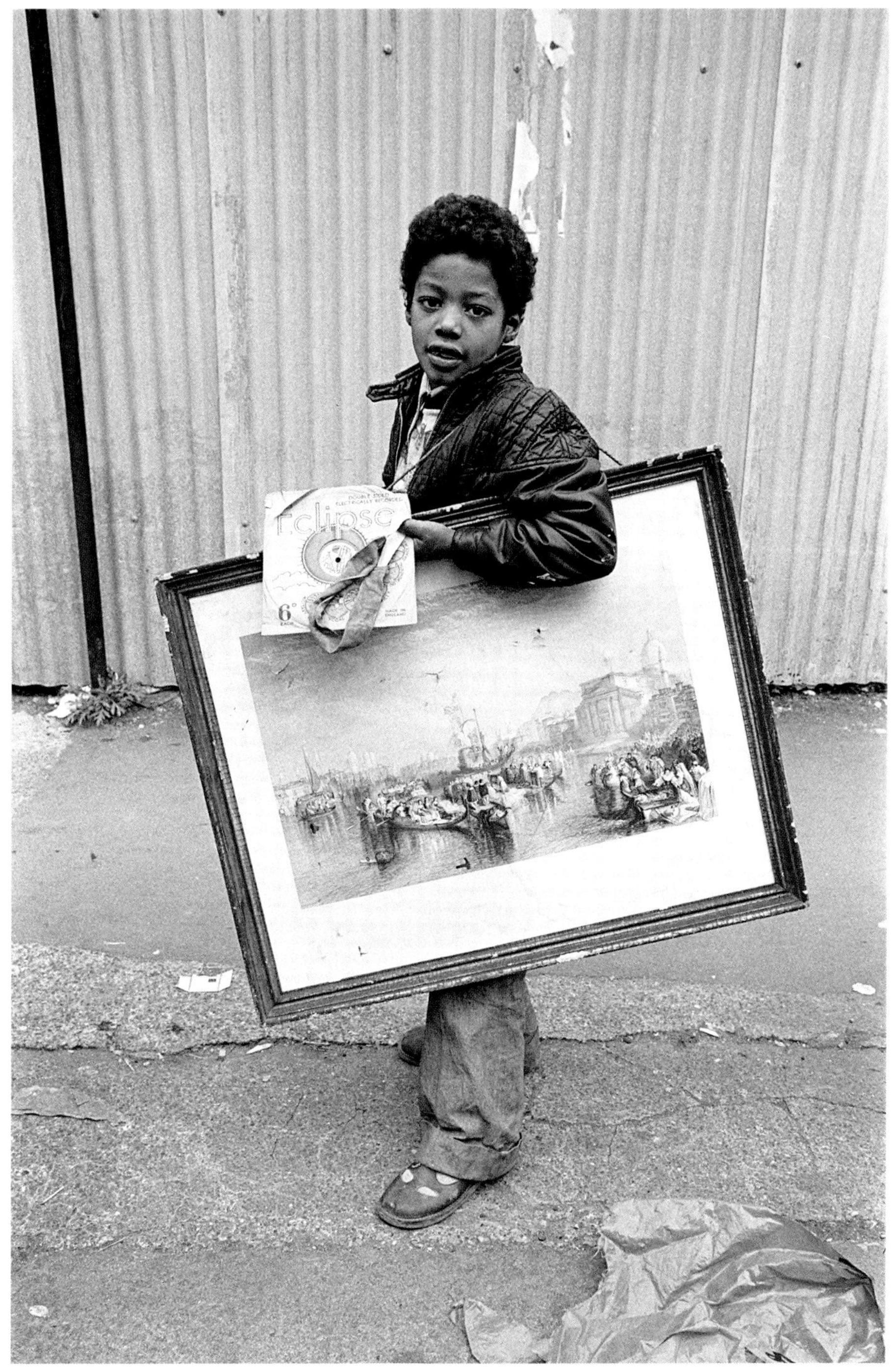

Bacon Street, London E1, 1974

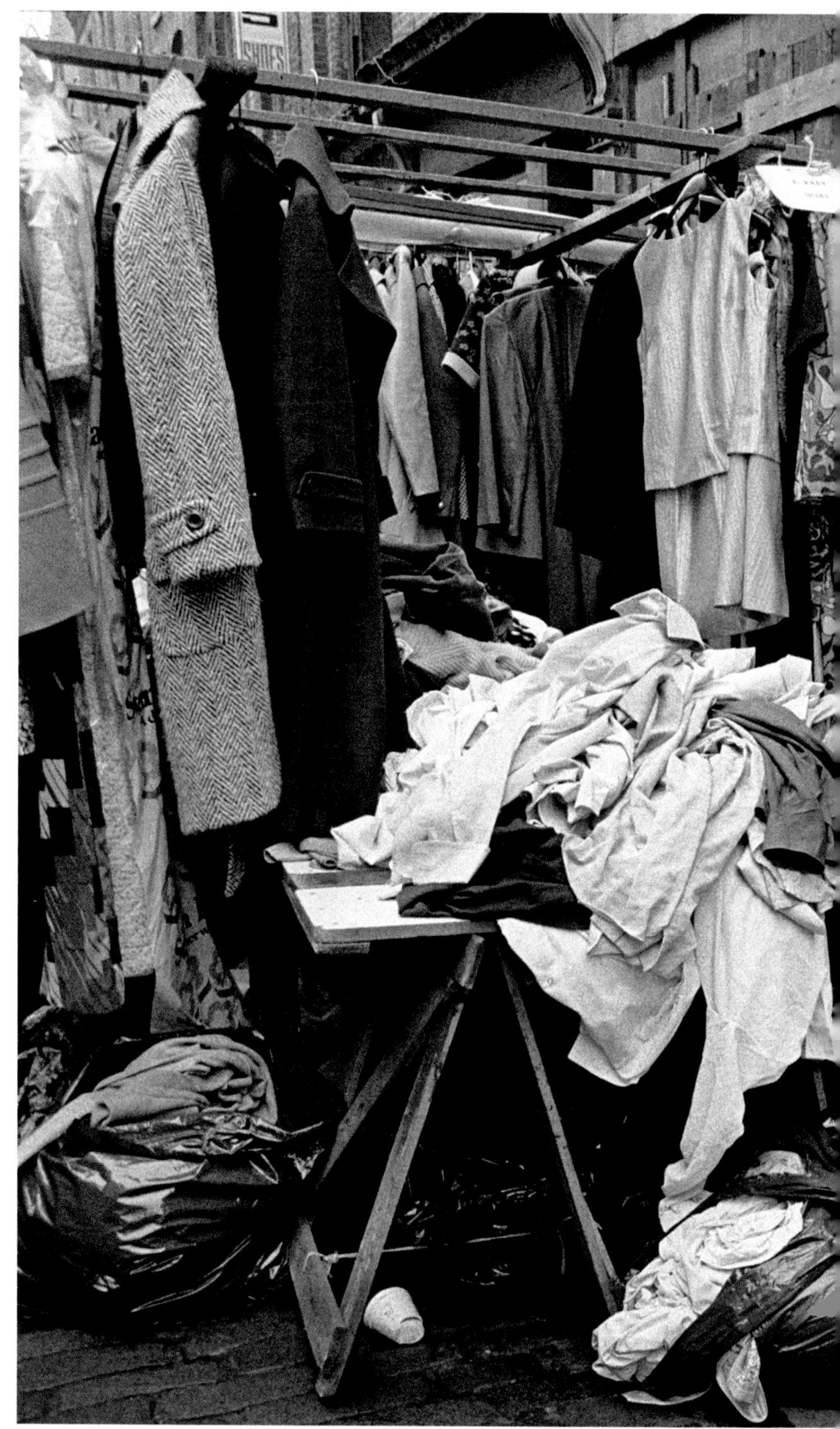

Cheshire Street, London E2, 1978

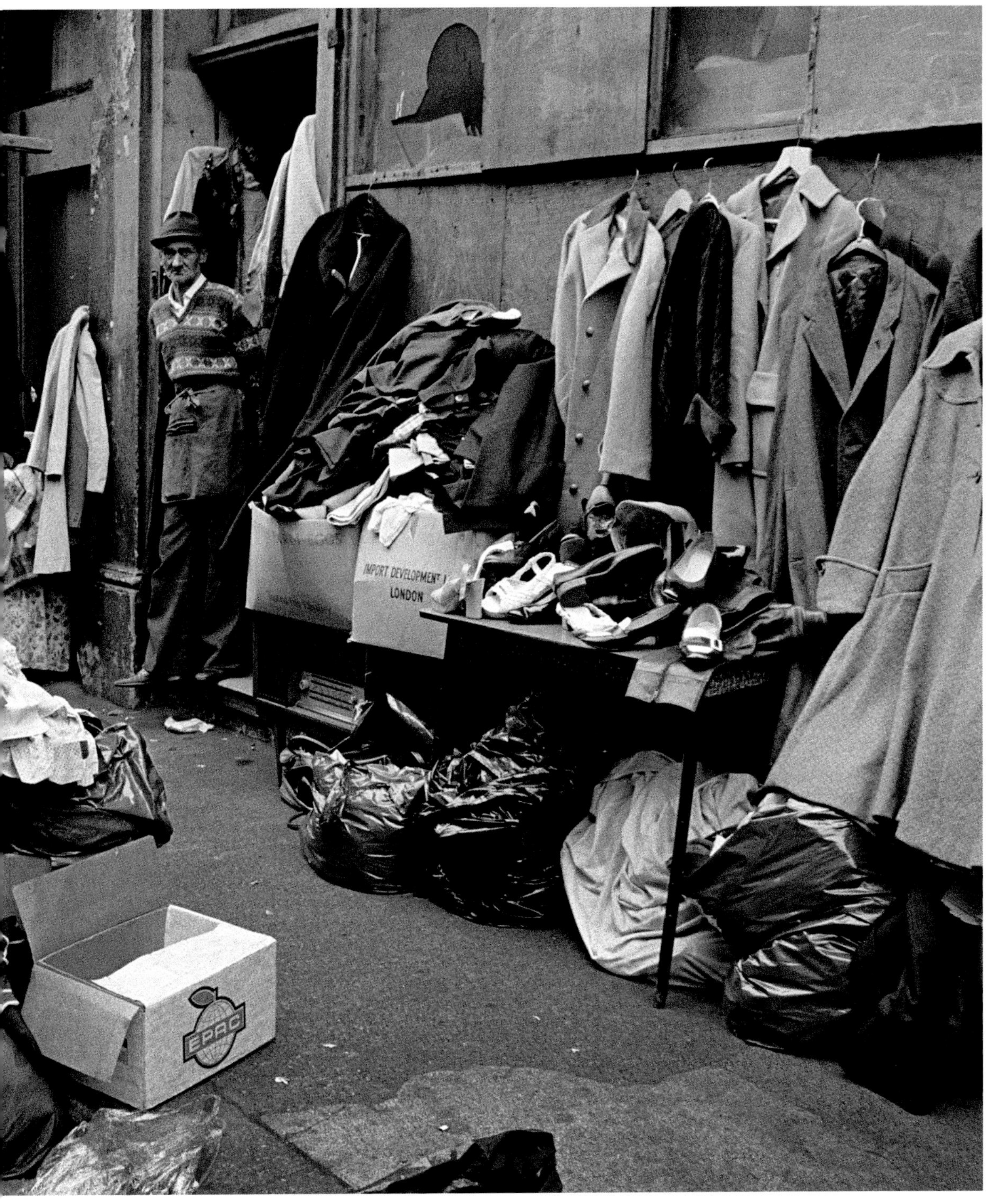

IMPORT DEVELOPMENT
LONDON
EPAC

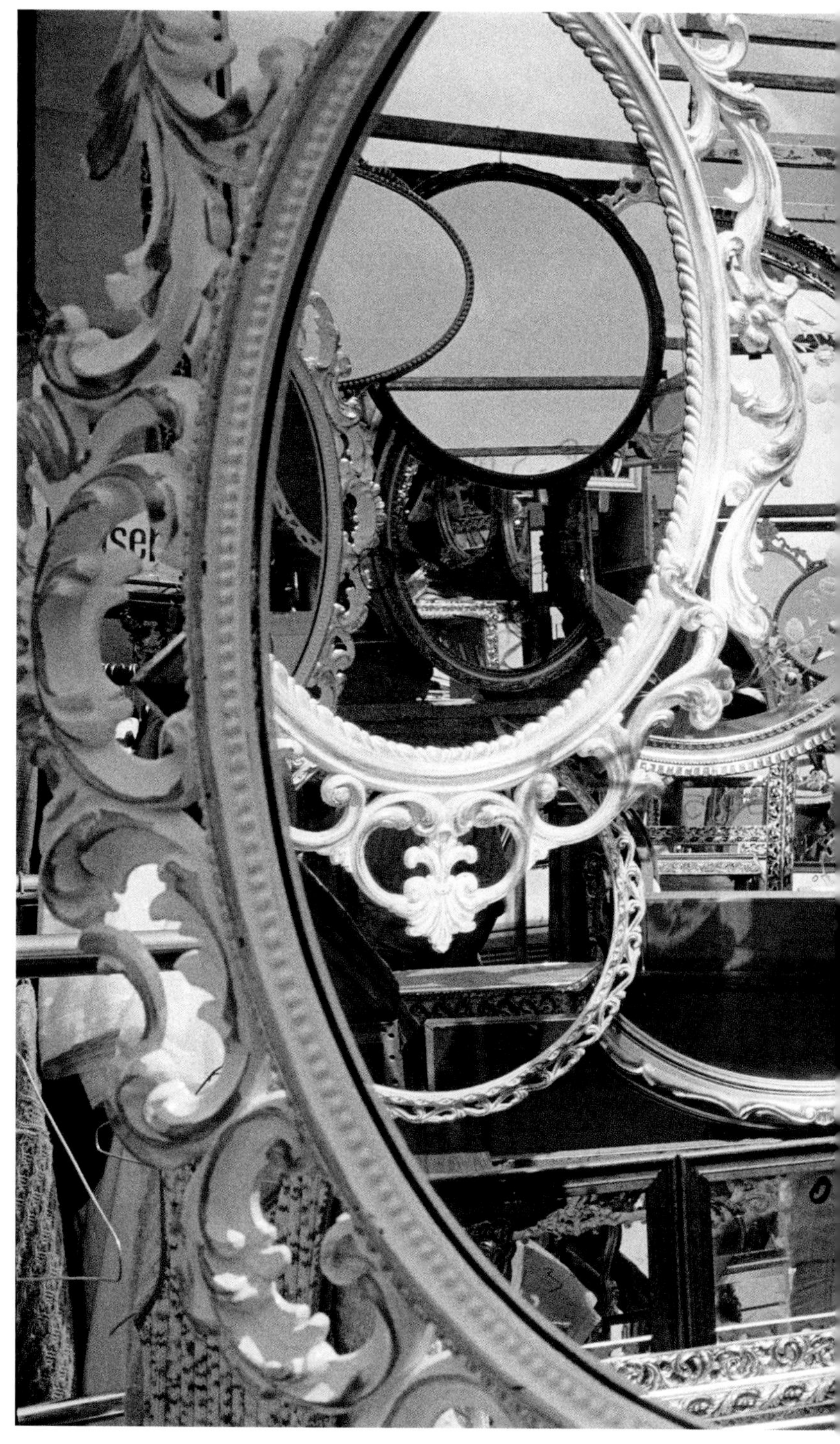

Cygnet Street, London E1, 1982

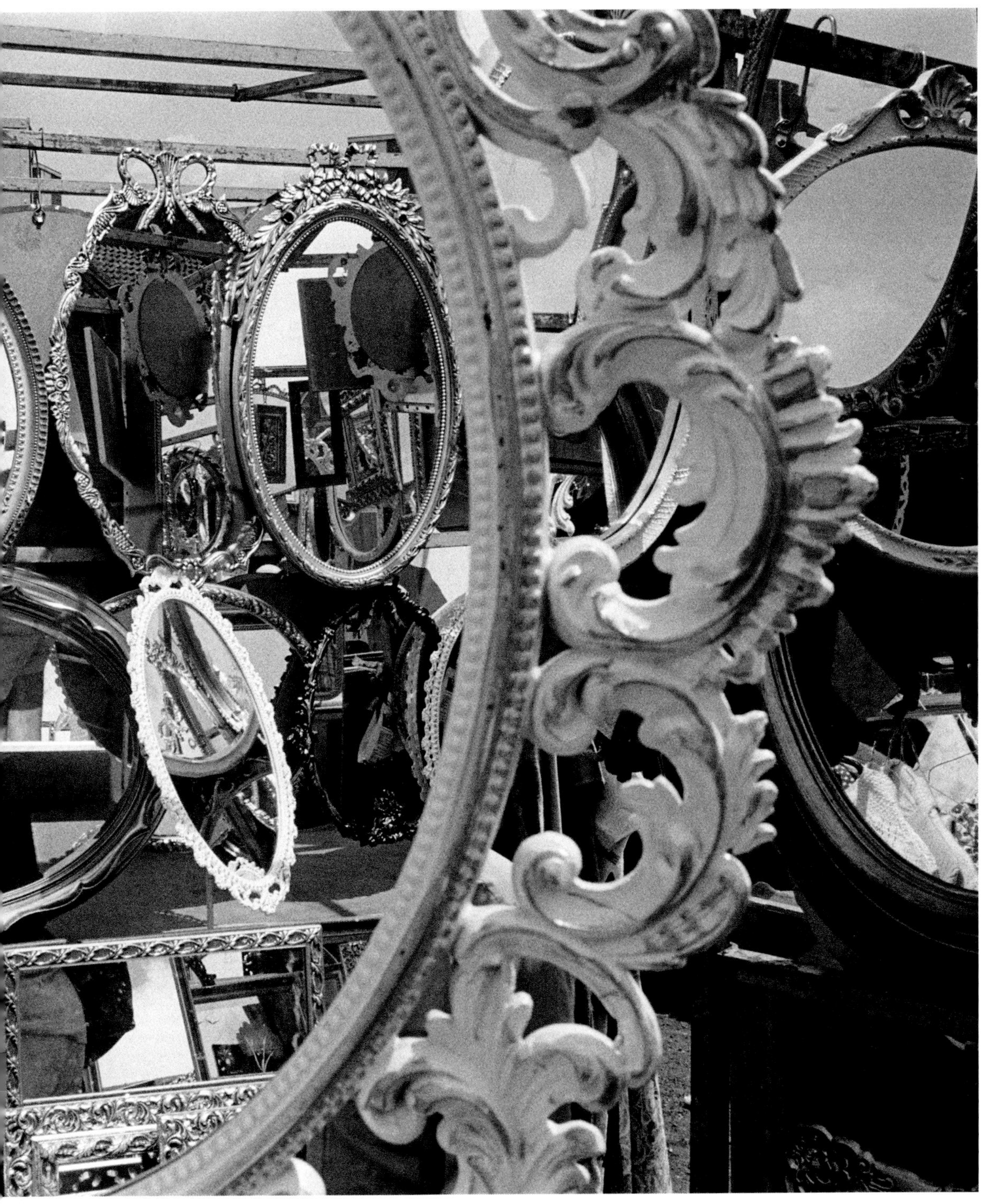

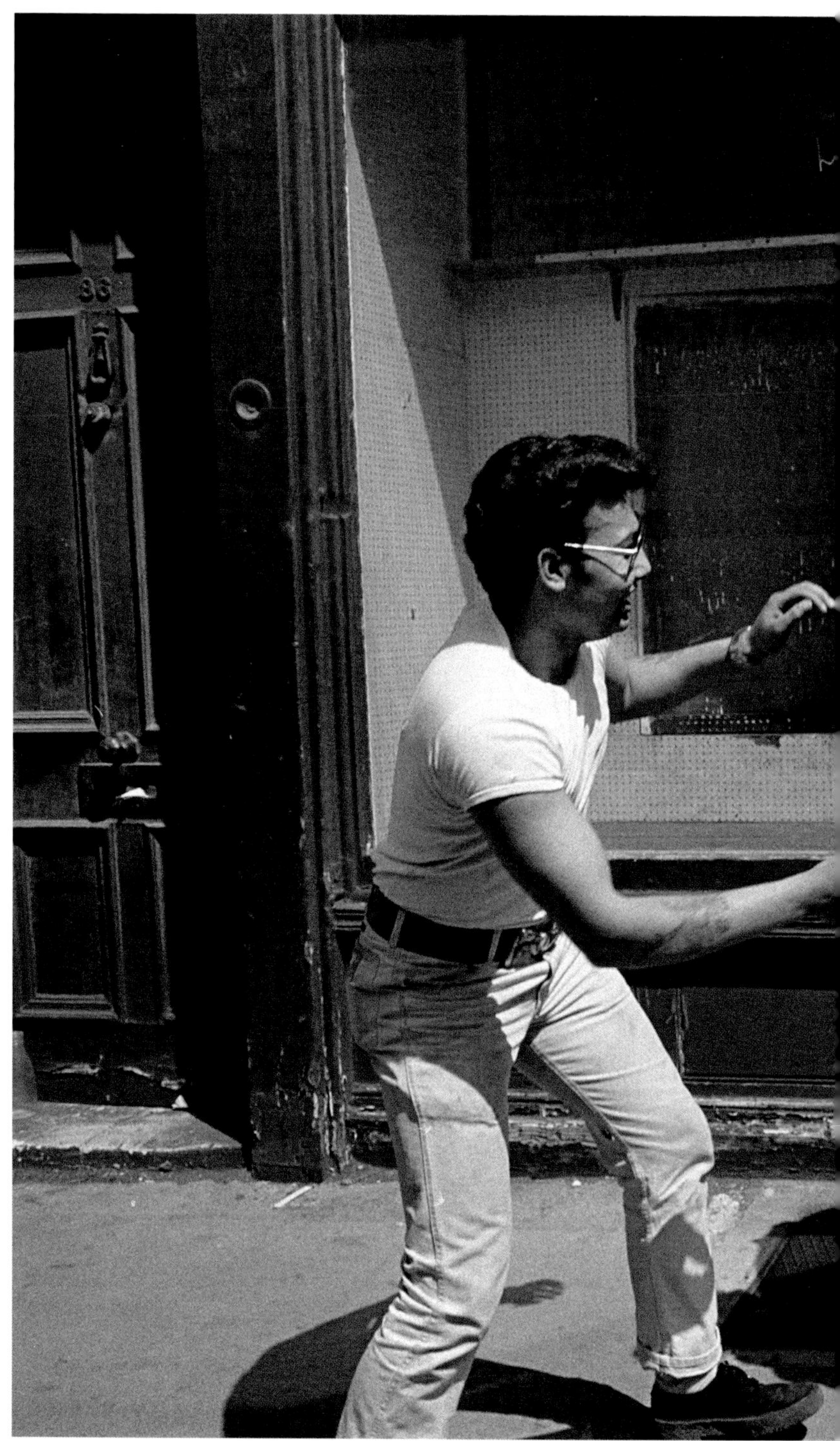

Commercial Street,
London E1, 1977

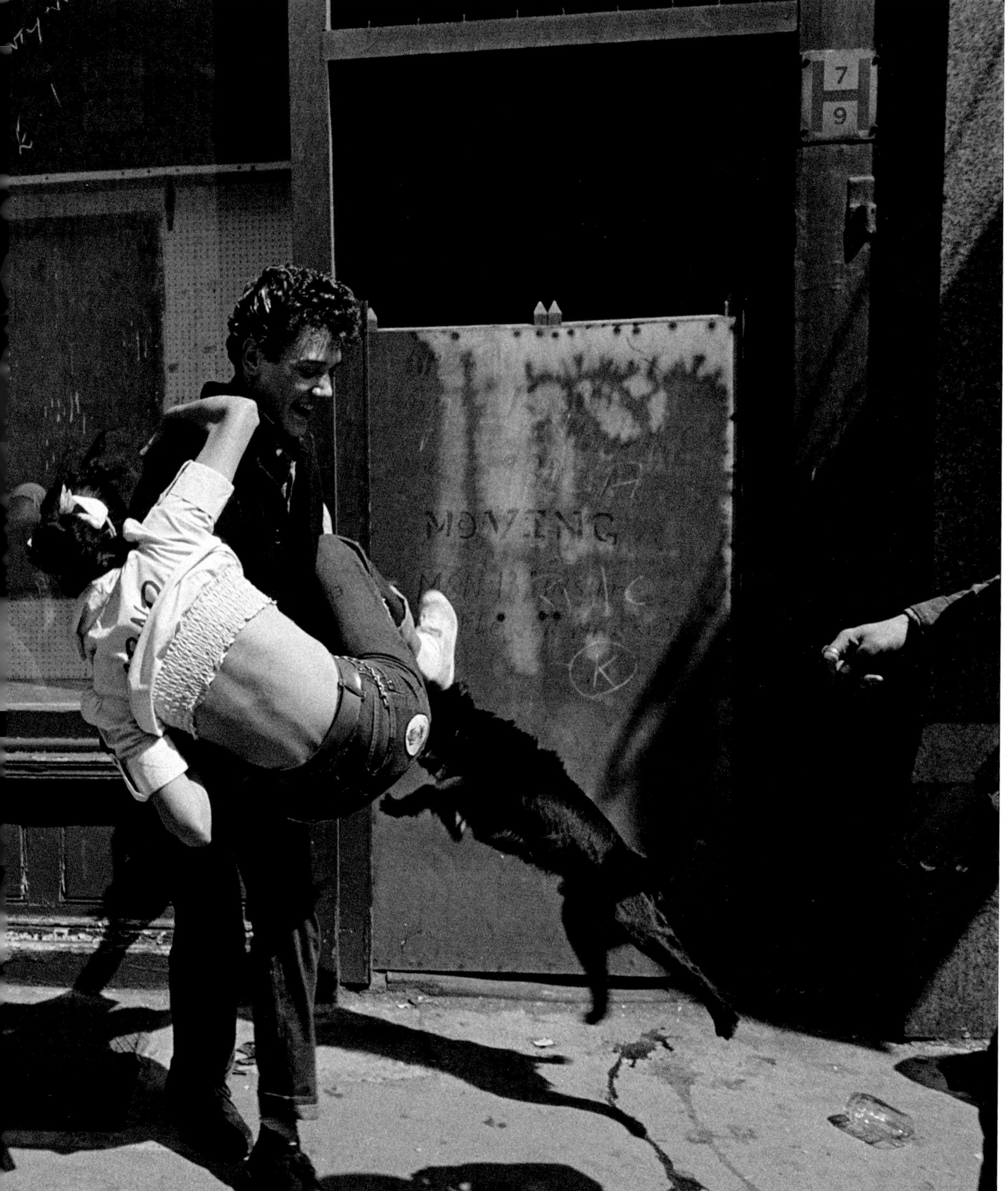

7
9
MOVING

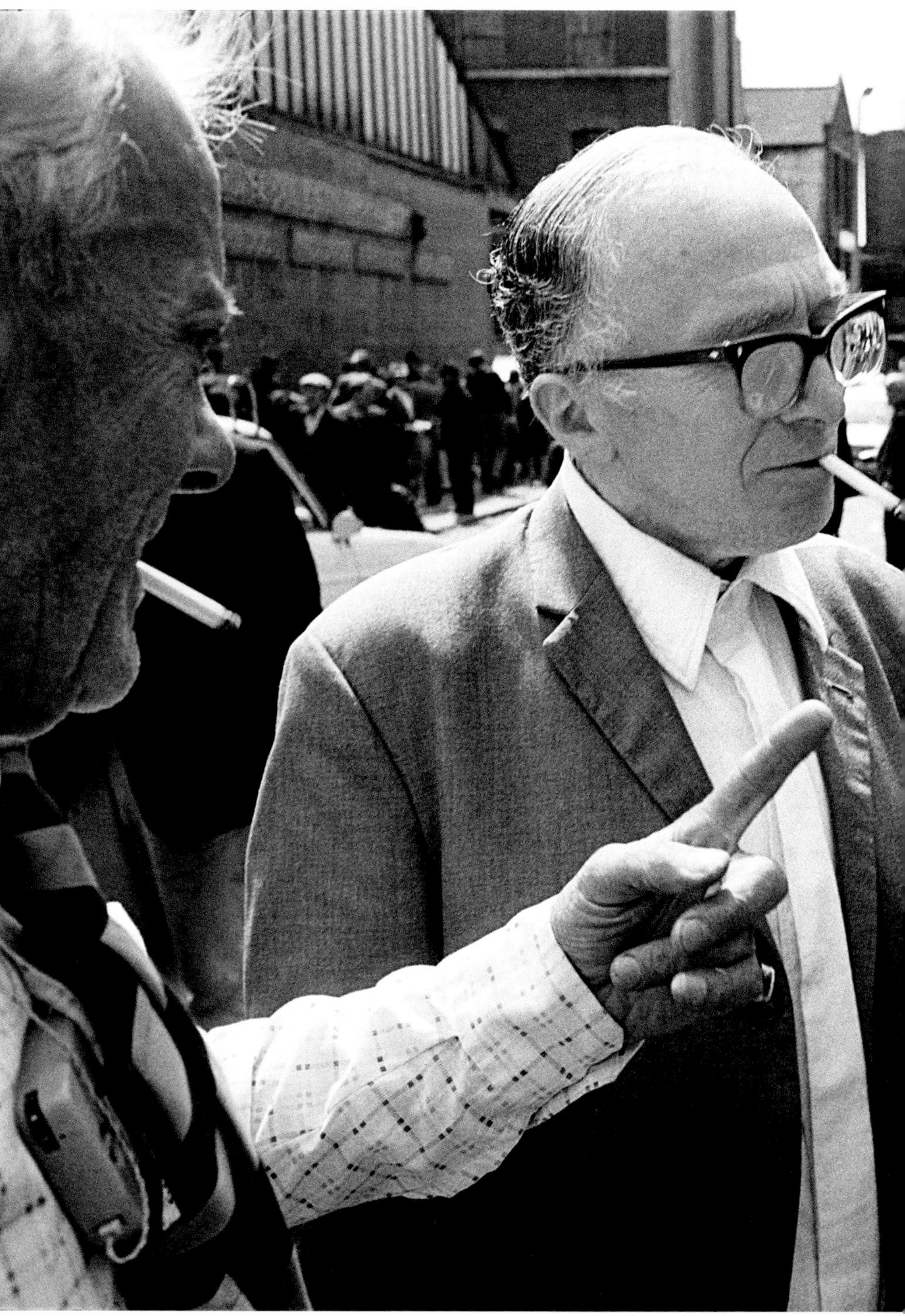

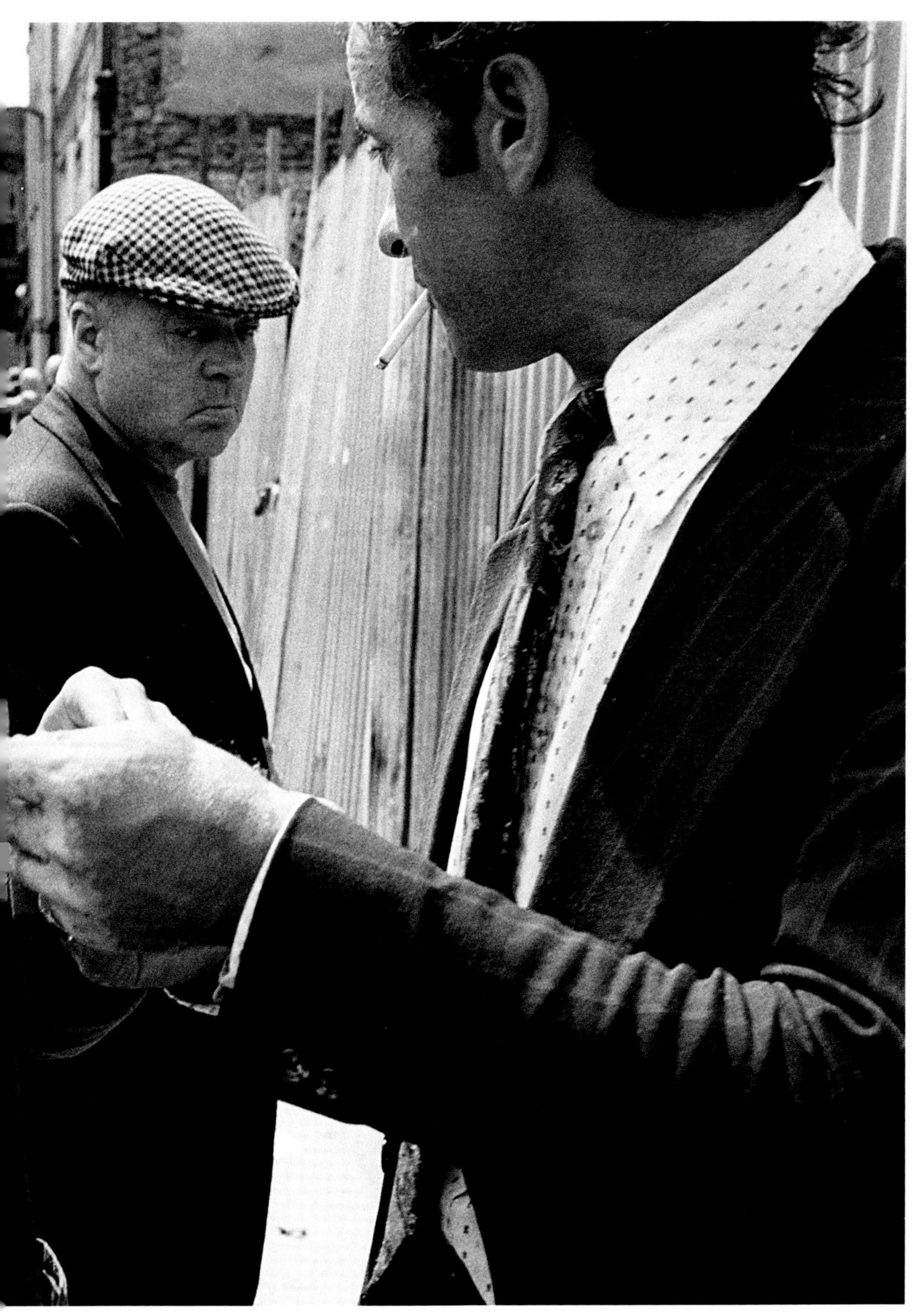

Chilton Street,
London E2, 1977

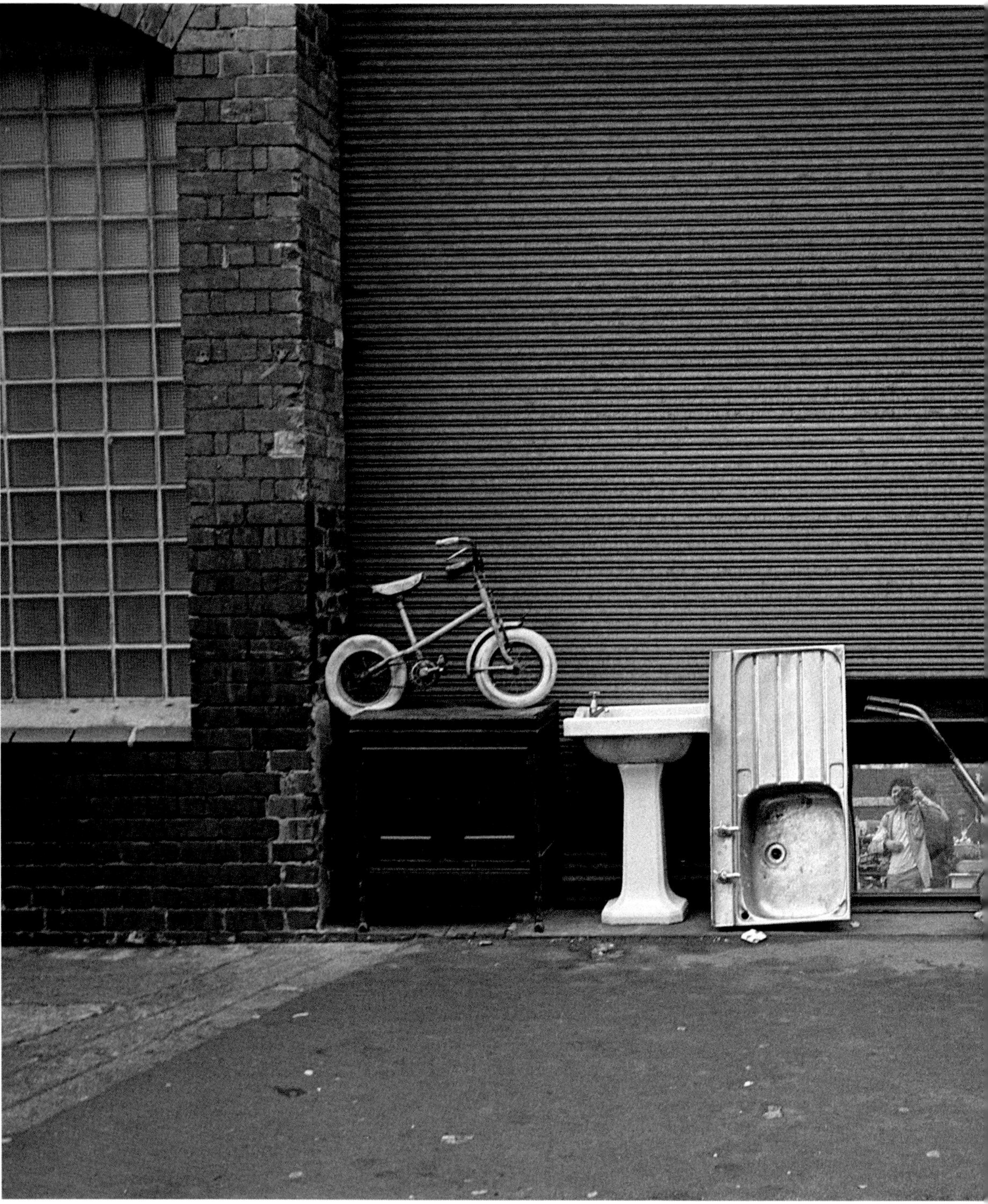

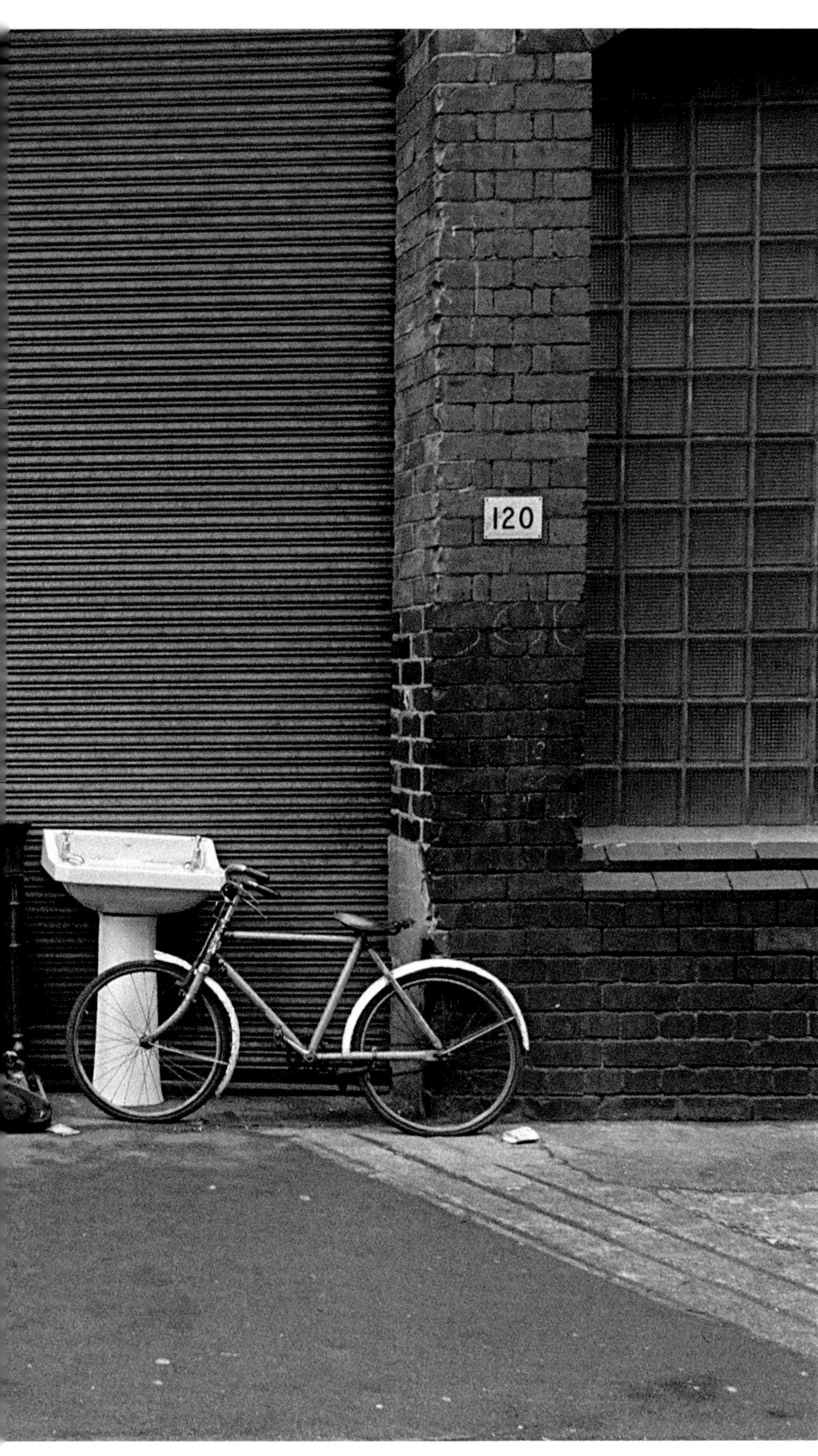

Cheshire Street, London E2, 1974

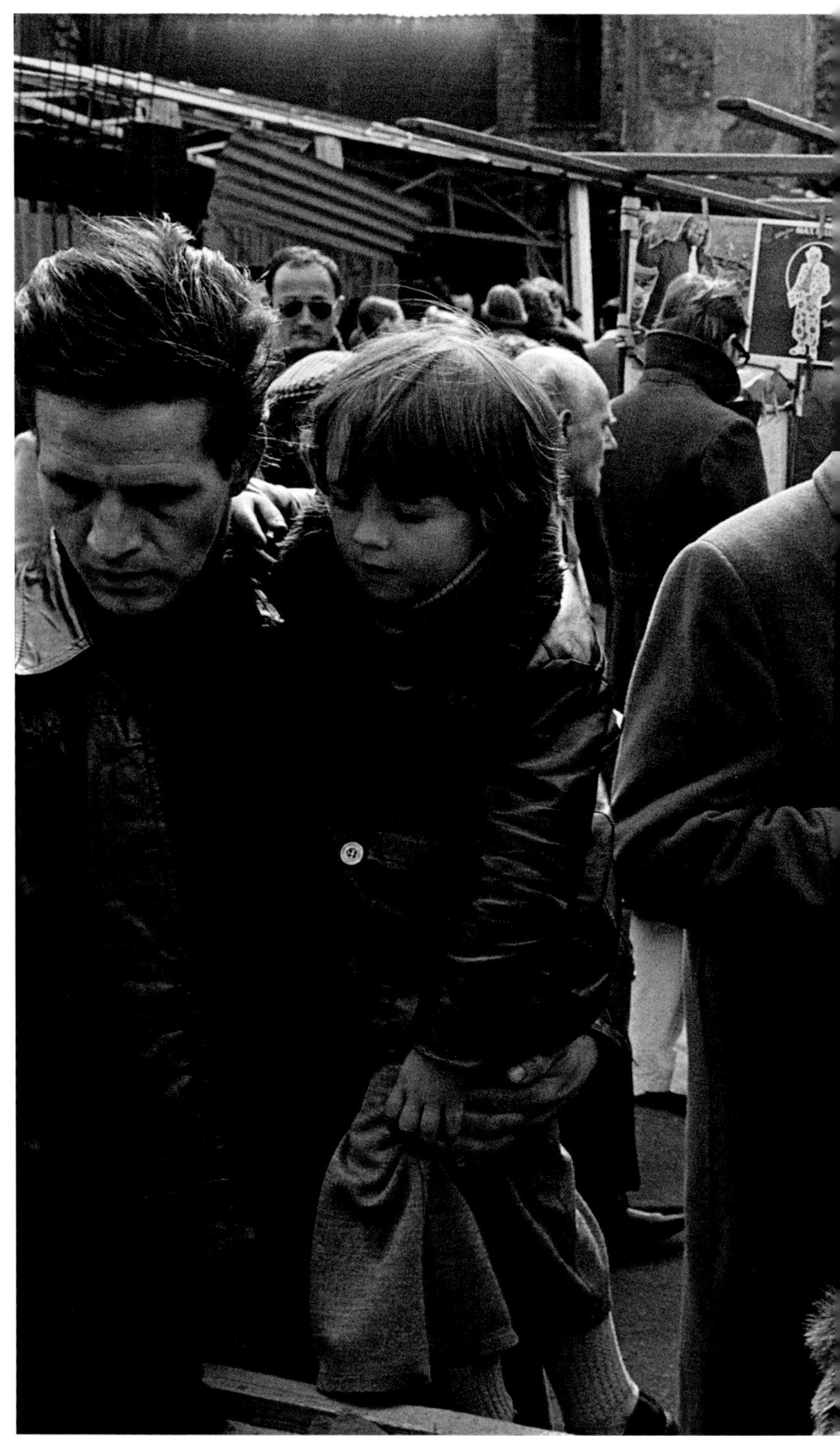

Cheshire Street, London E2, 1977

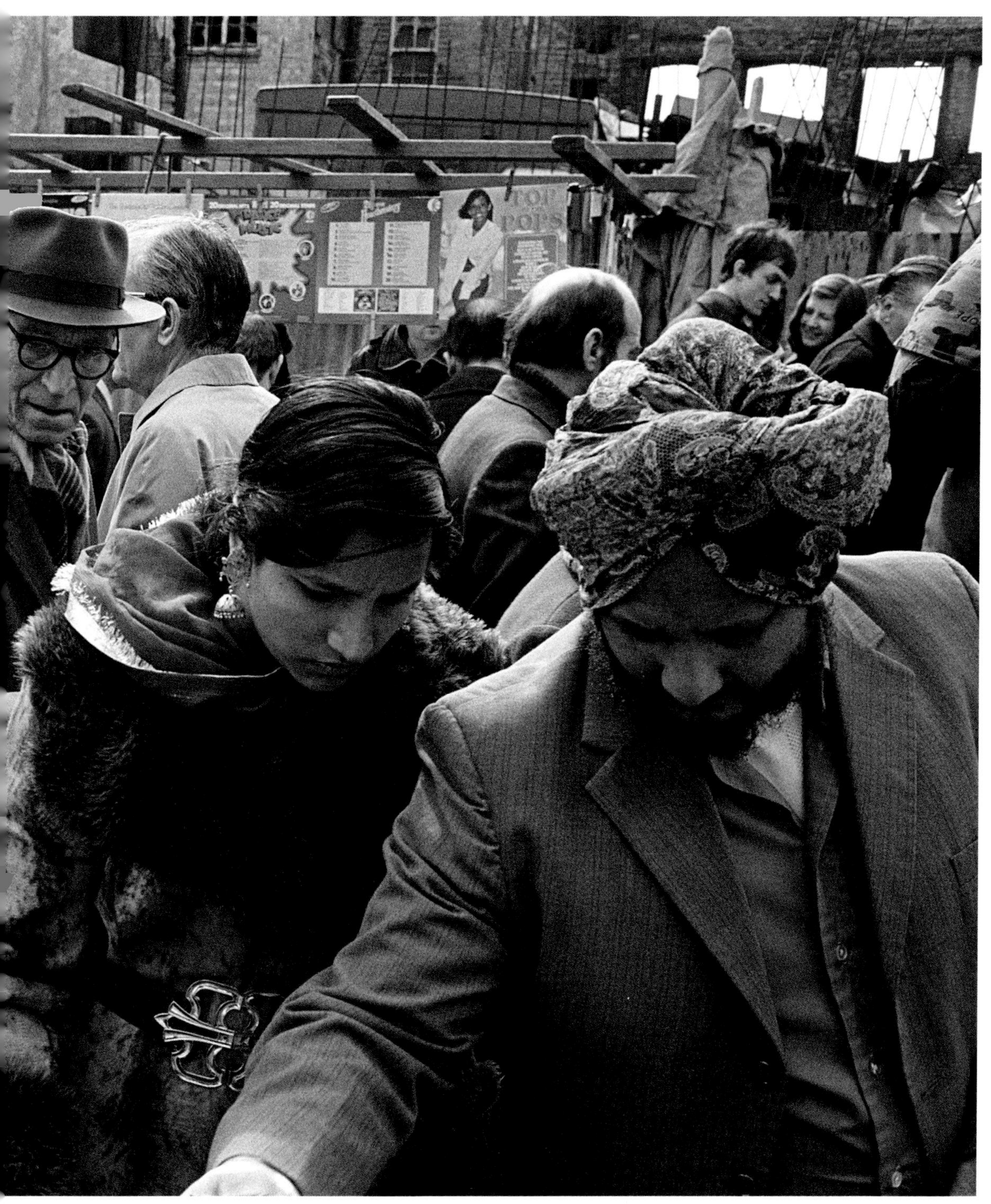

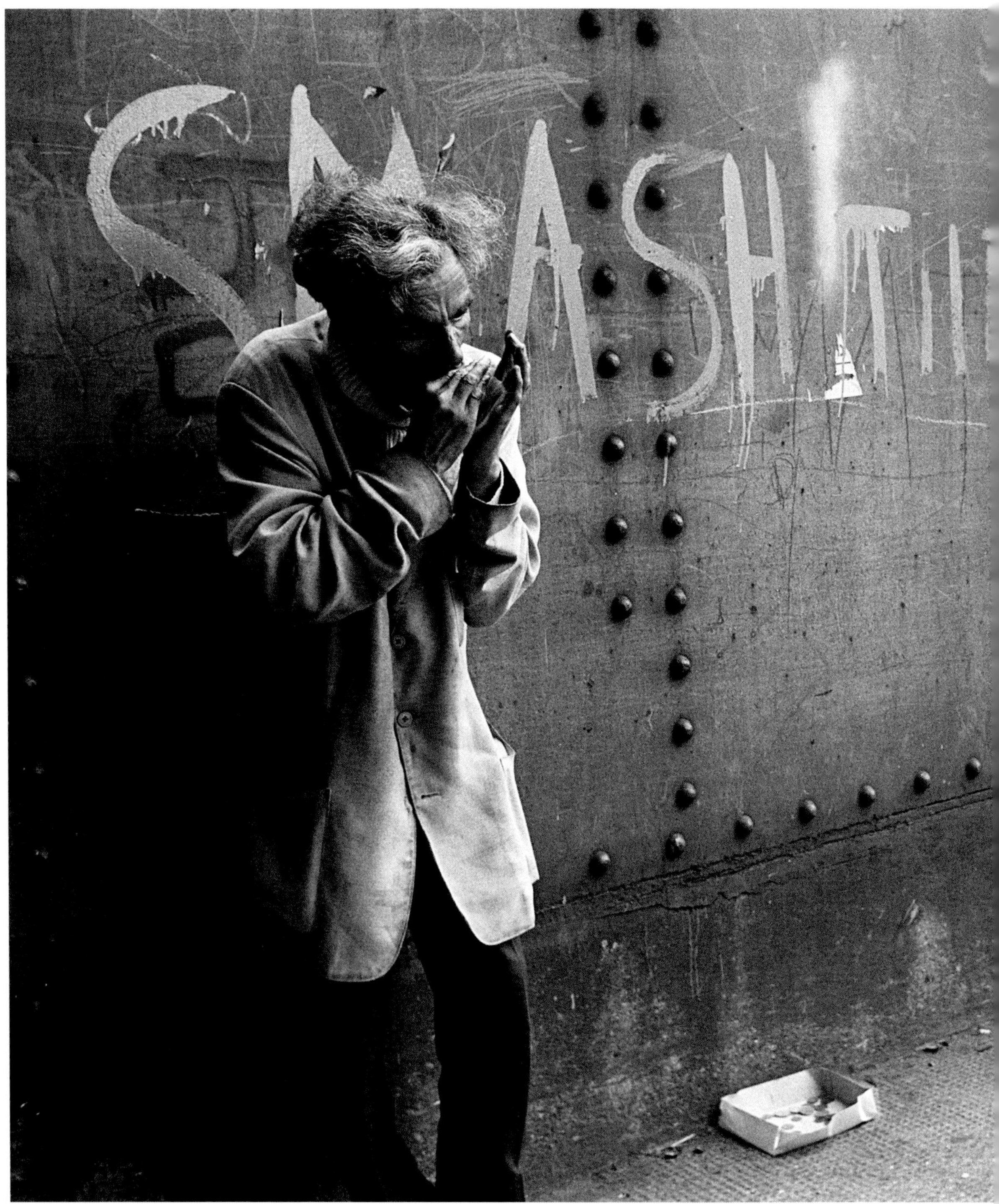

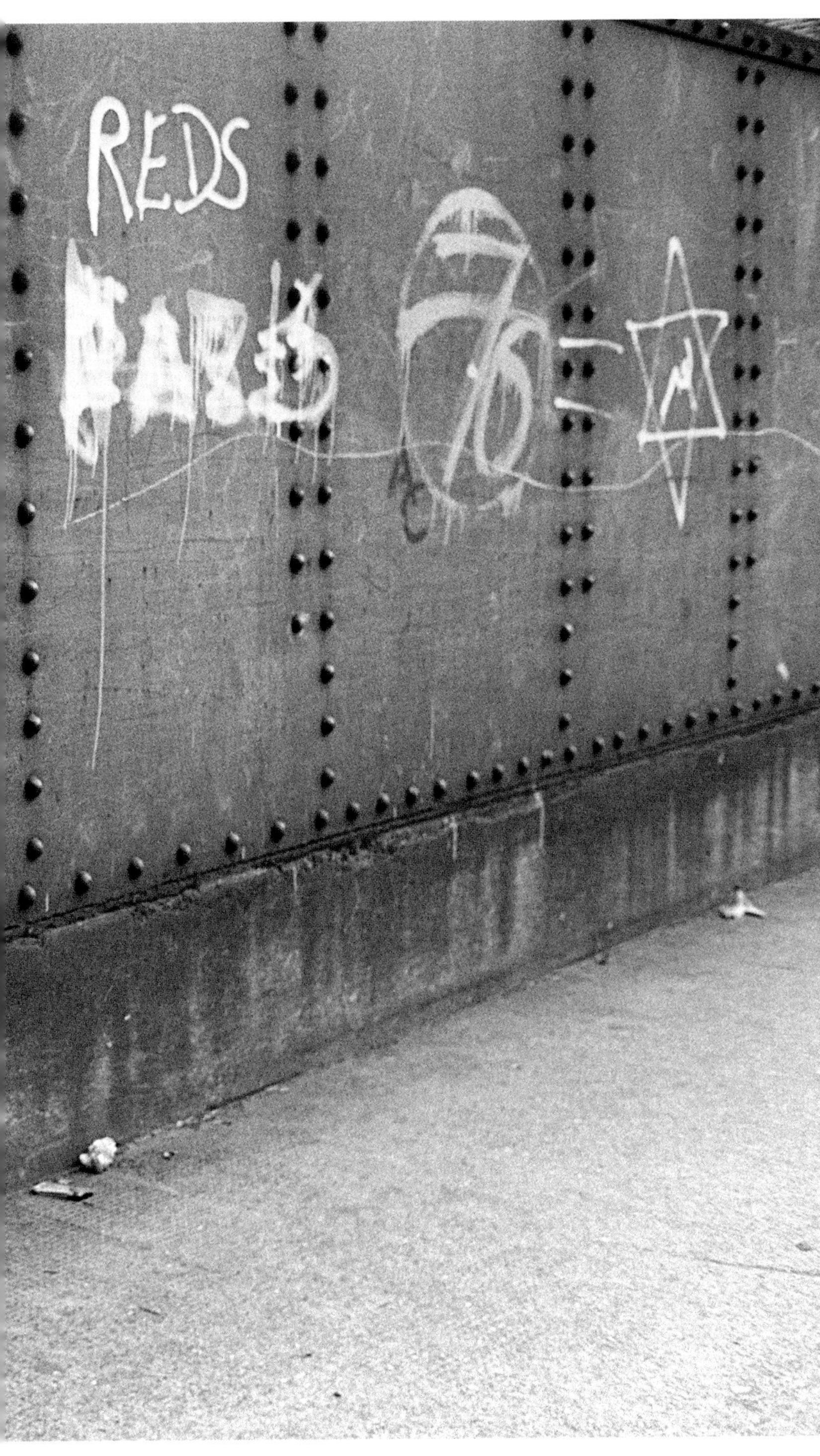

Brick Lane, London E1, 1977

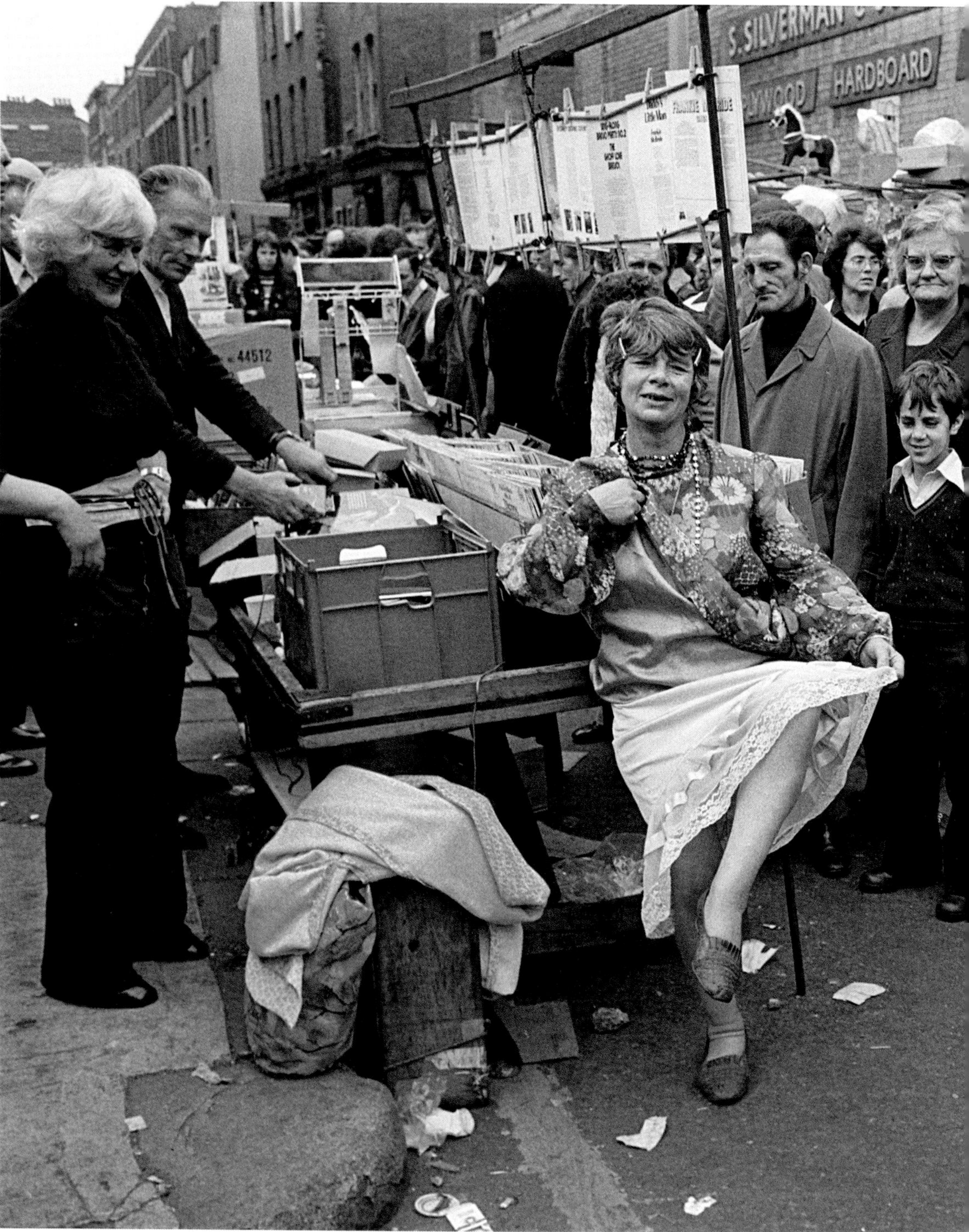

S. SILVERMAN & SONS
HARDBOARD

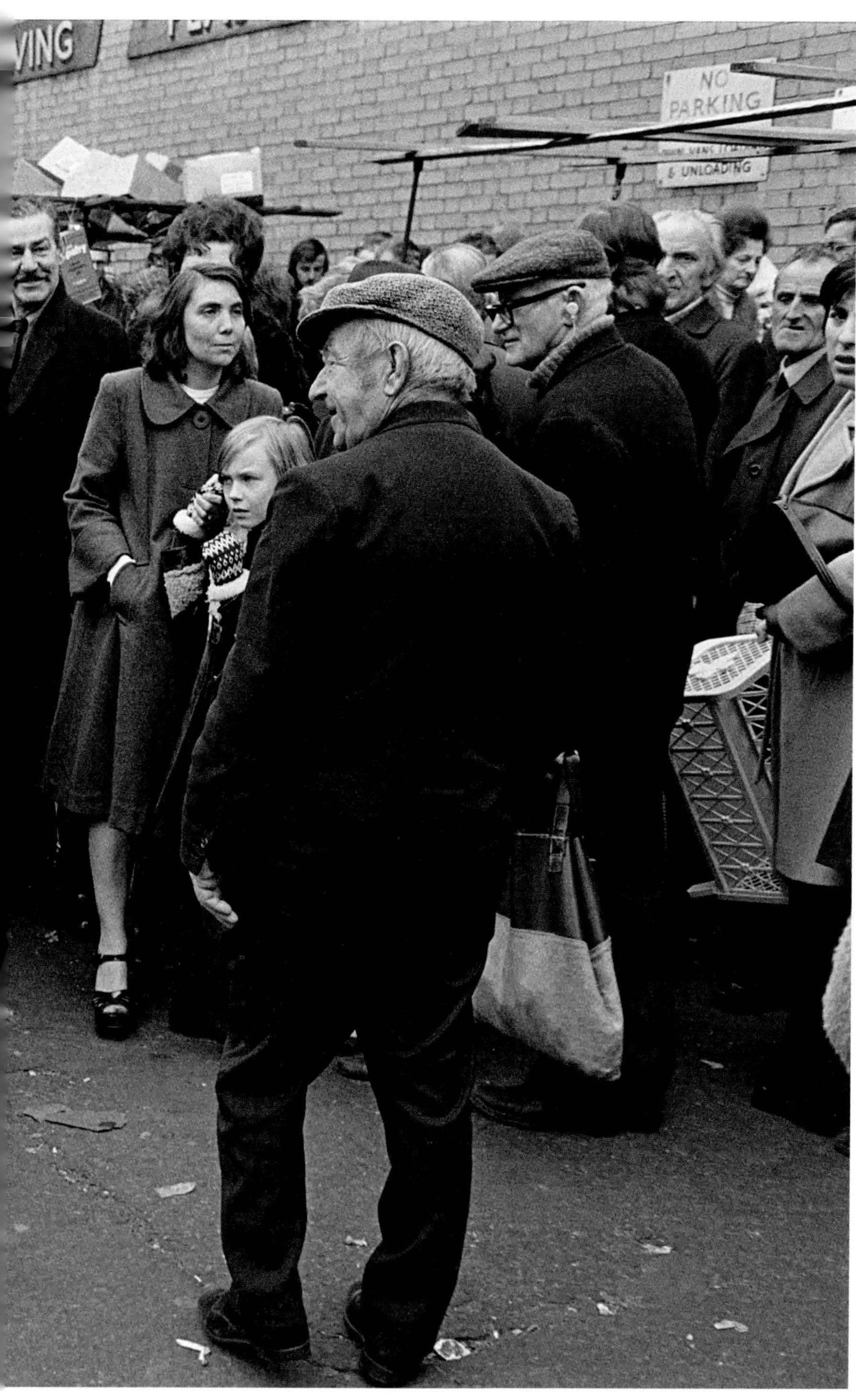

Cheshire Street,
London E2, 1975

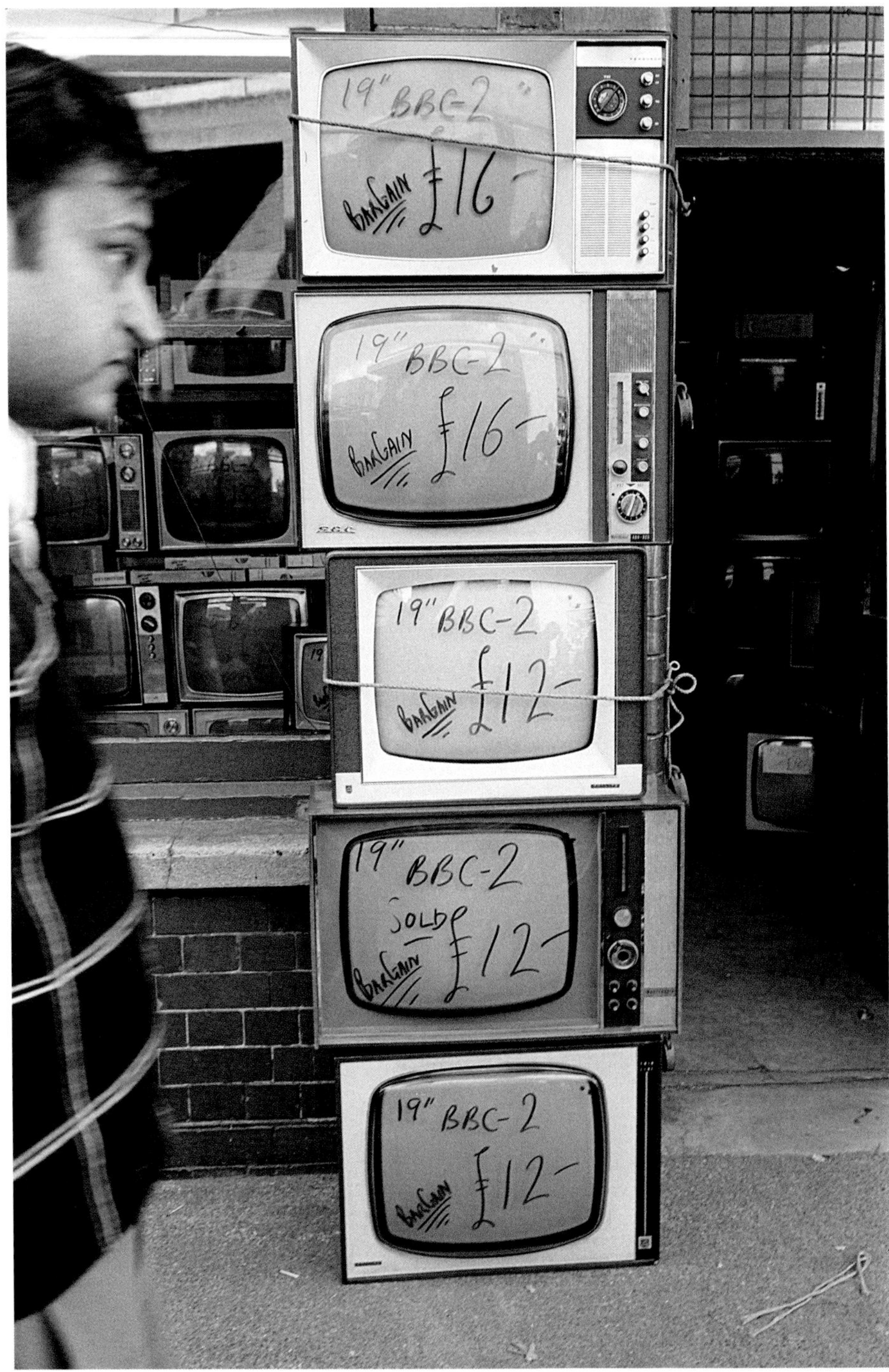

Cheshire Street, London E2, 1974

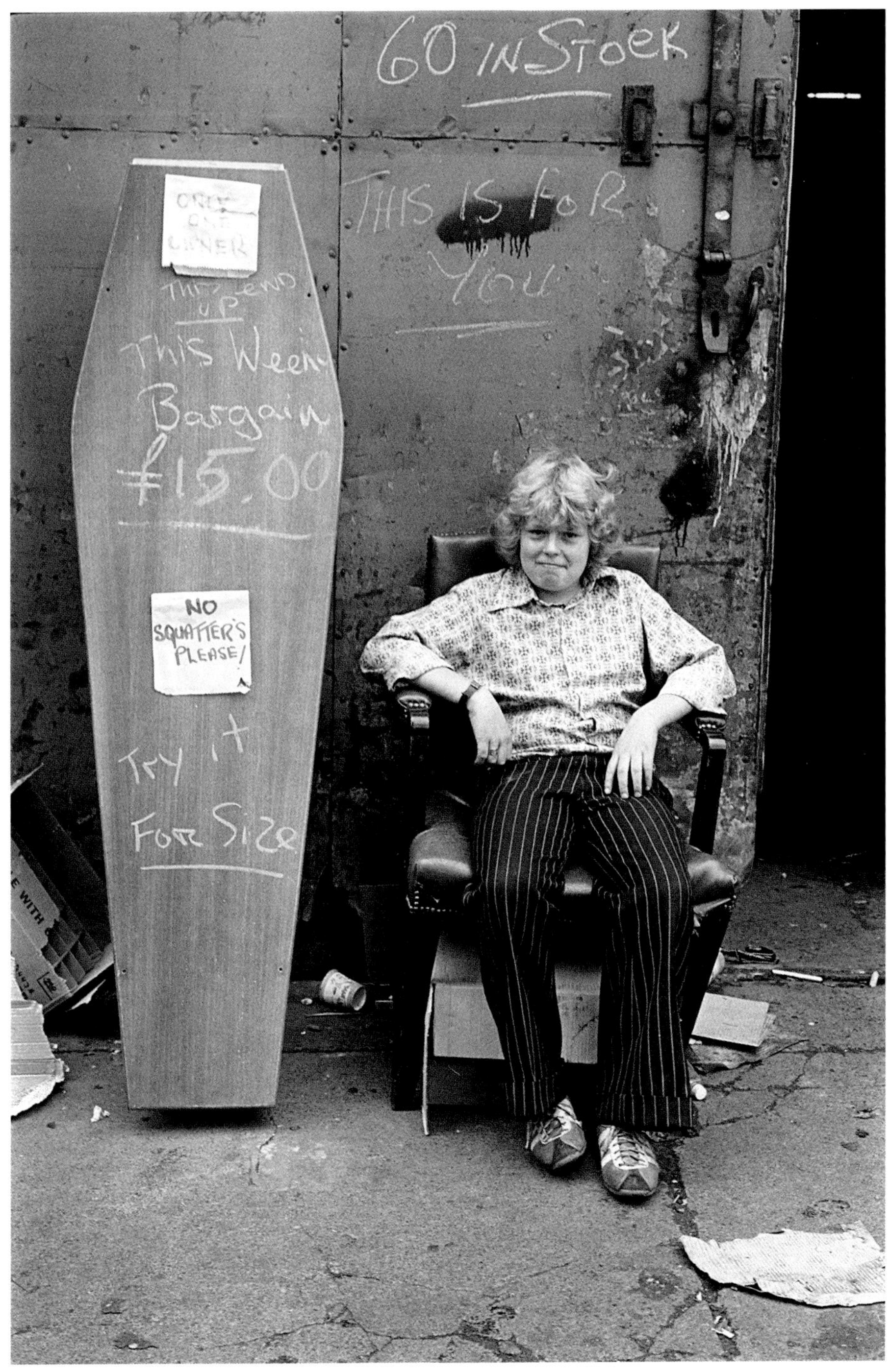

Bacon Street, London E1, 1974

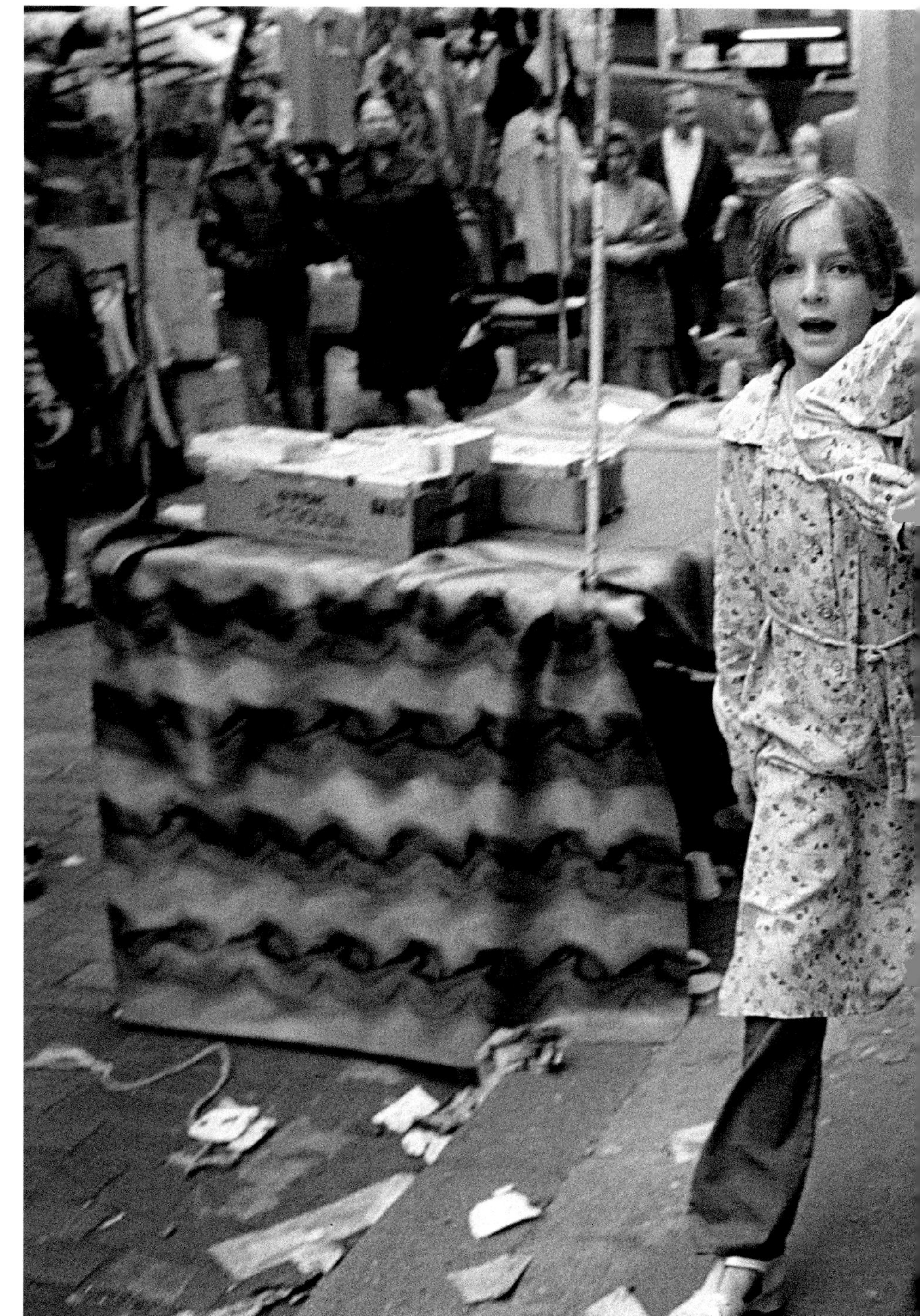

Cheshire Street,
London E2, 1979

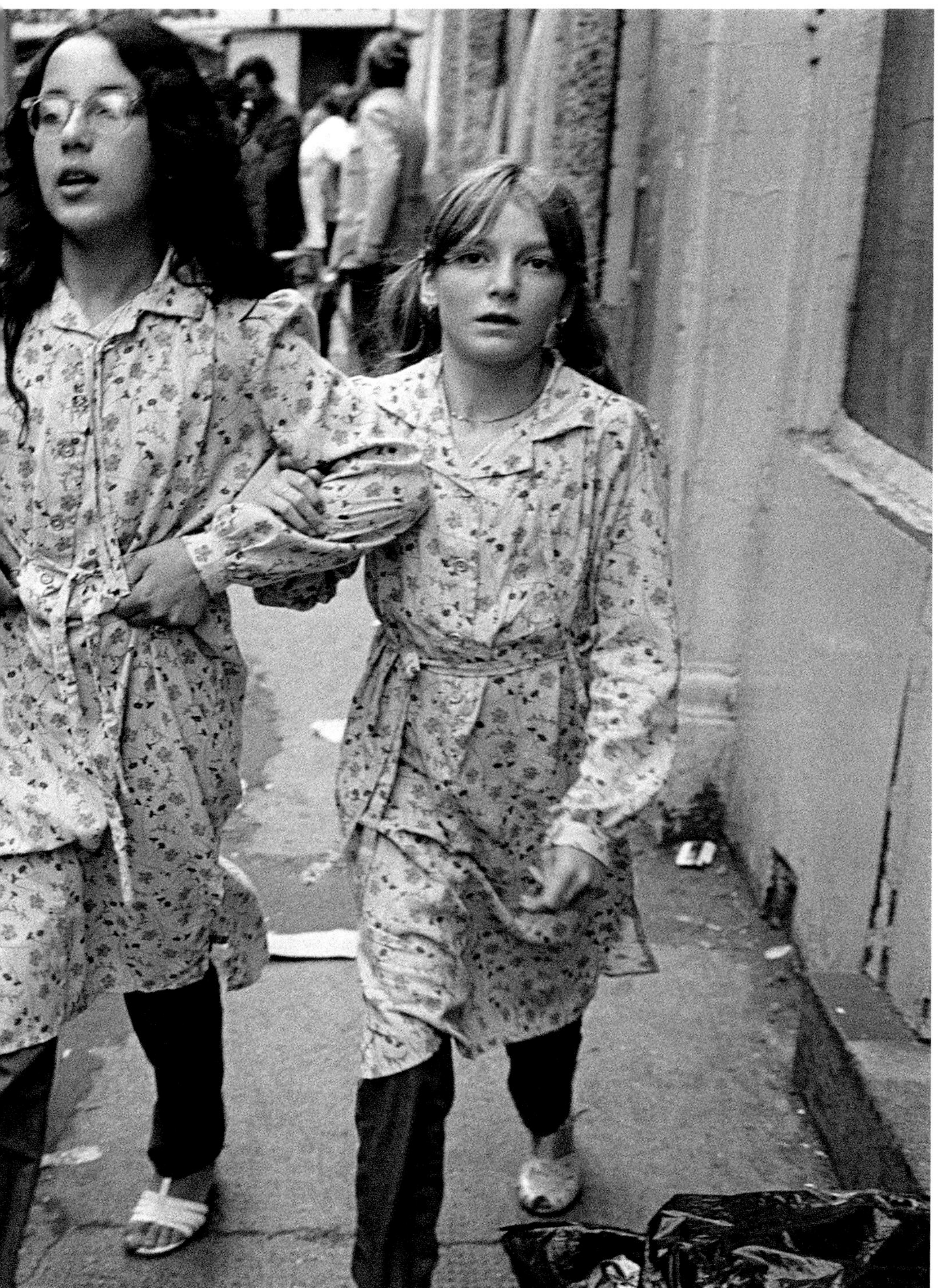

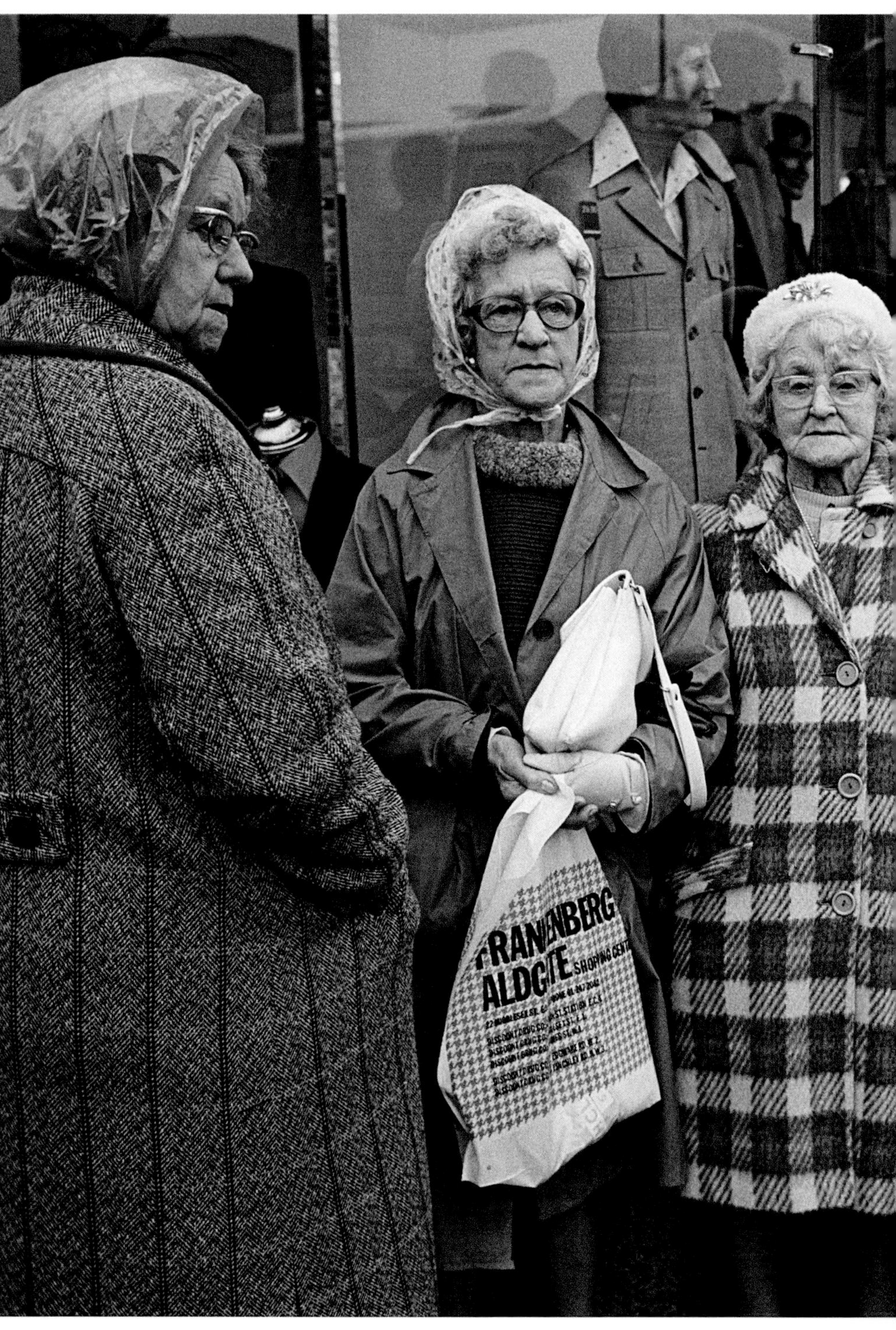
FRANENBERG
ALDGATE SHOPPING CENTRE

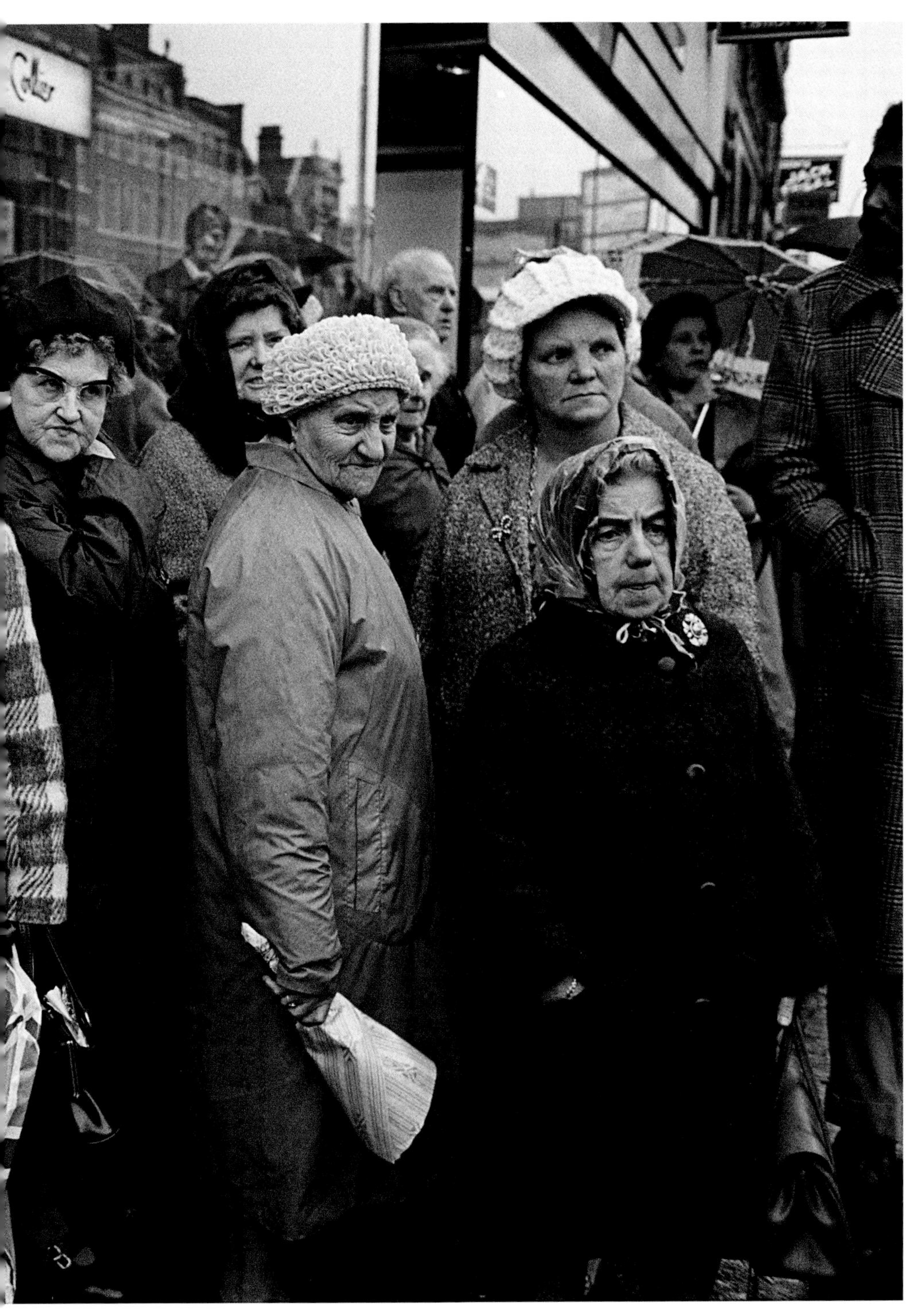

Whitechapel
High Street,
London E1, 1977

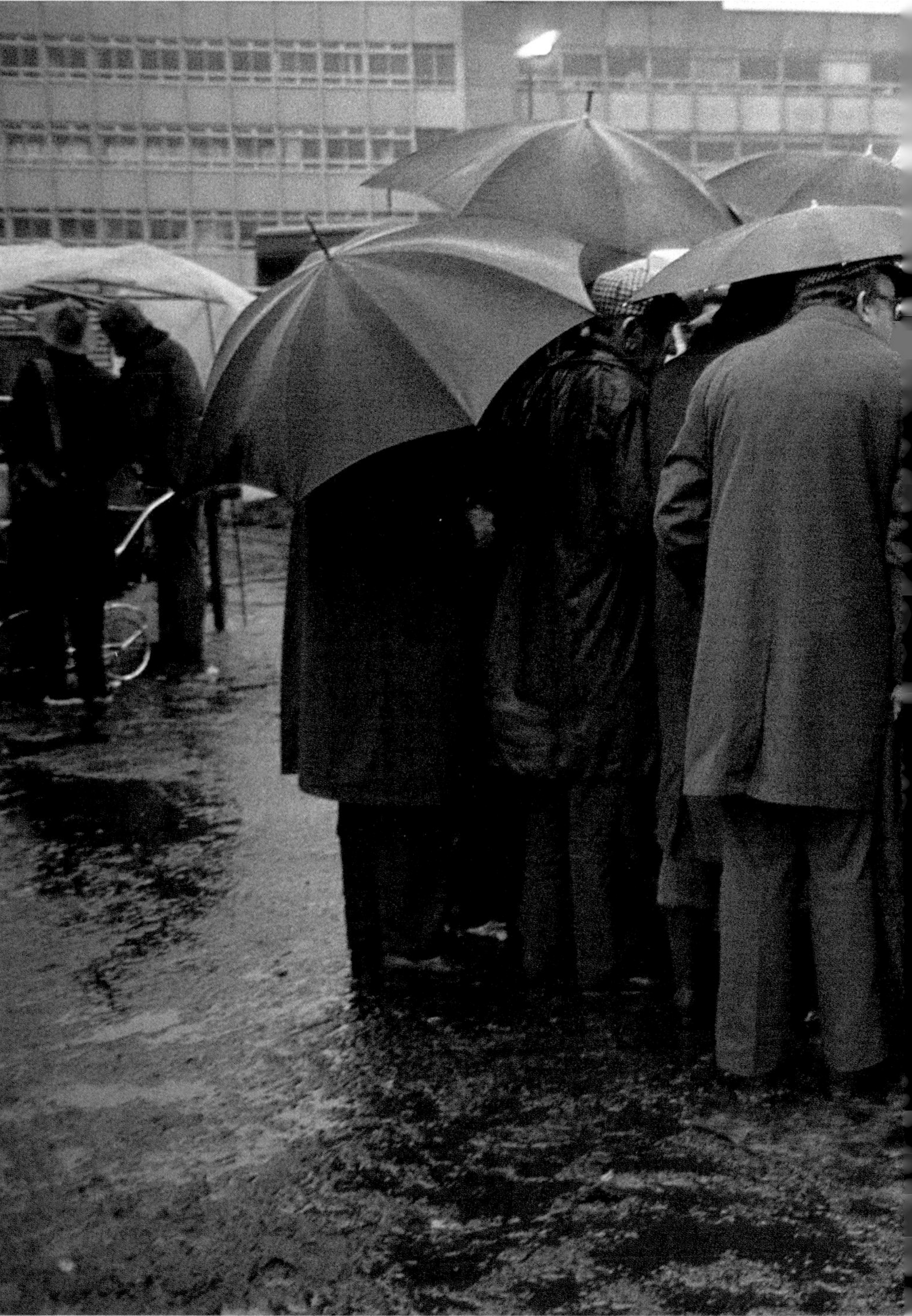

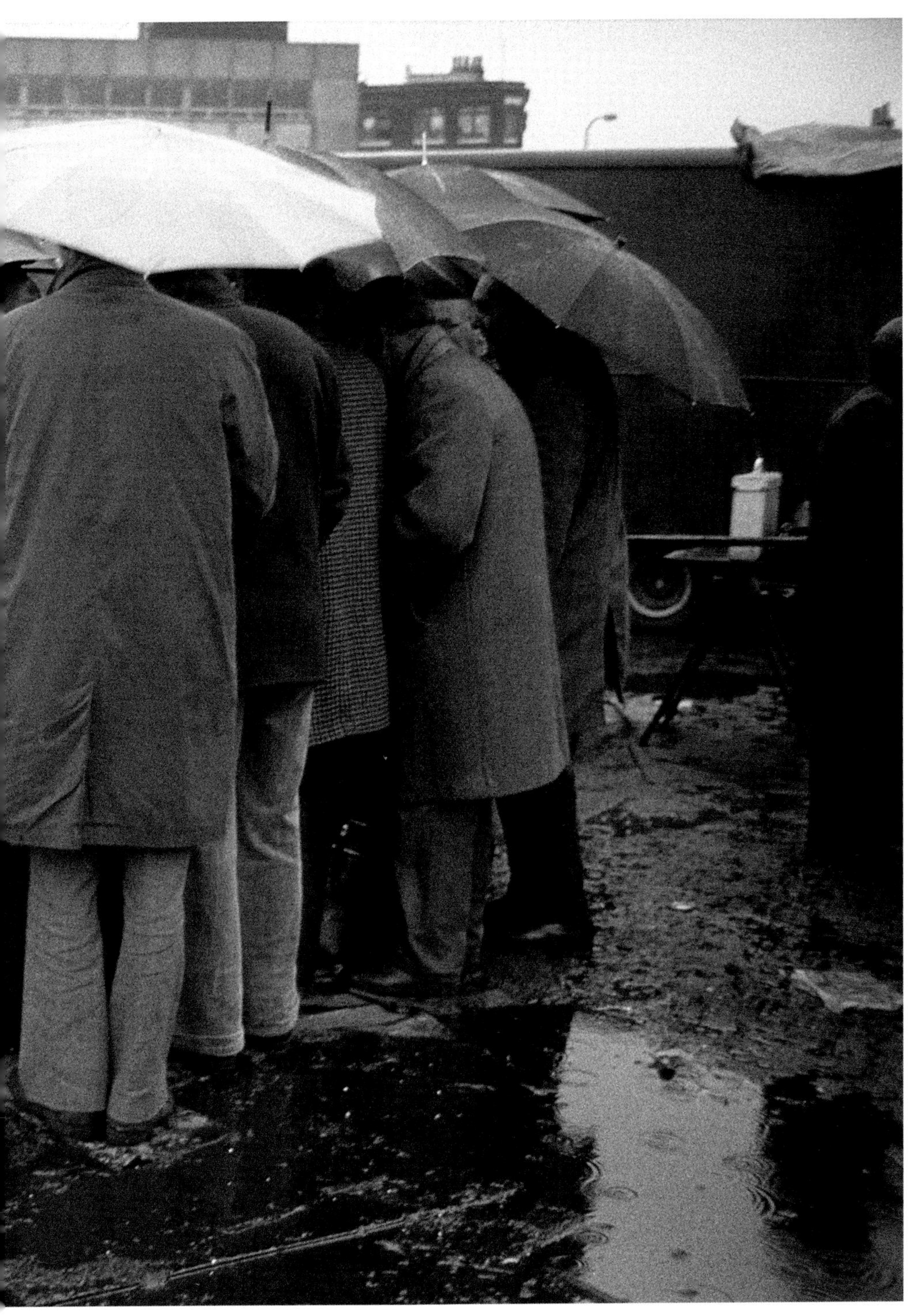

Sclater Street,
London E1, 1977

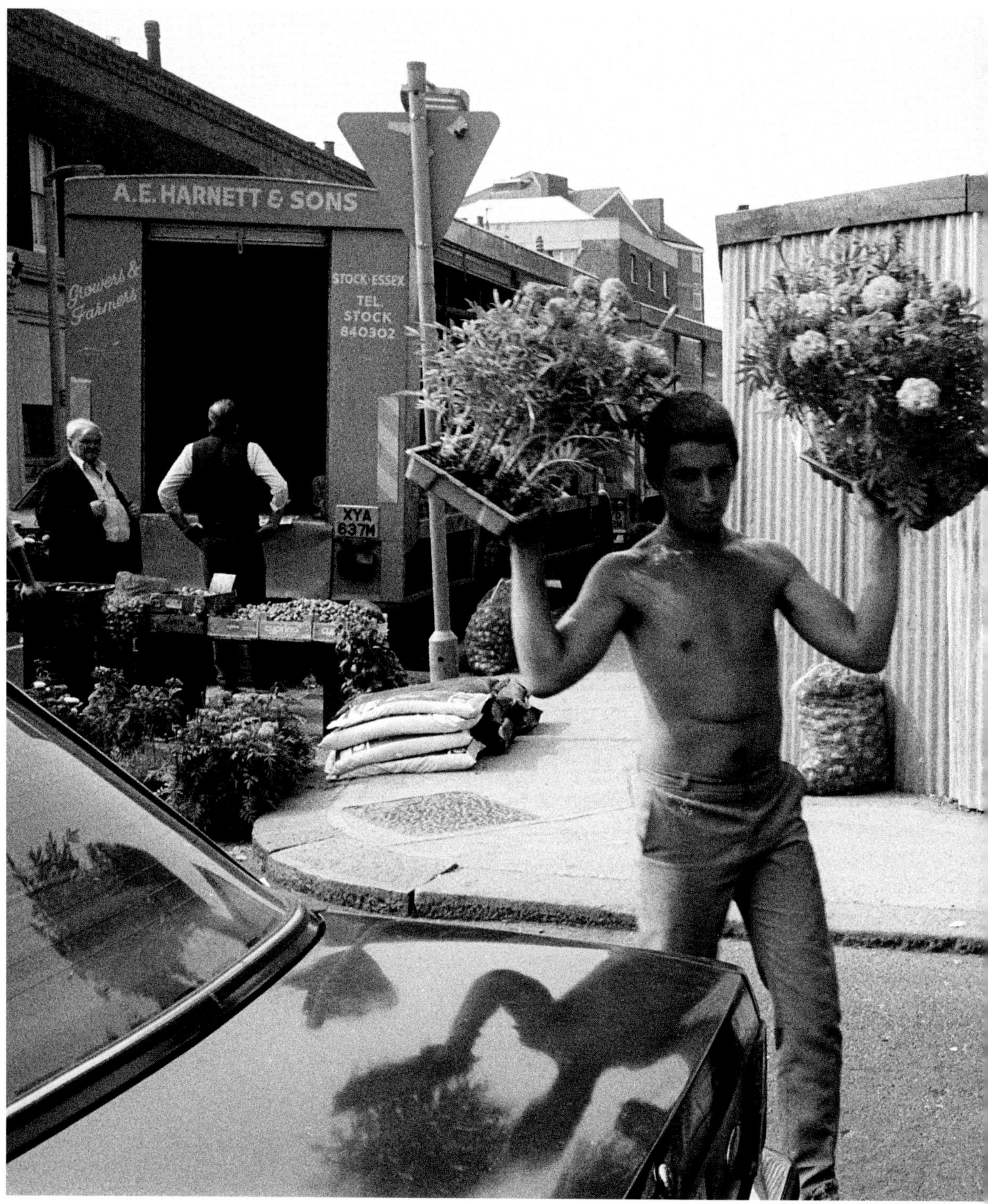

A.E. HARNETT & SONS
Growers & Farmers
STOCK·ESSEX
TEL.
STOCK
840302
XYA
637M

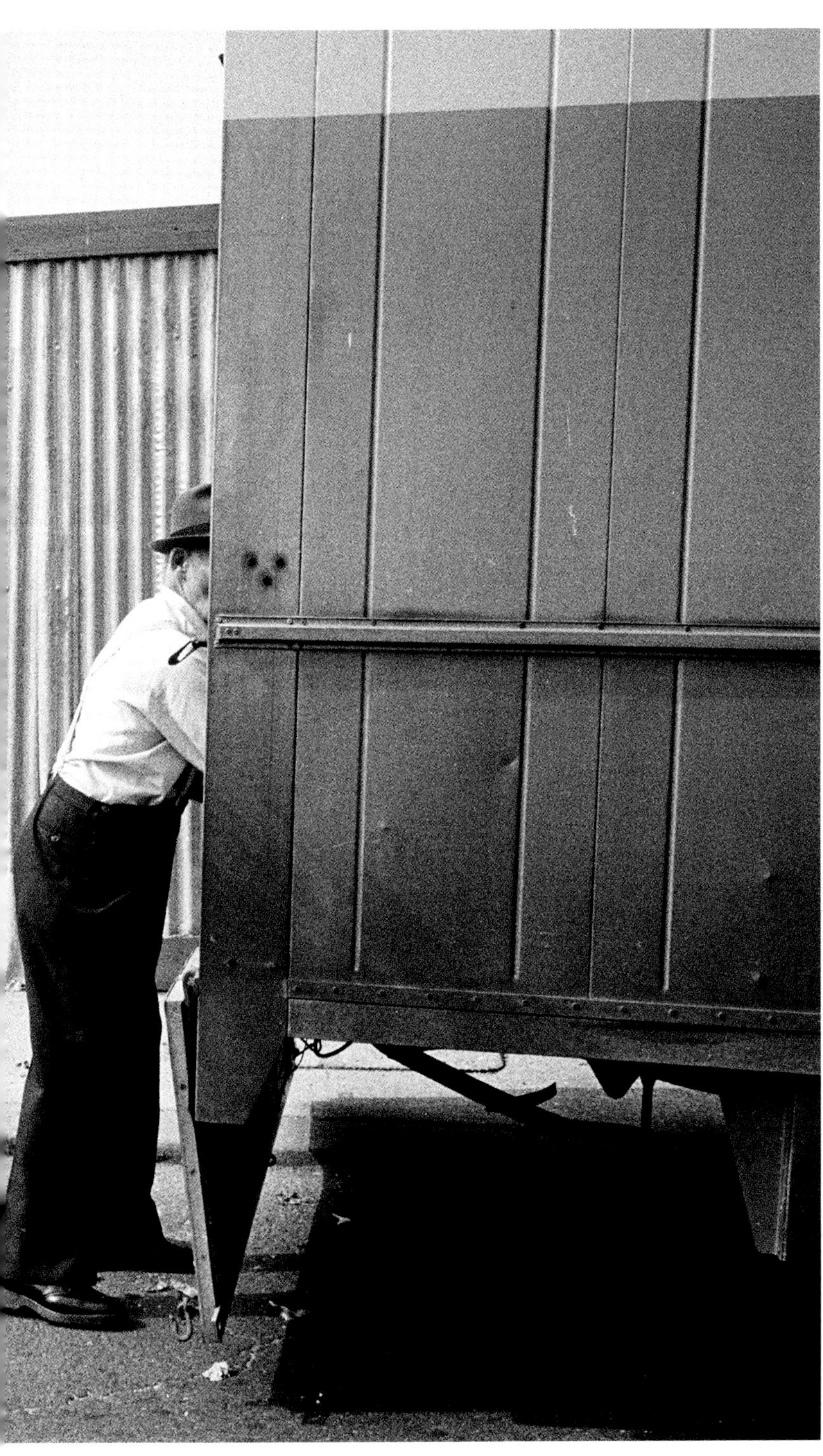

Columbia Road, London E2, 1984

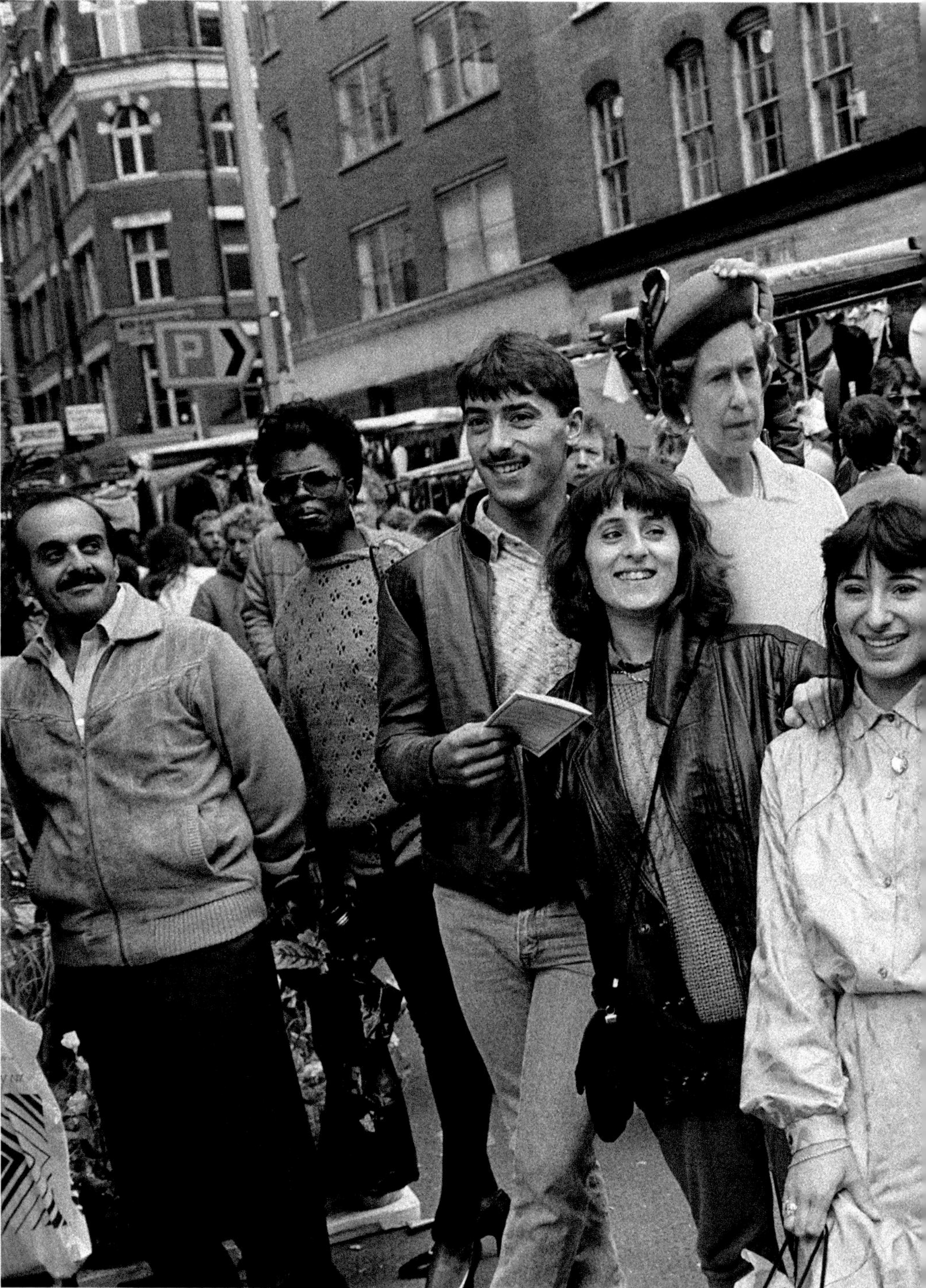

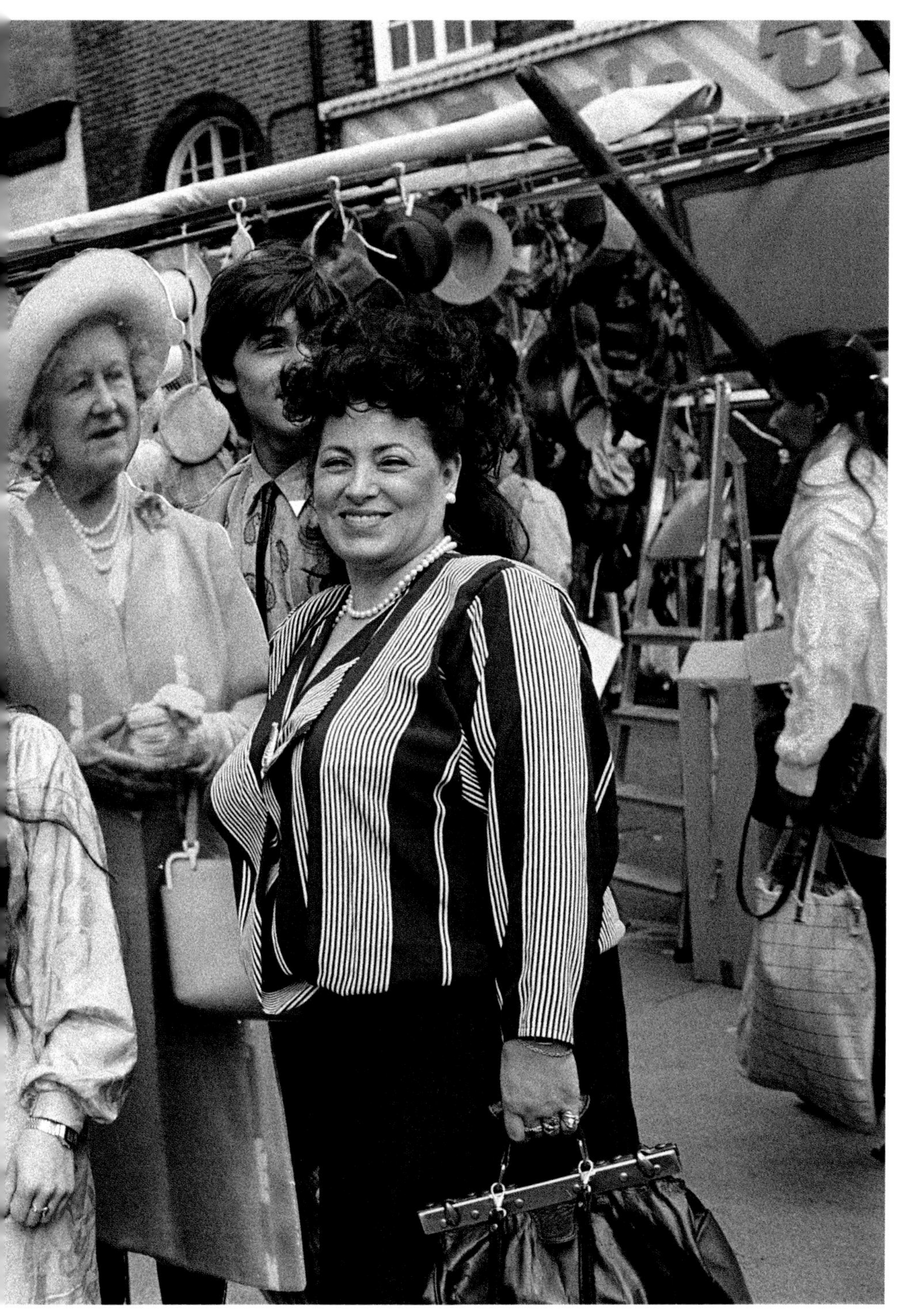

Middlesex Street,
London E1, 1986

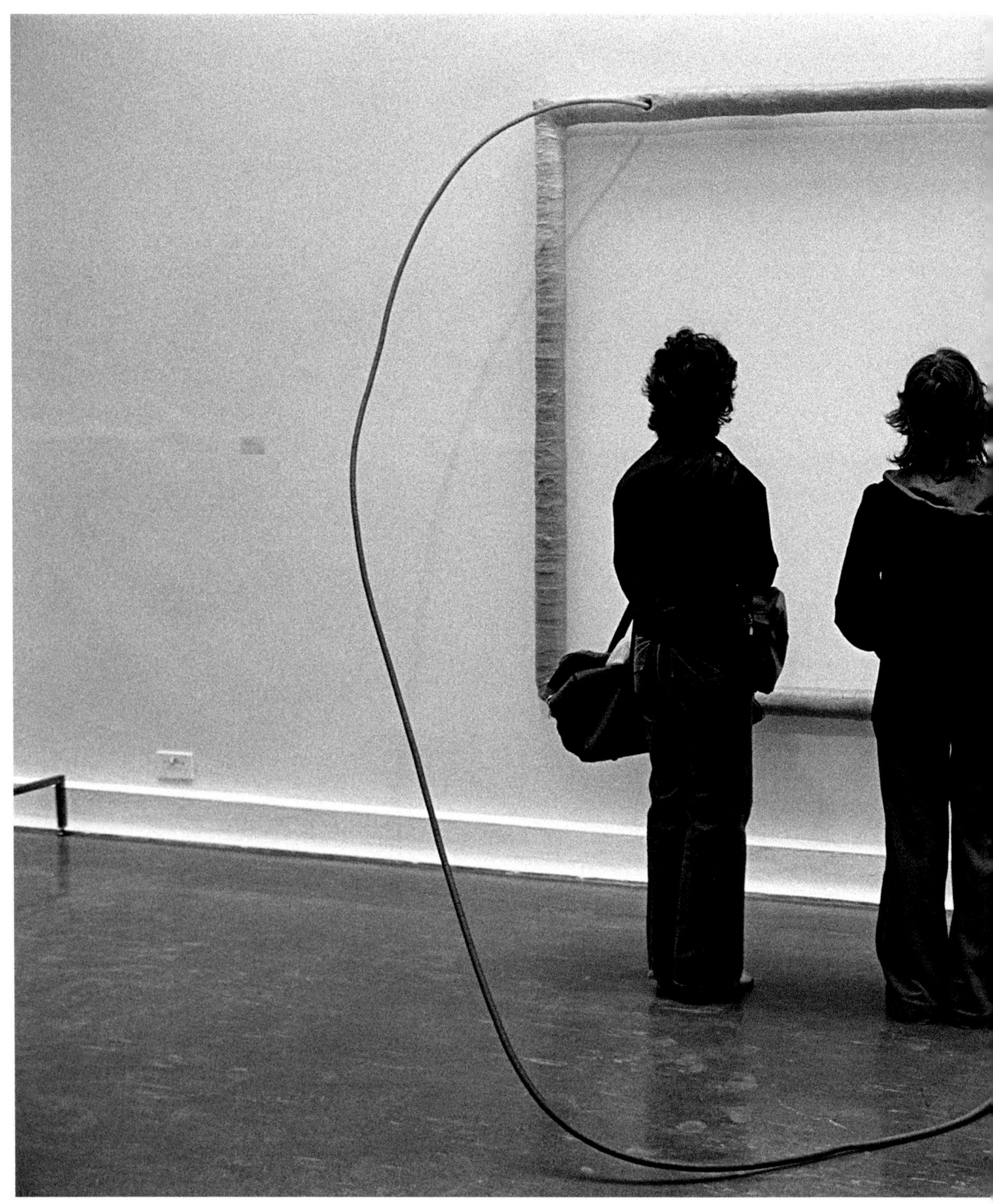

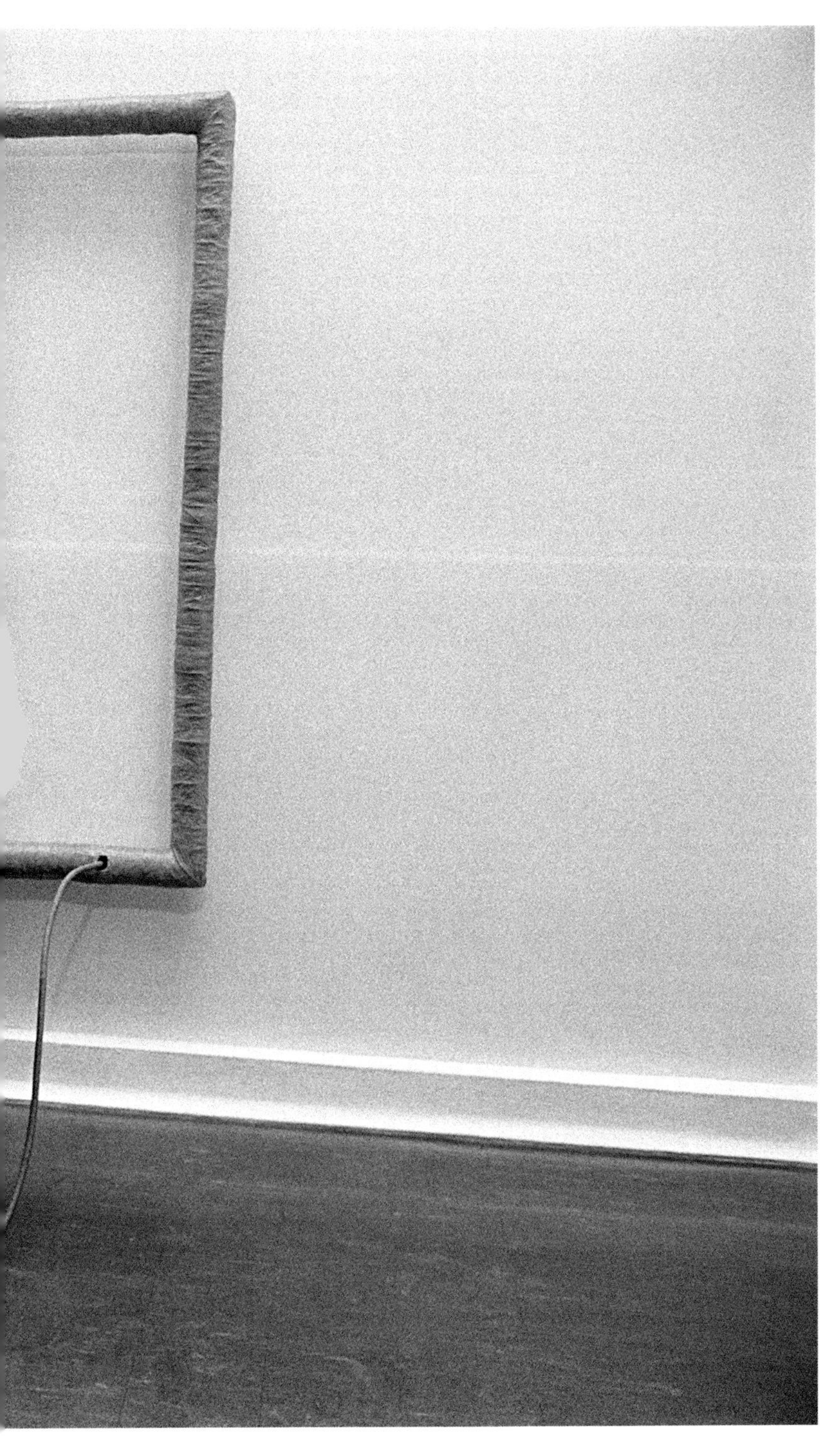

Whitechapel Gallery, Whitechapel
High Street, London E1, 1979

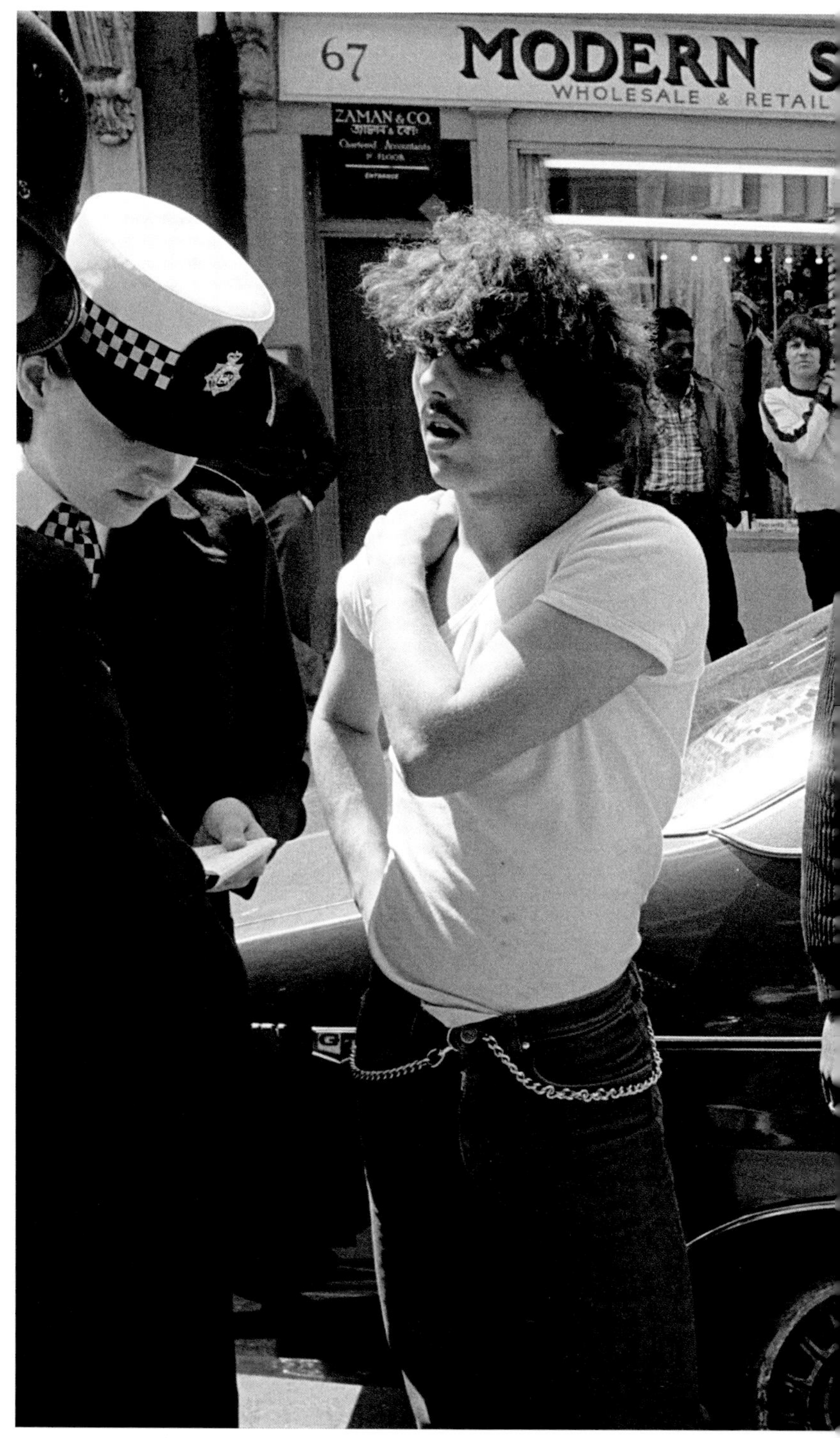

Brick Lane, London E1, 1981

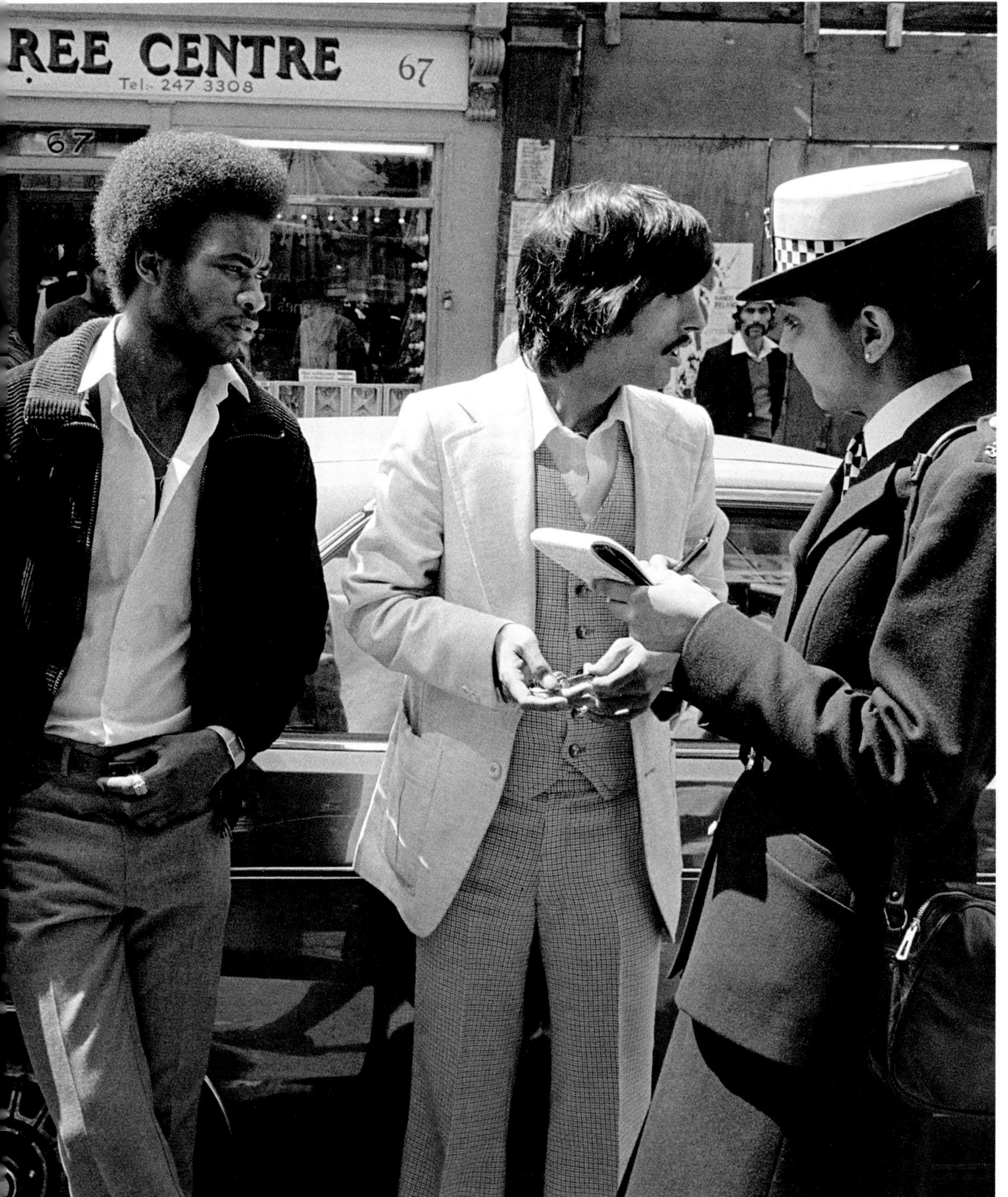
REE CENTRE
67
Tel:- 247 3308
67

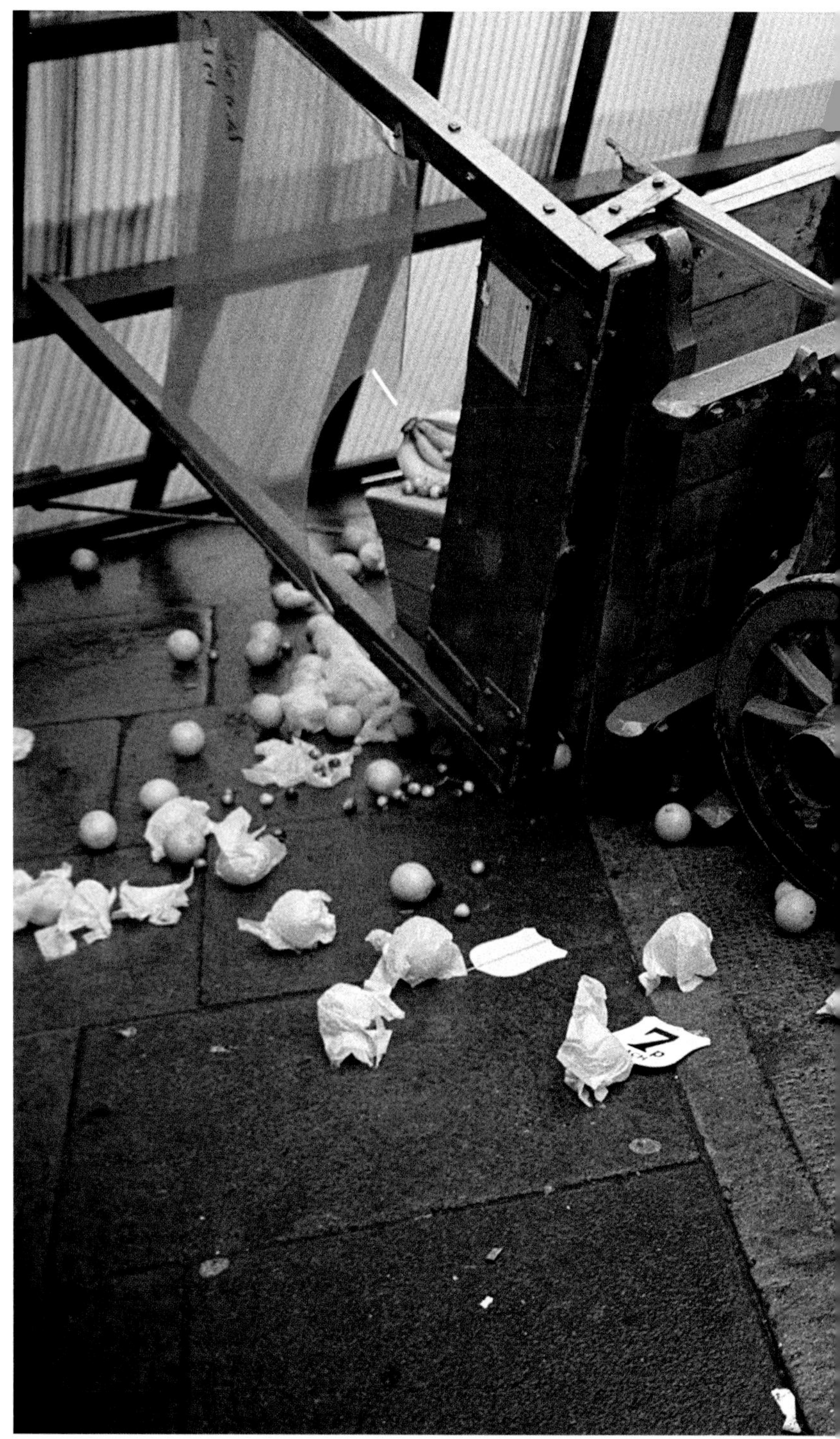

Brick Lane, London E1, 1978

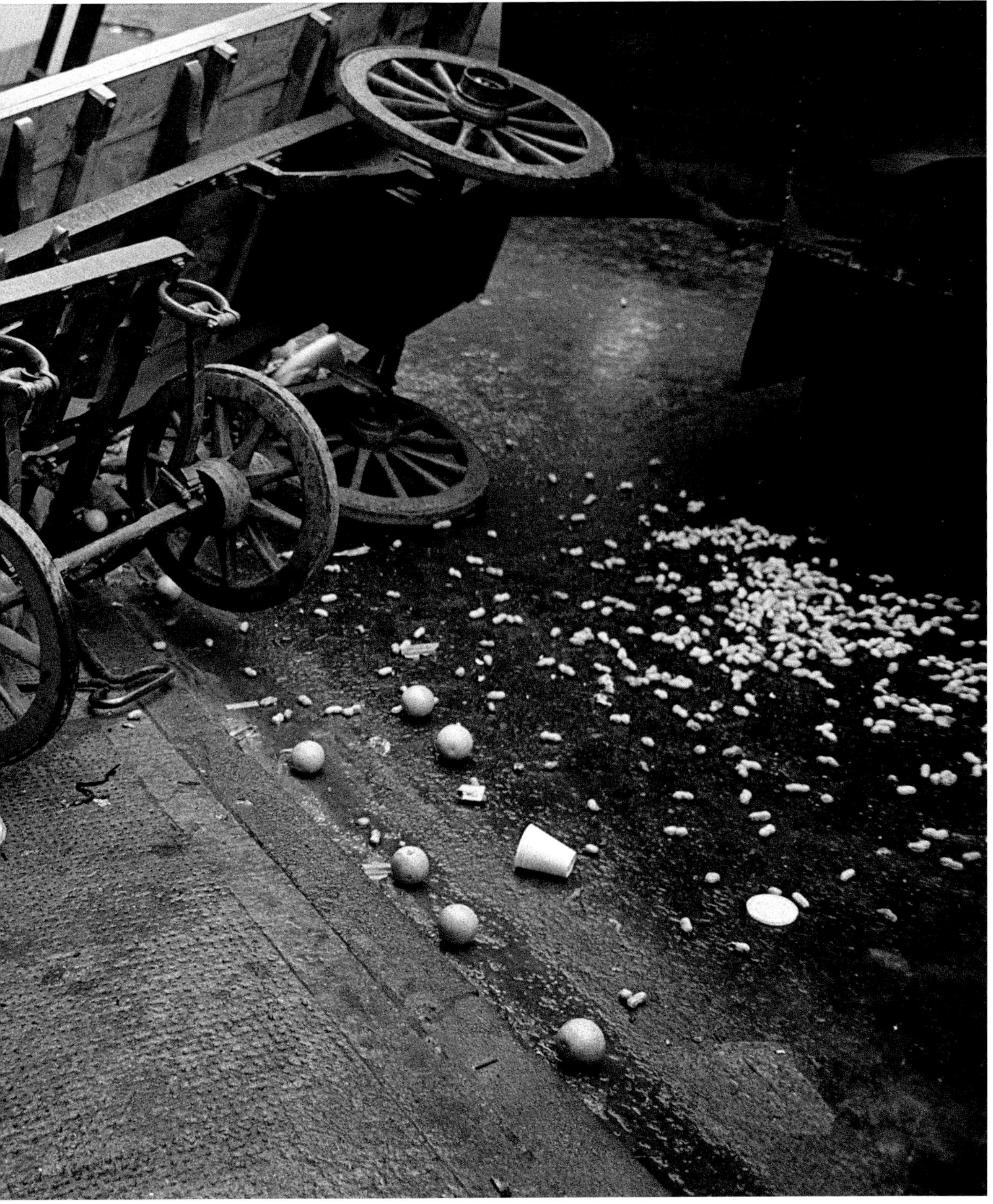

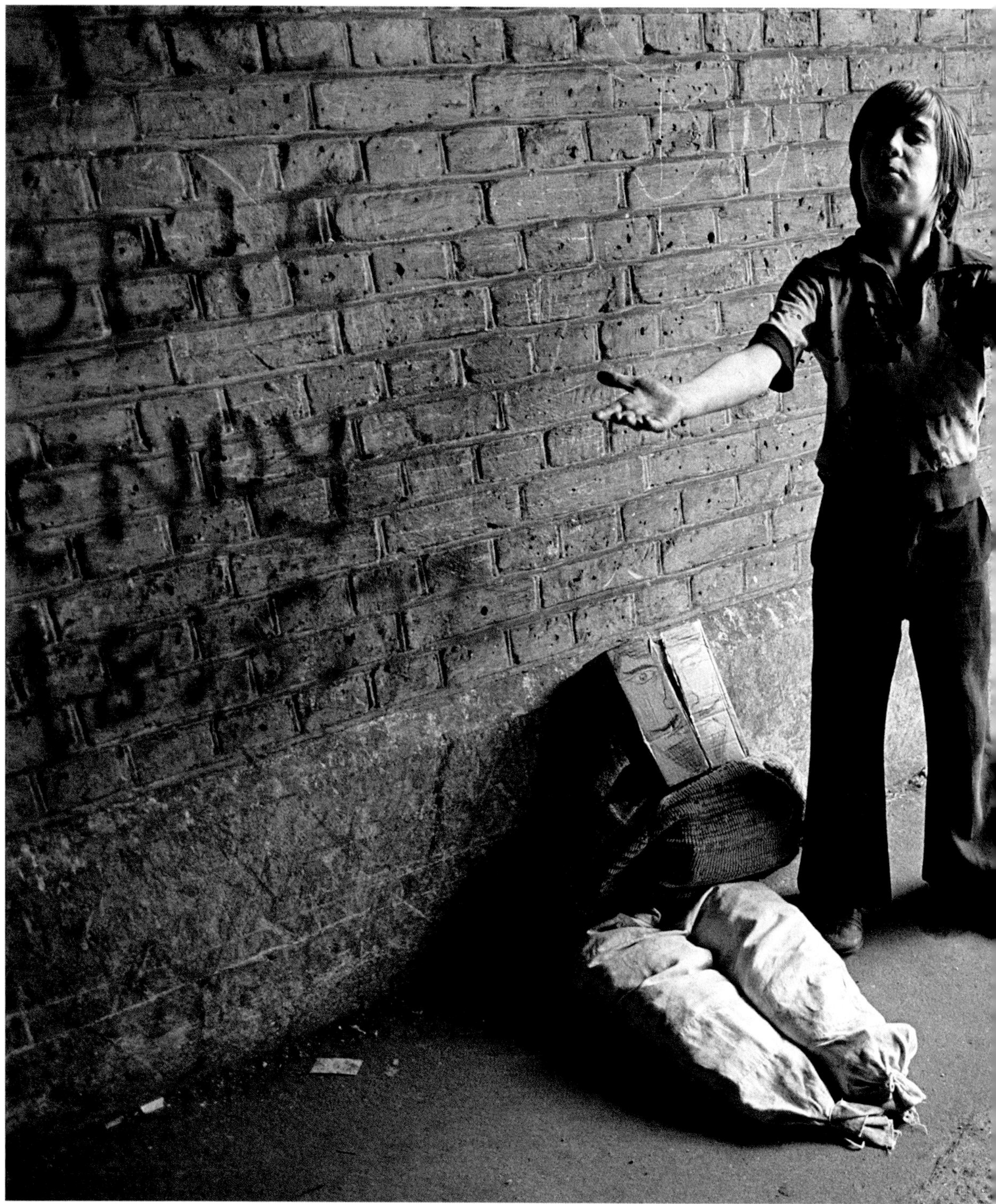

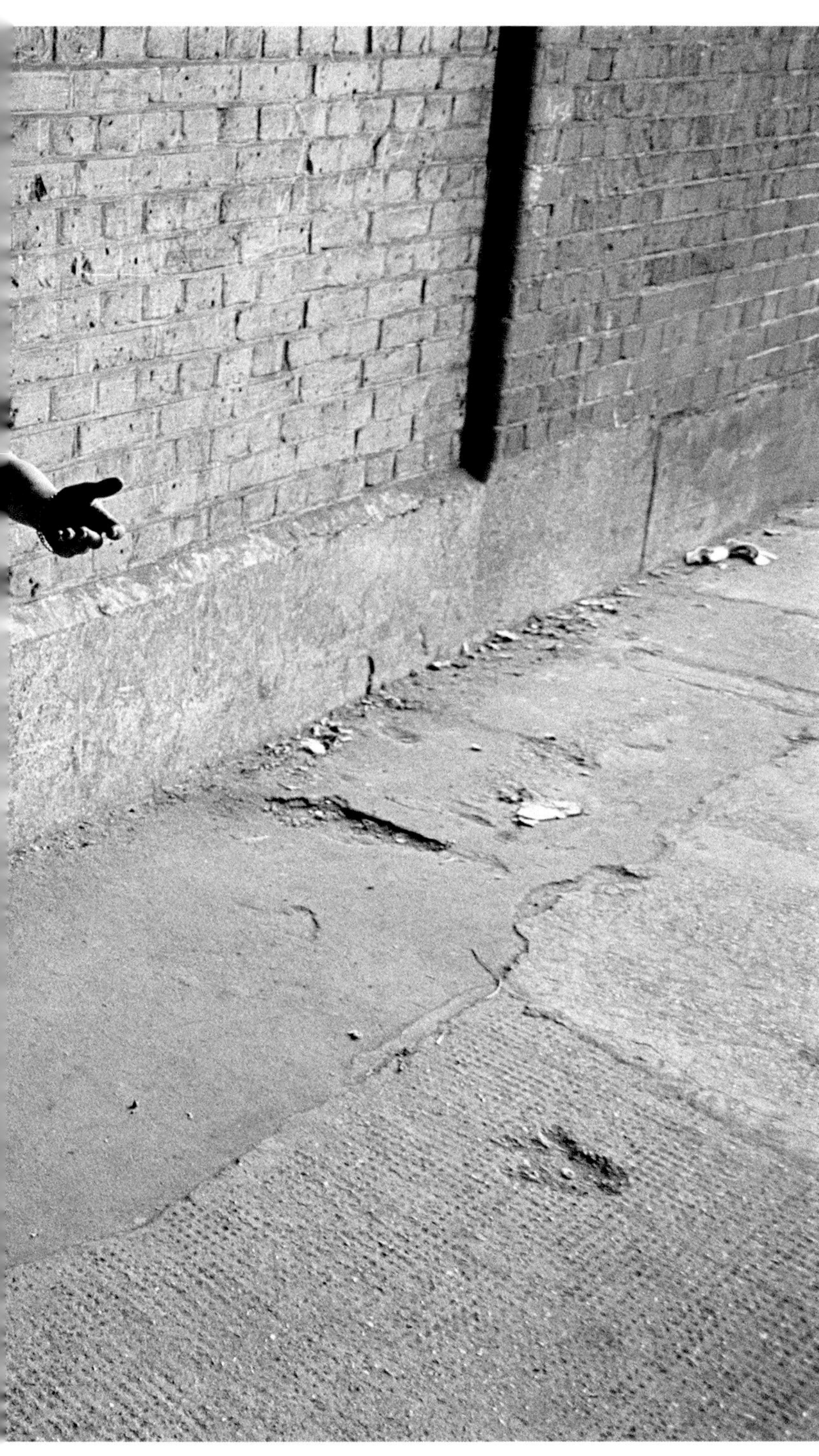

Brick Lane, London E1, 1977

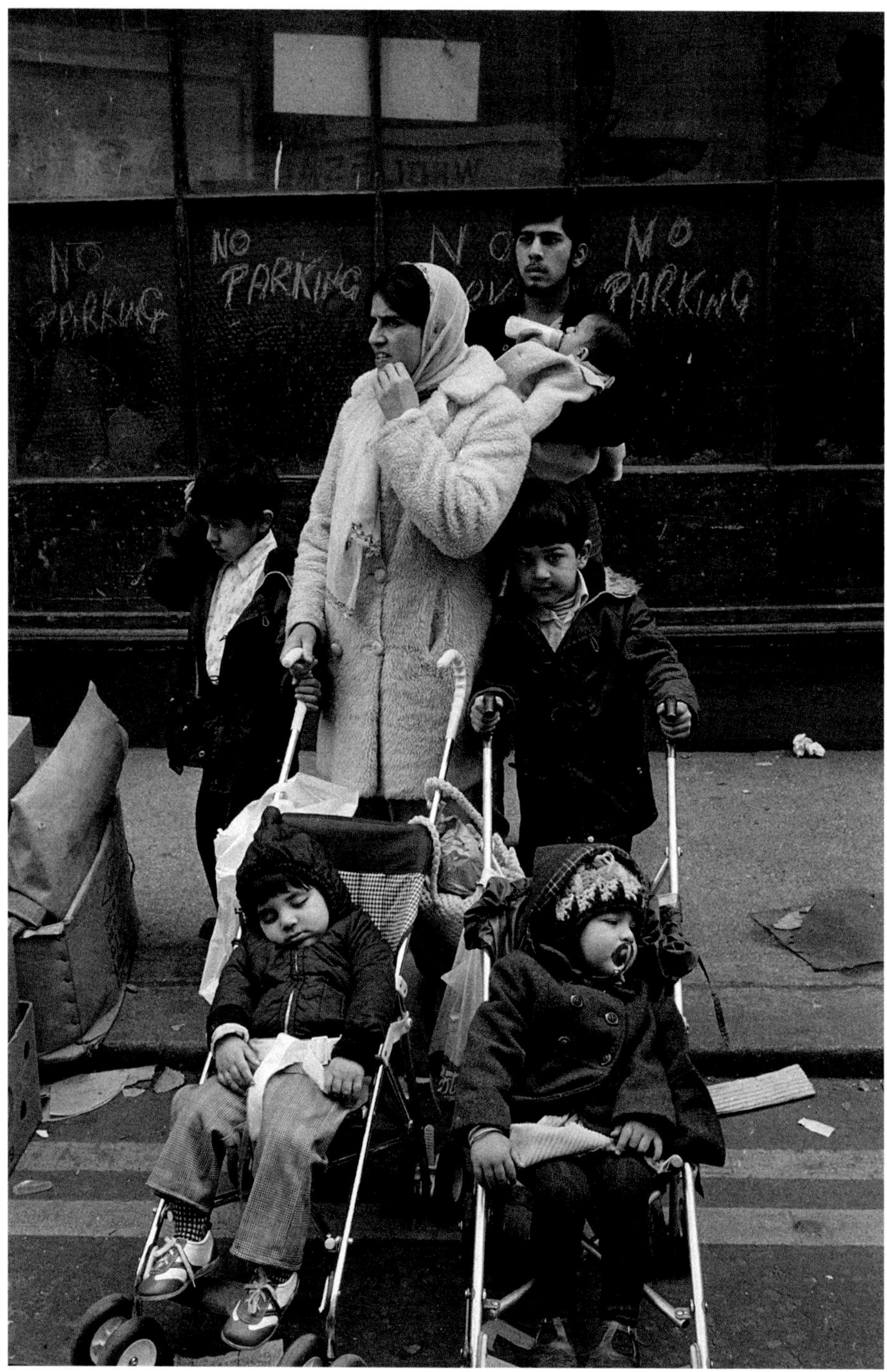

Cheshire Street, London E2, 1983

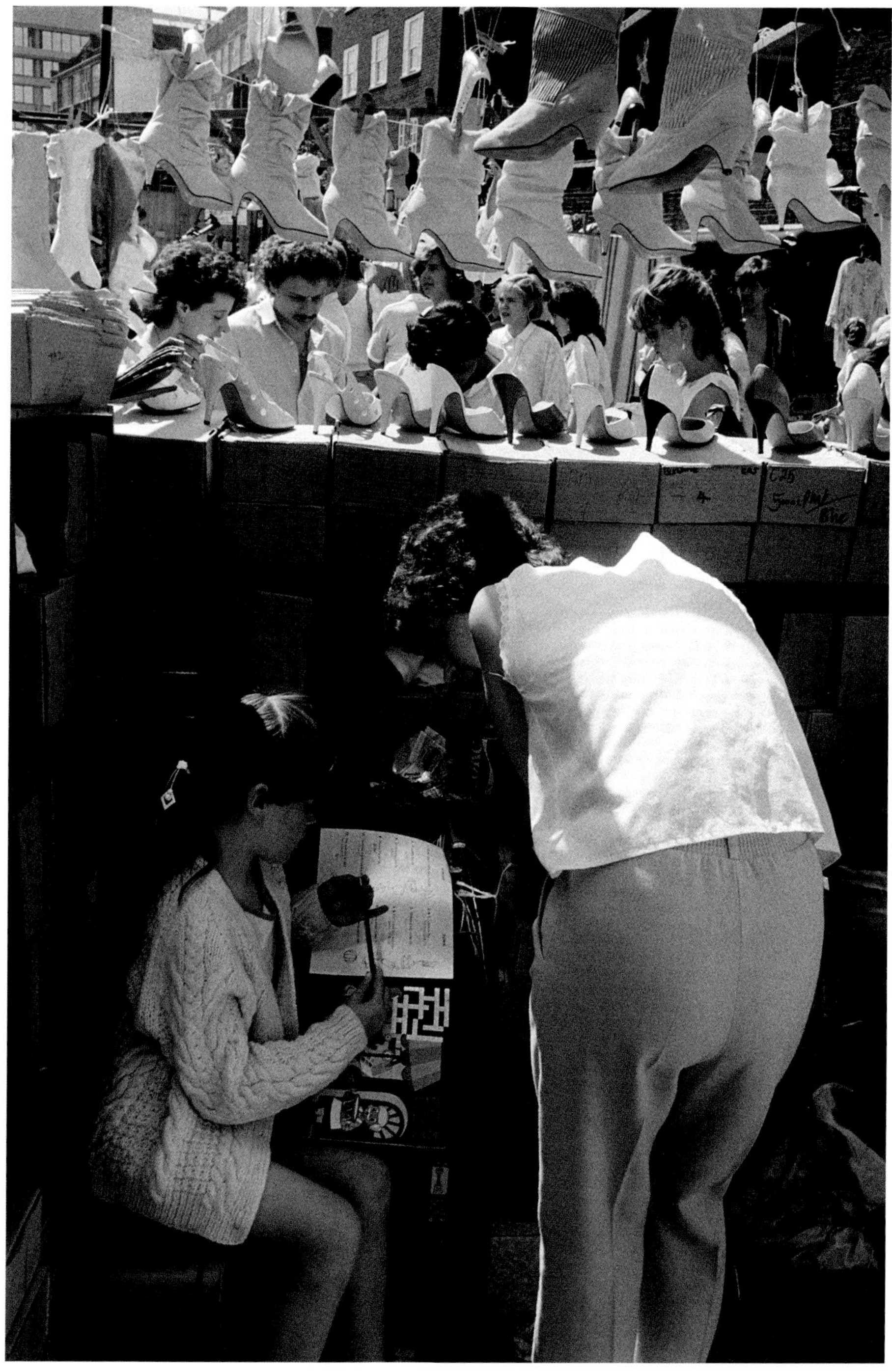

Goulston Street, London E1, 1985

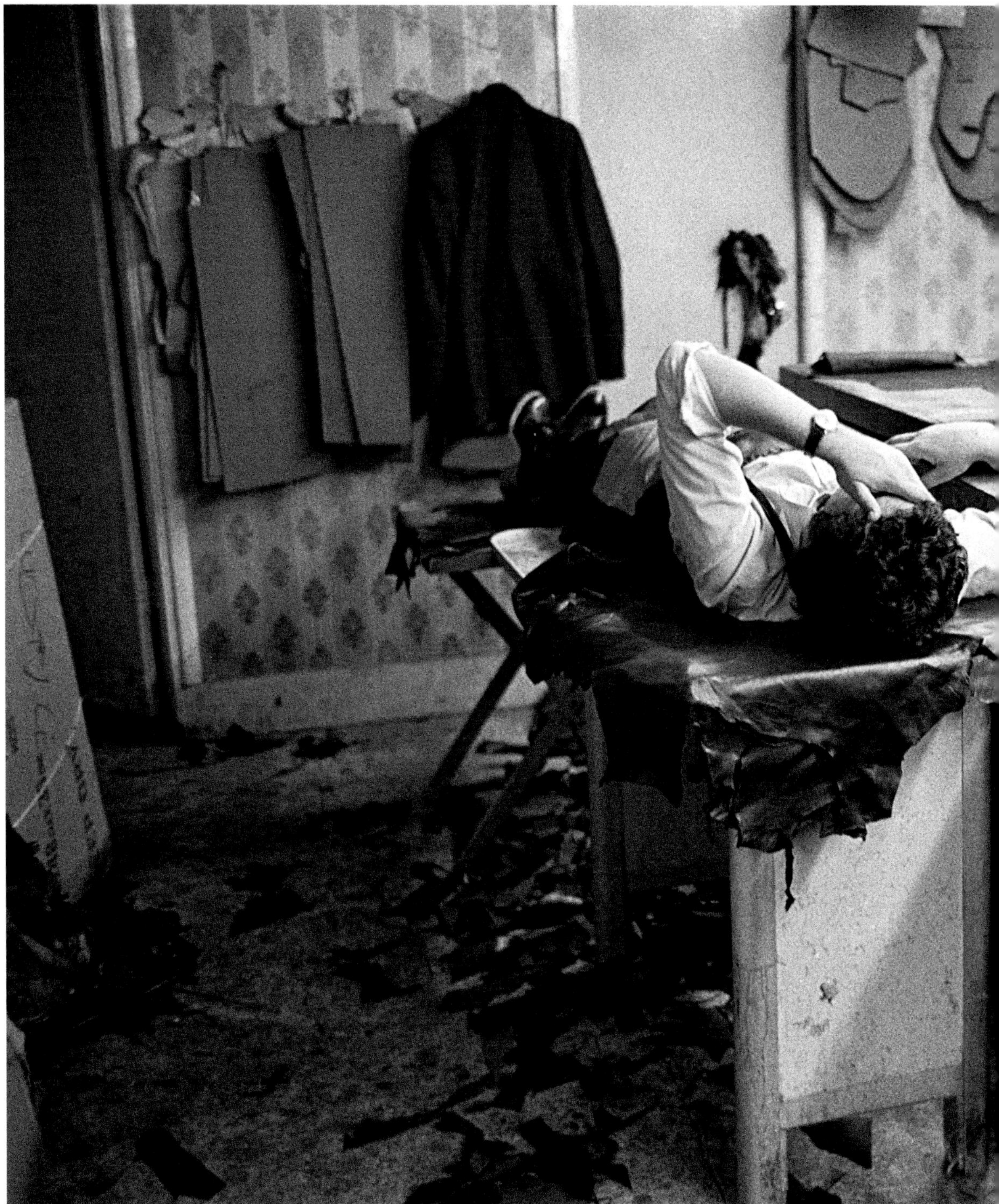

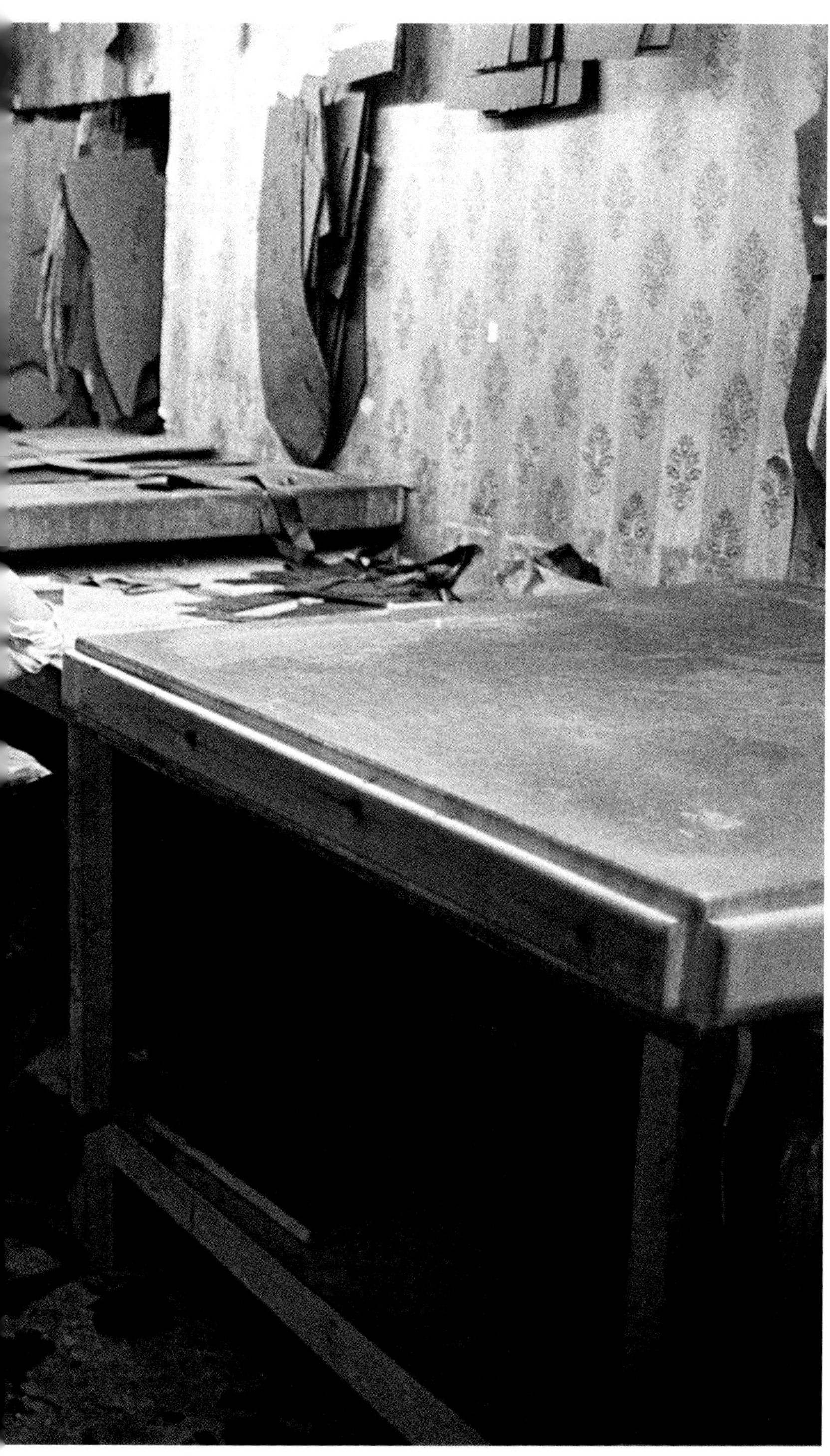

Hanbury Street, London E1, 1978

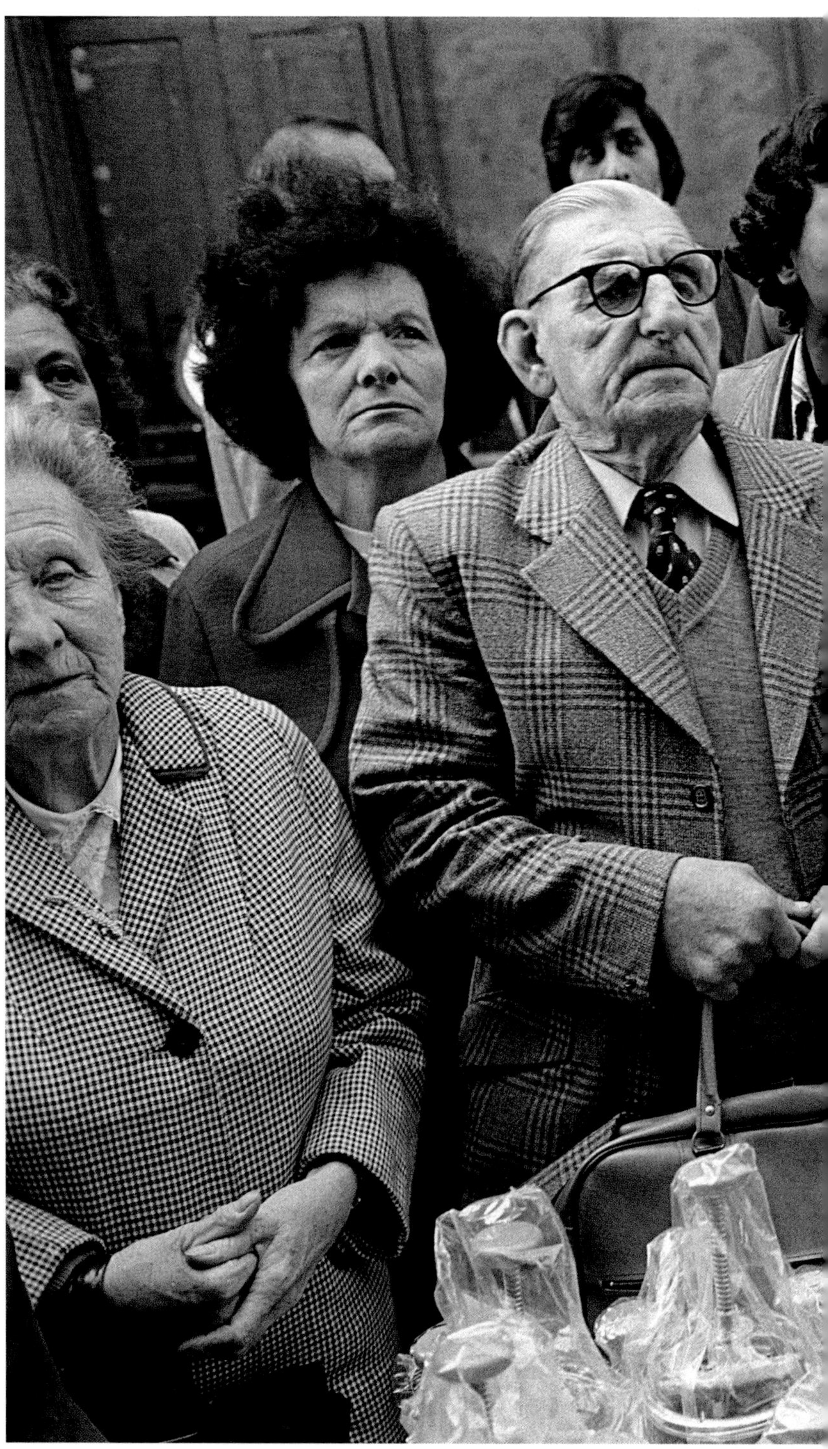

Cheshire Street, London E2, 1978

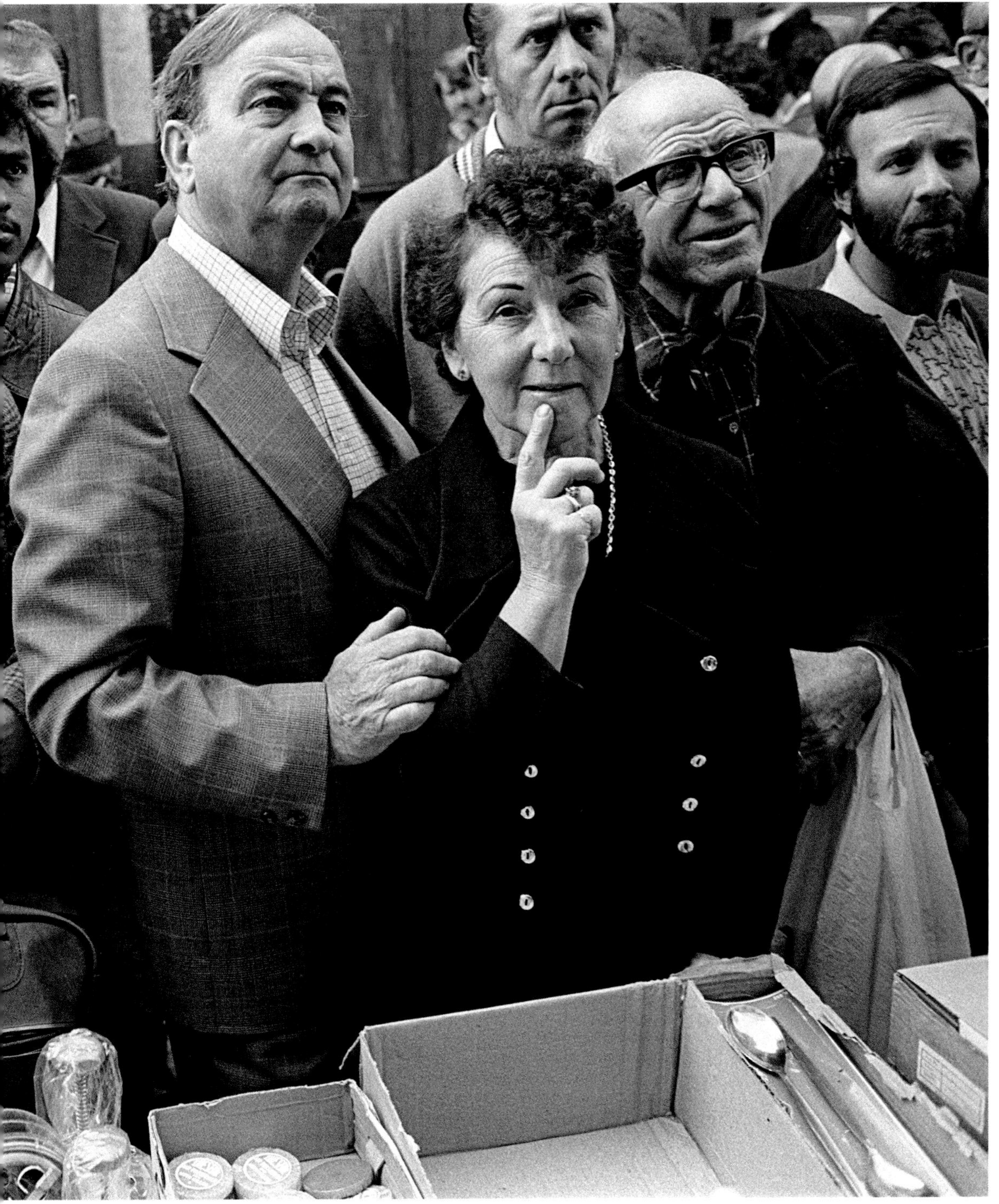

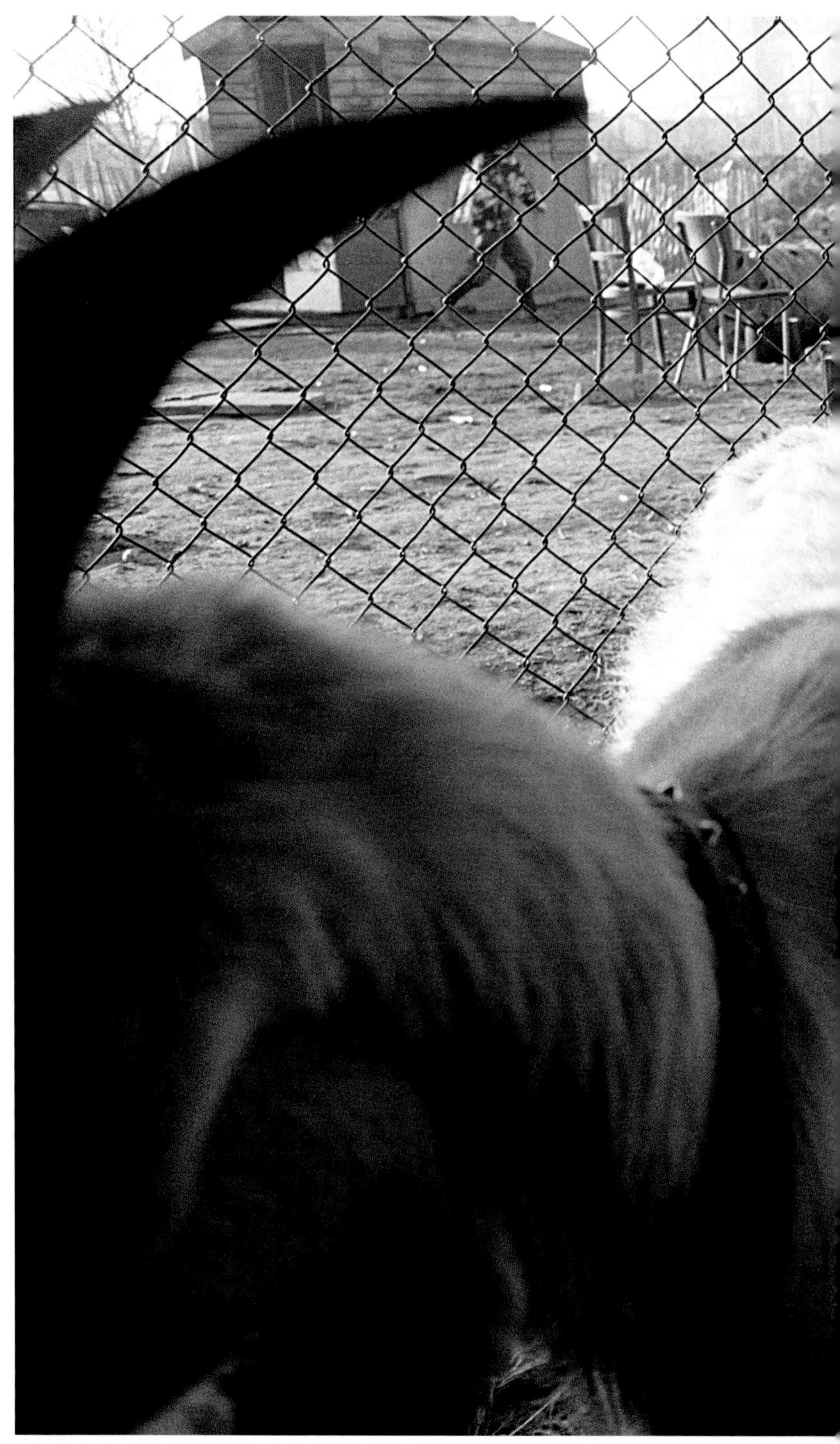

Spitalfields City Farm,
Weaver Street, London E1, 1979

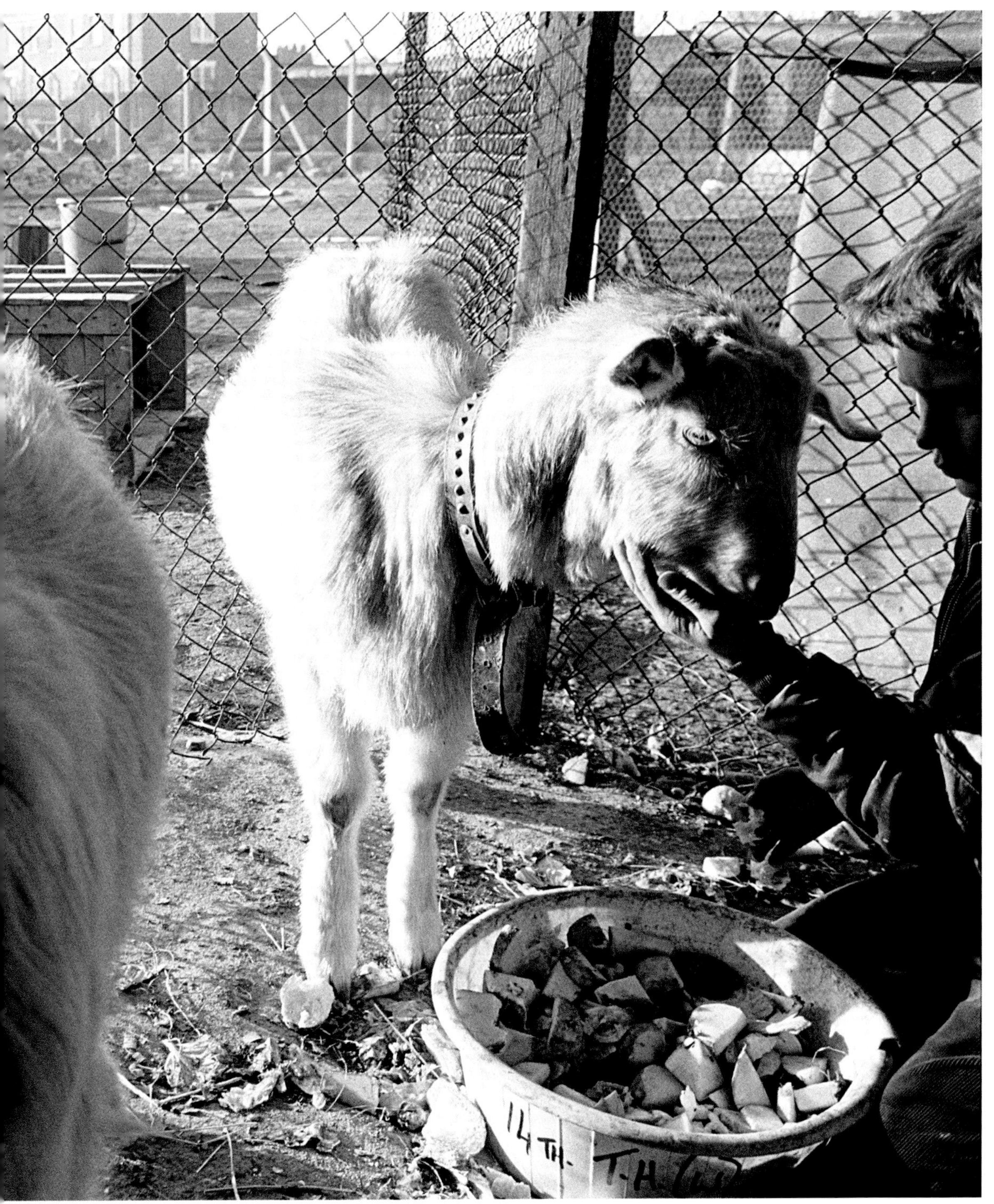

14TH. T.H.

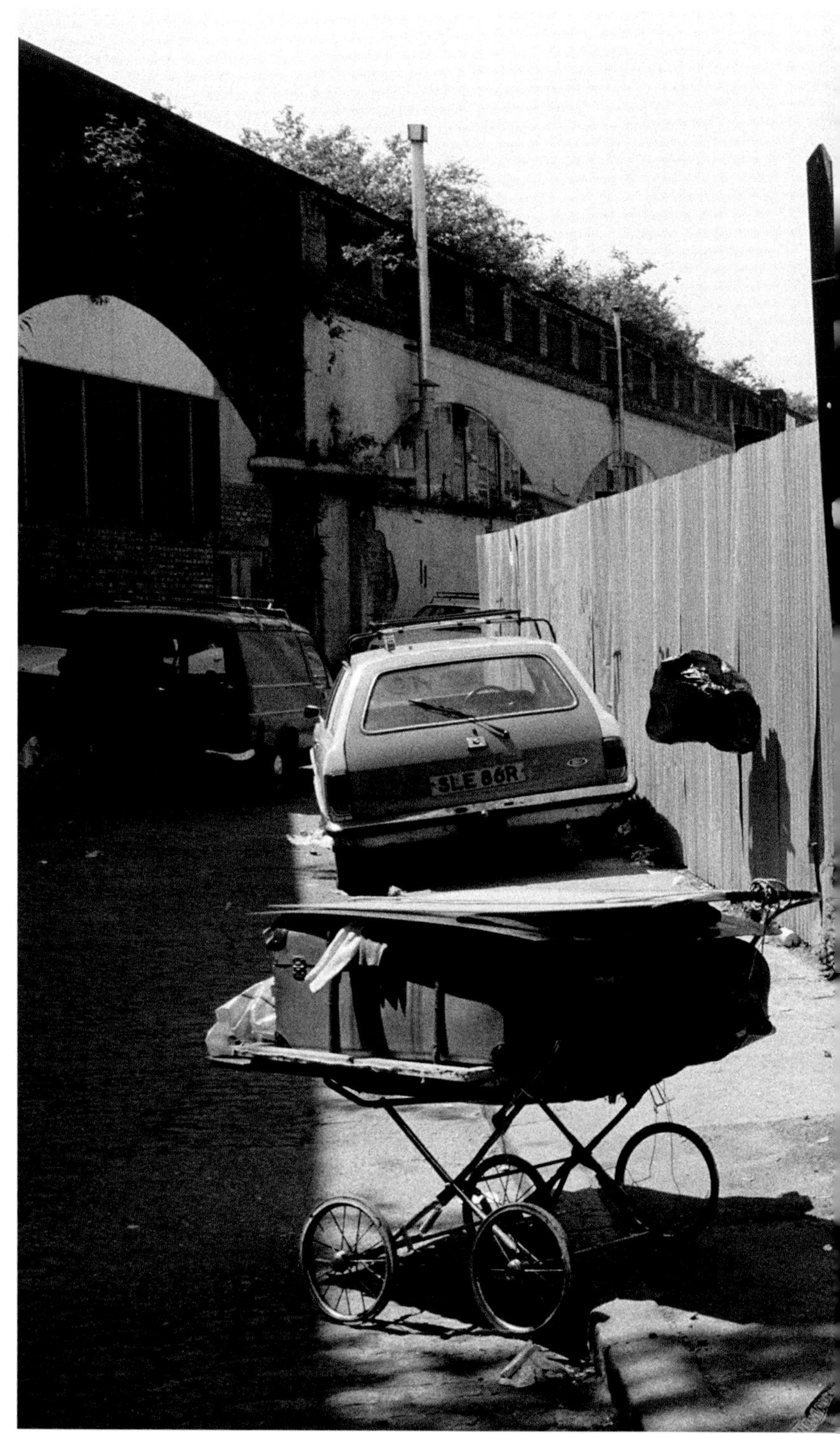

Grimsby Street, London E2, 1985

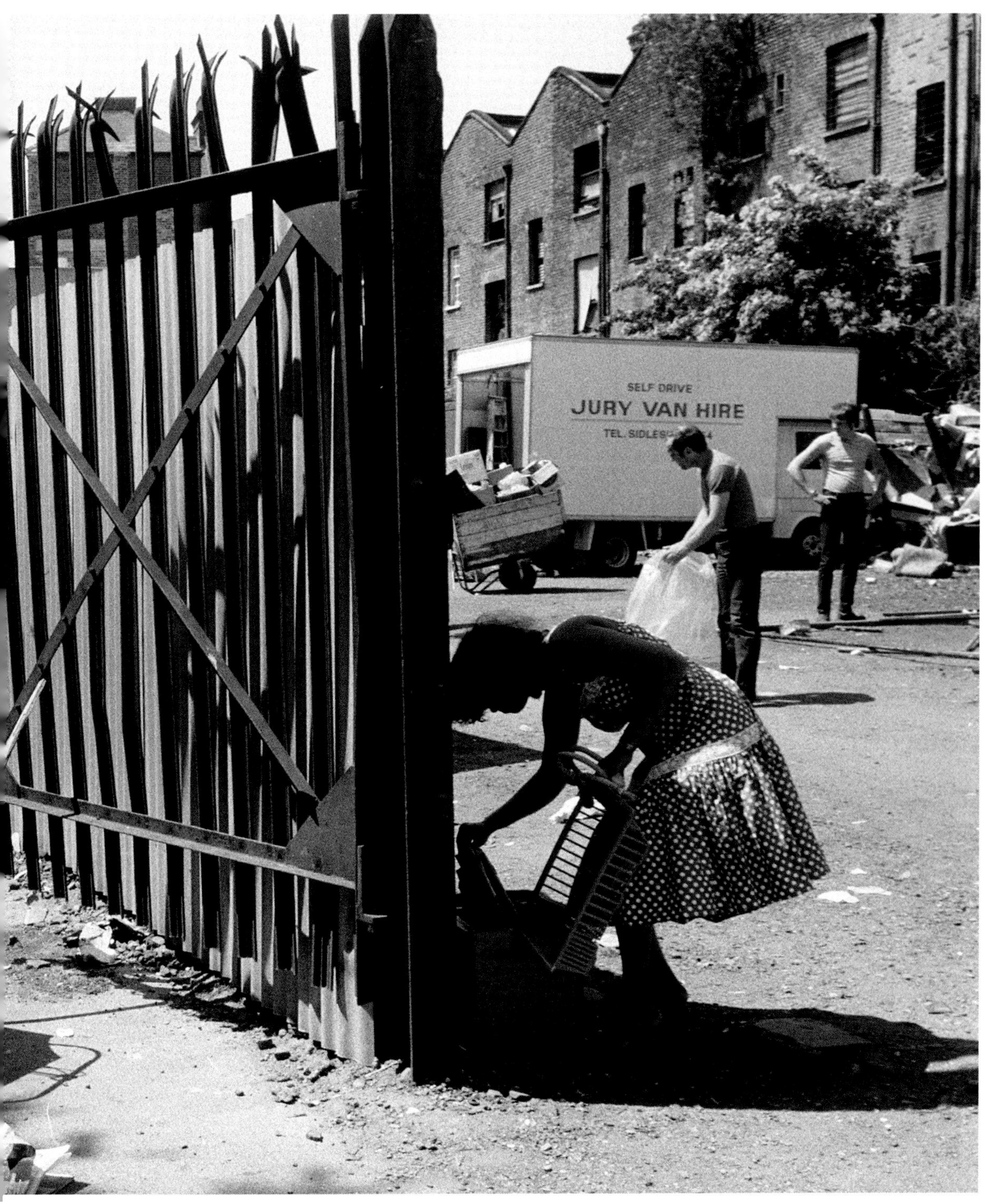
SELF DRIVE
JURY VAN HIRE
TEL. SIDLES

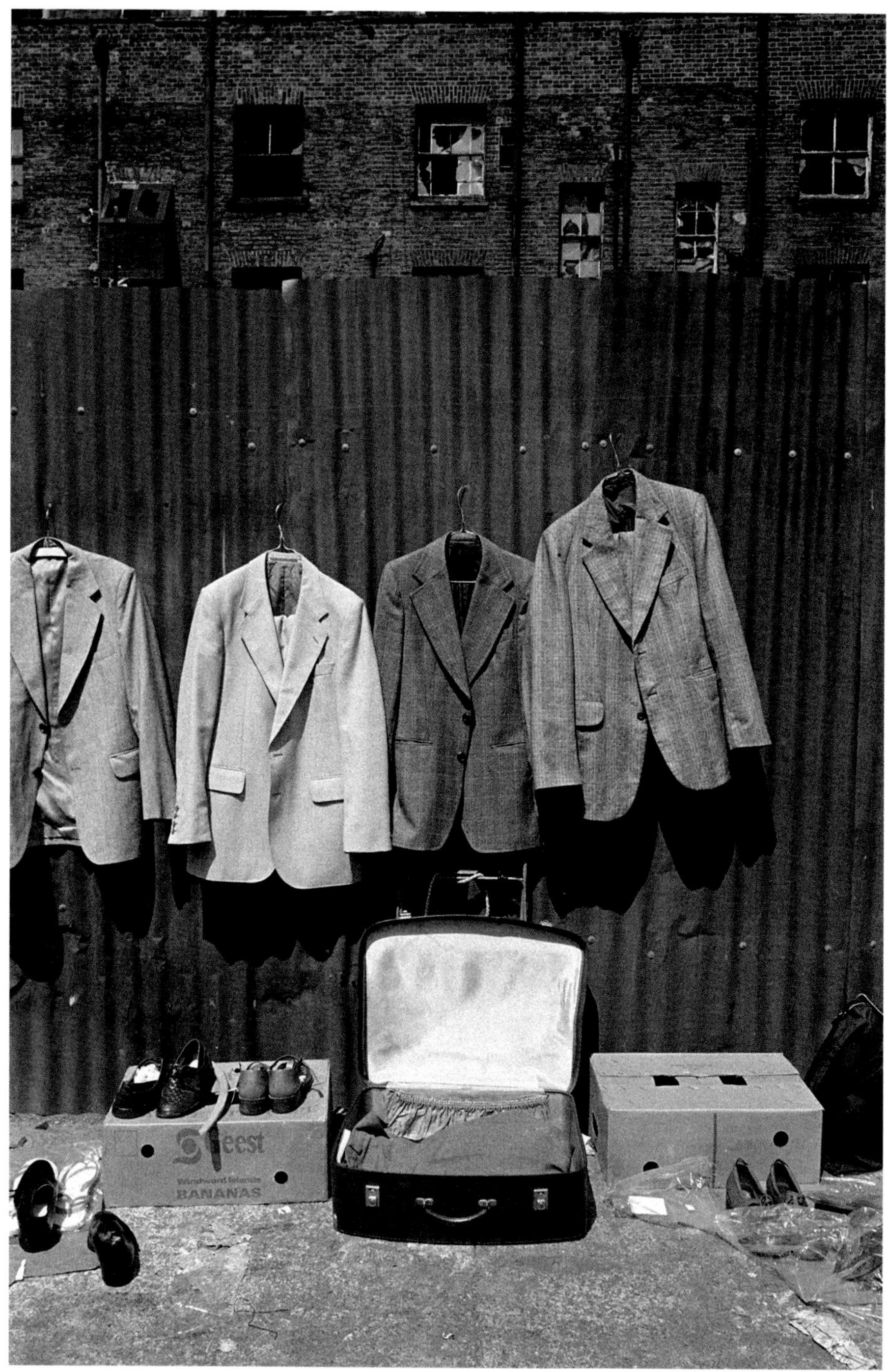

Grimsby Street, London E2, 1987

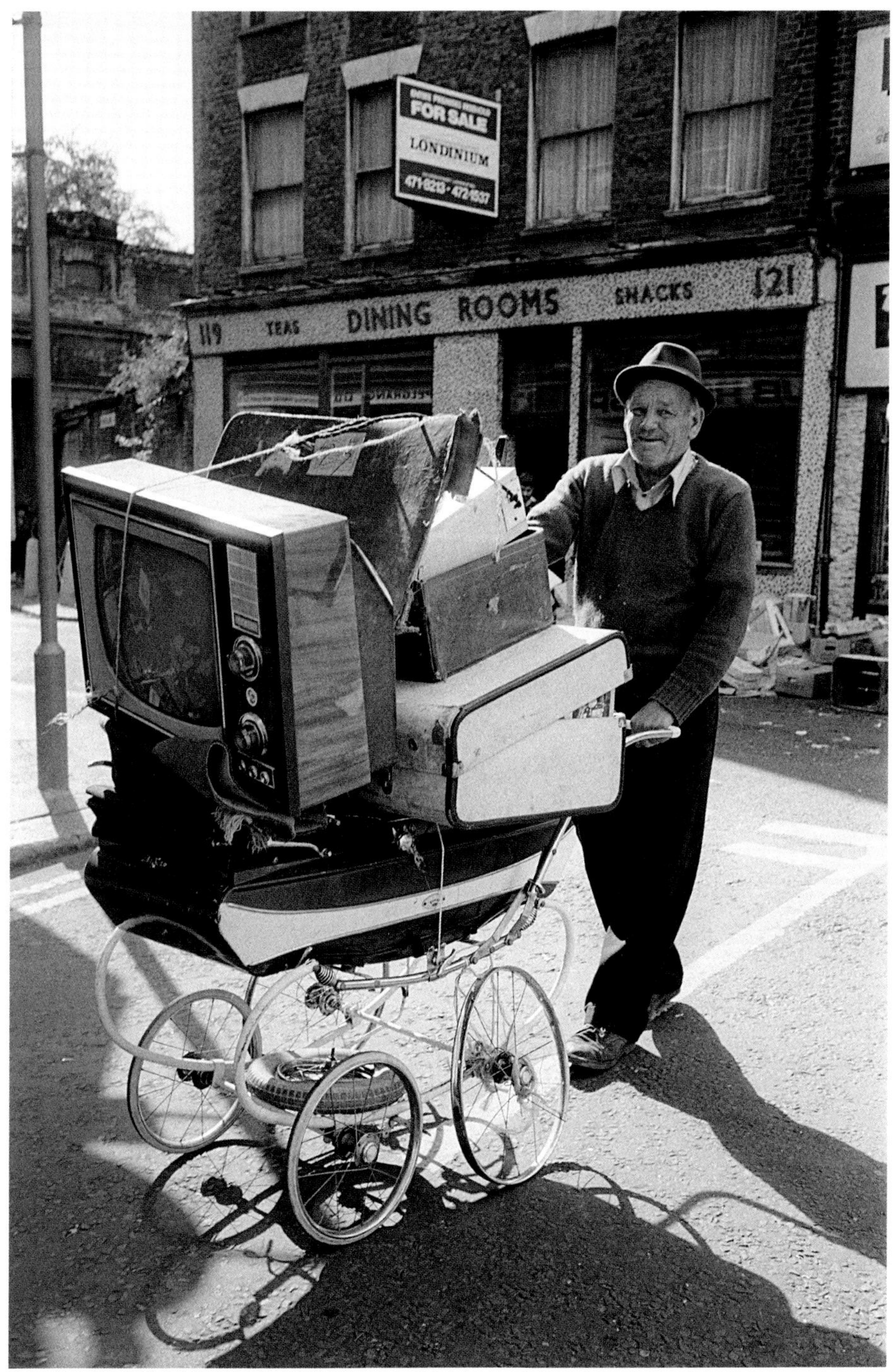

Cheshire Street, London E2, 1981

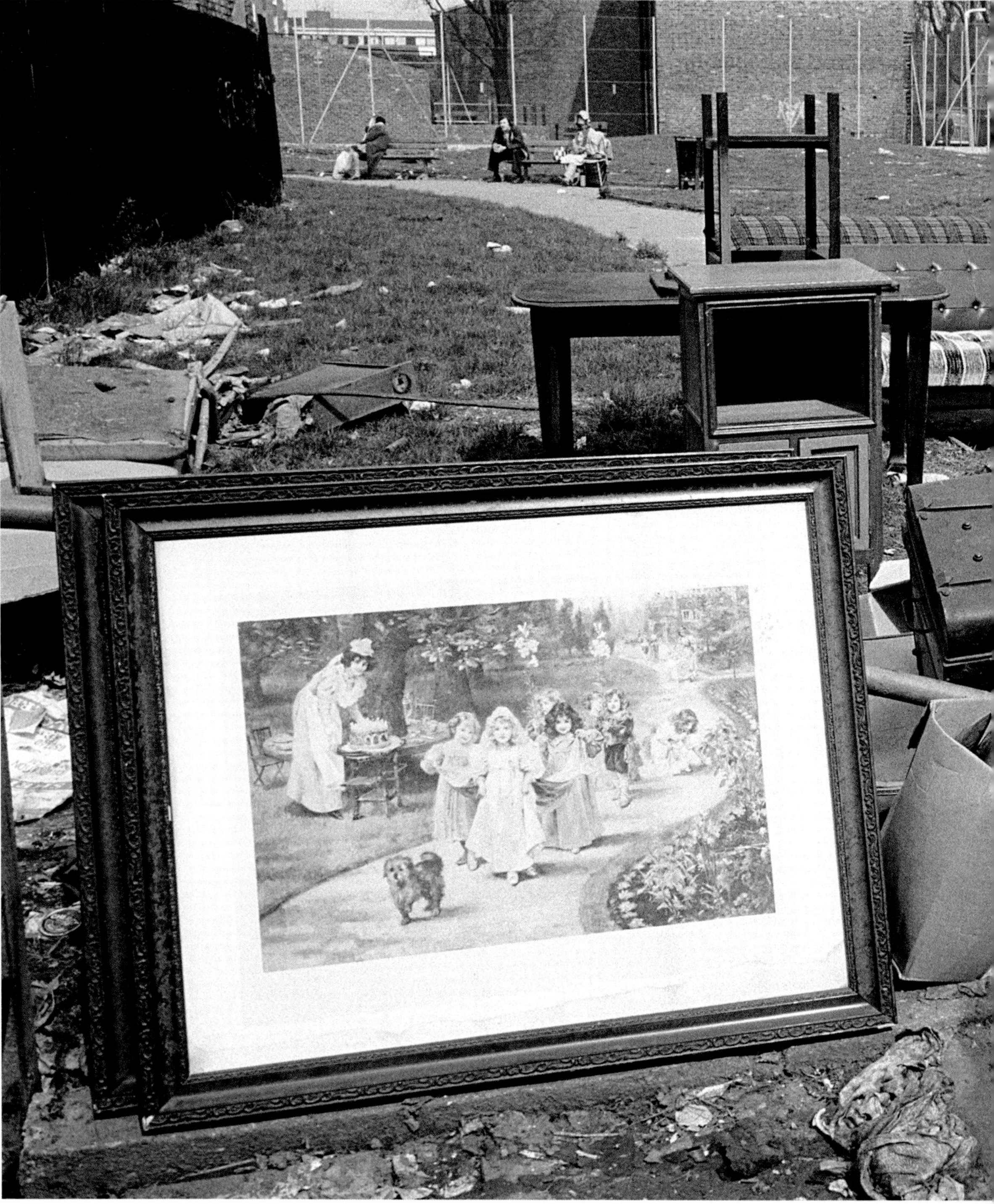

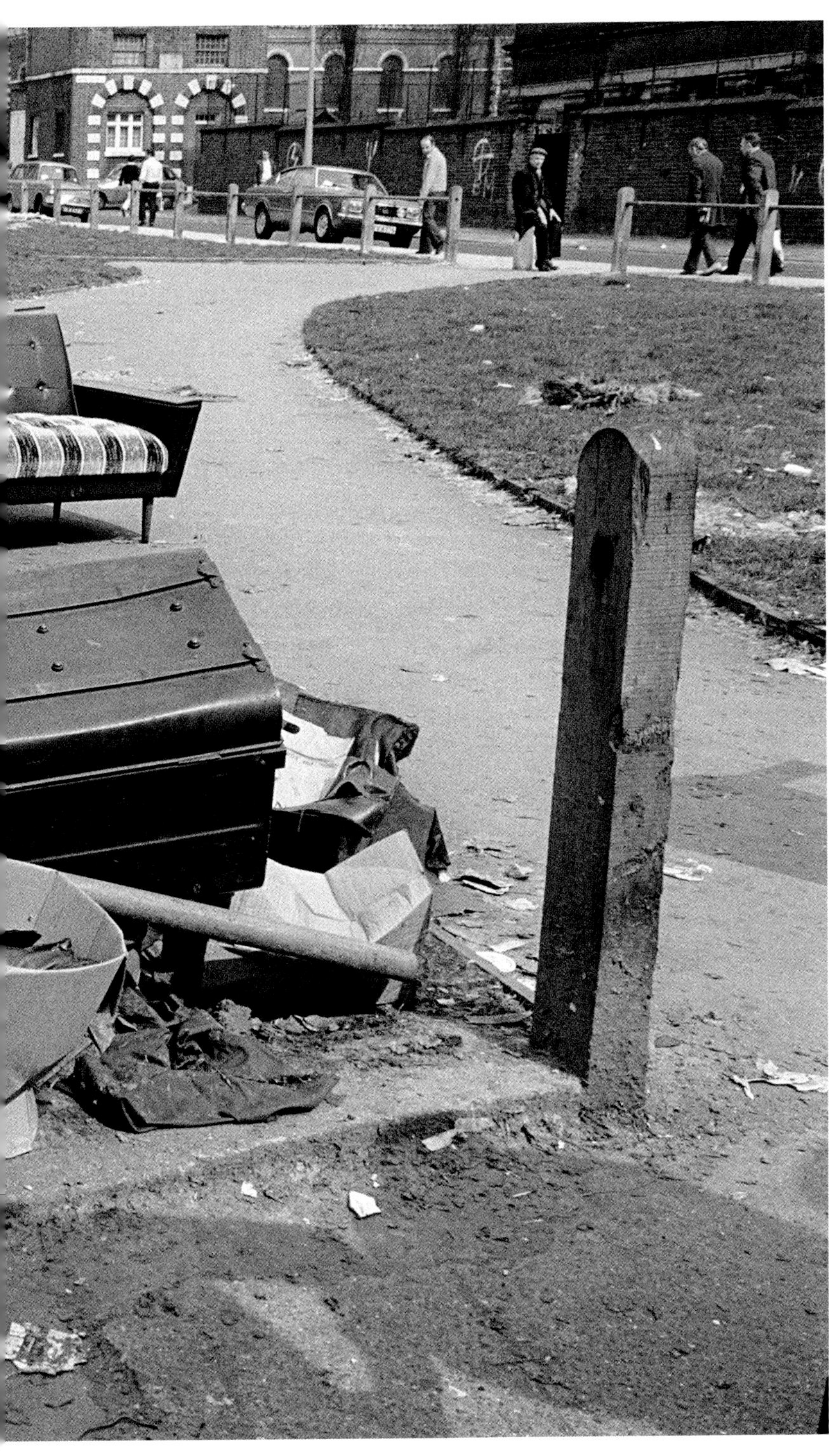

Cheshire Street, London E2, 1979

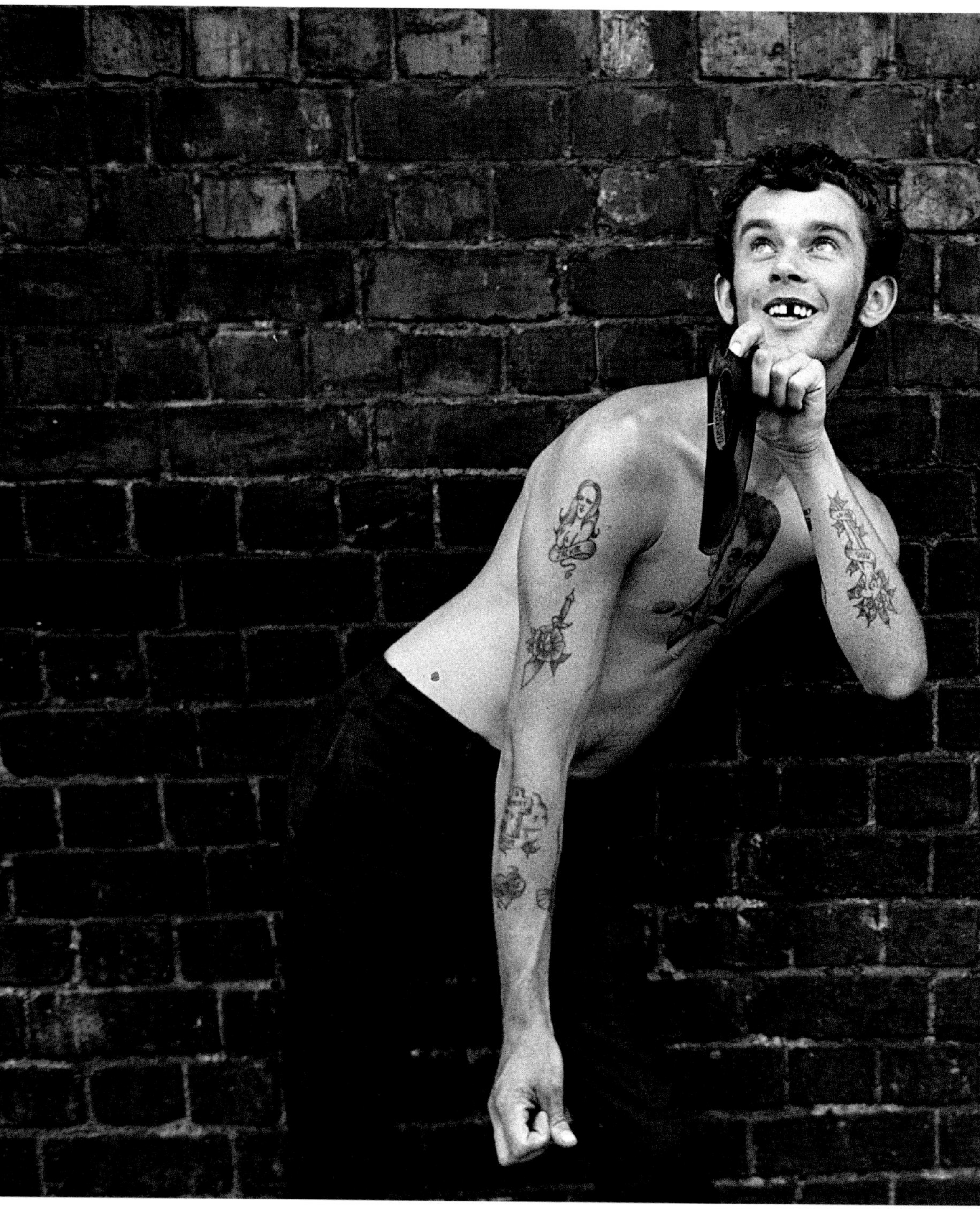

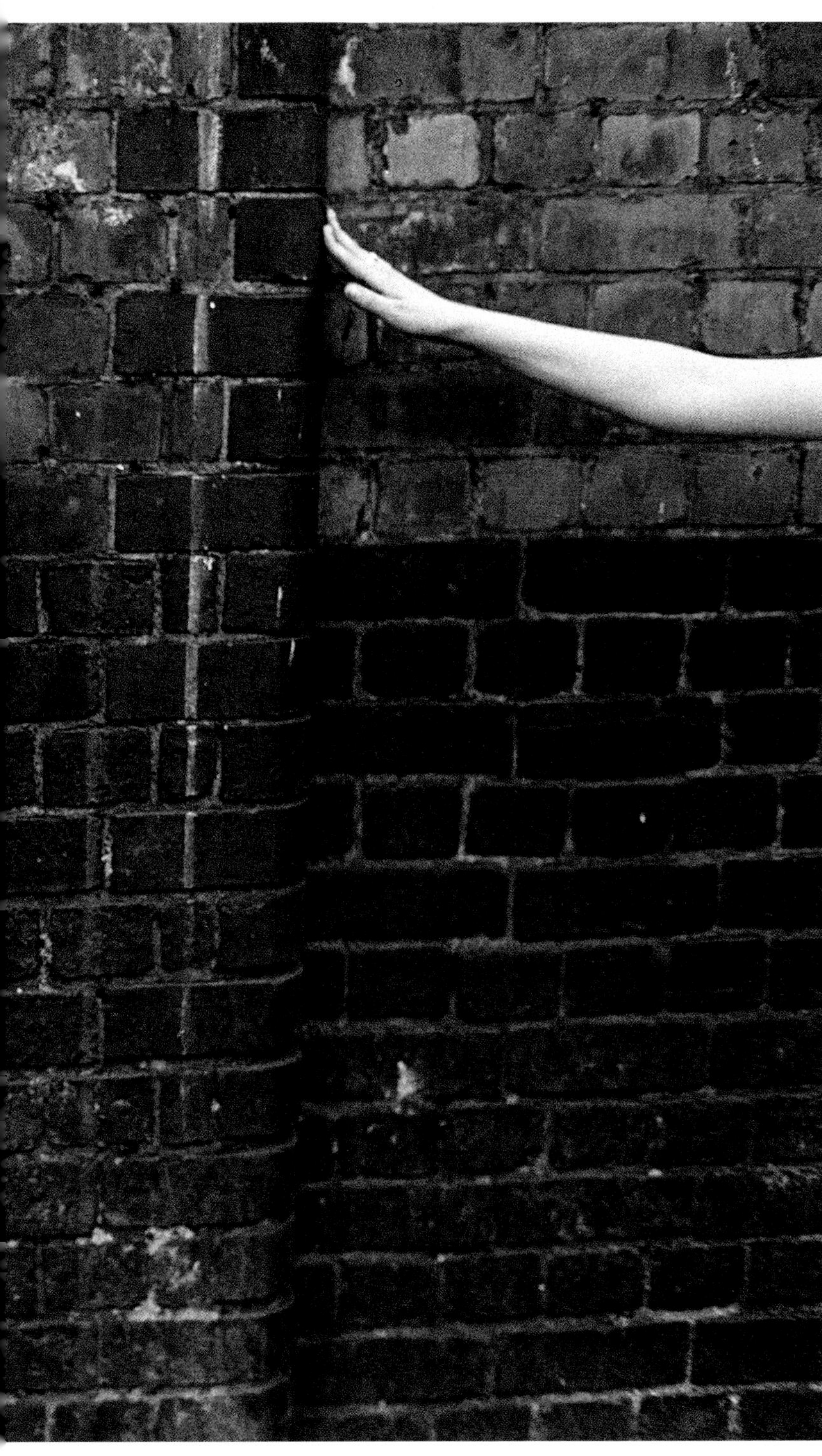

Sclater Street, London E1, 1977

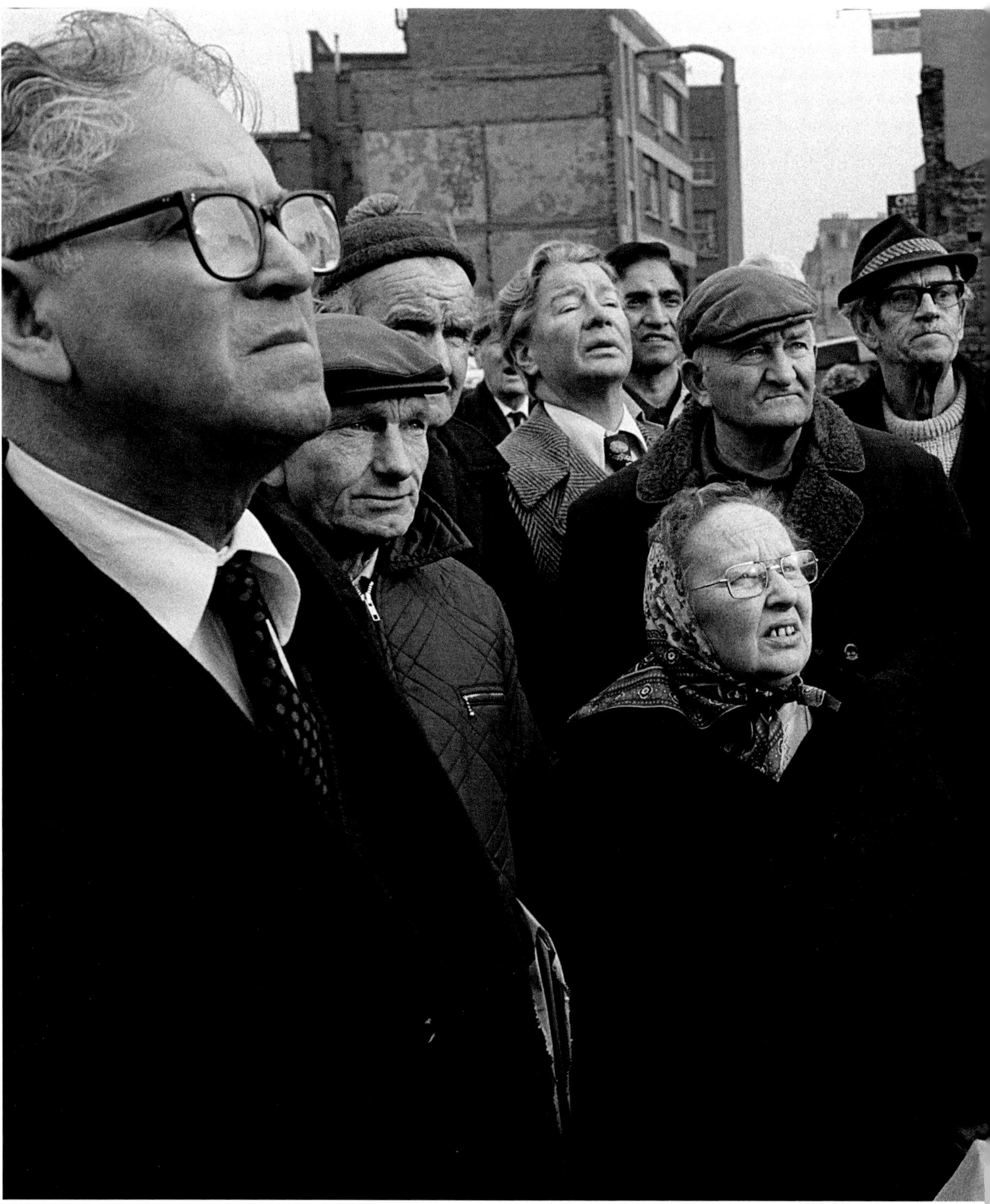

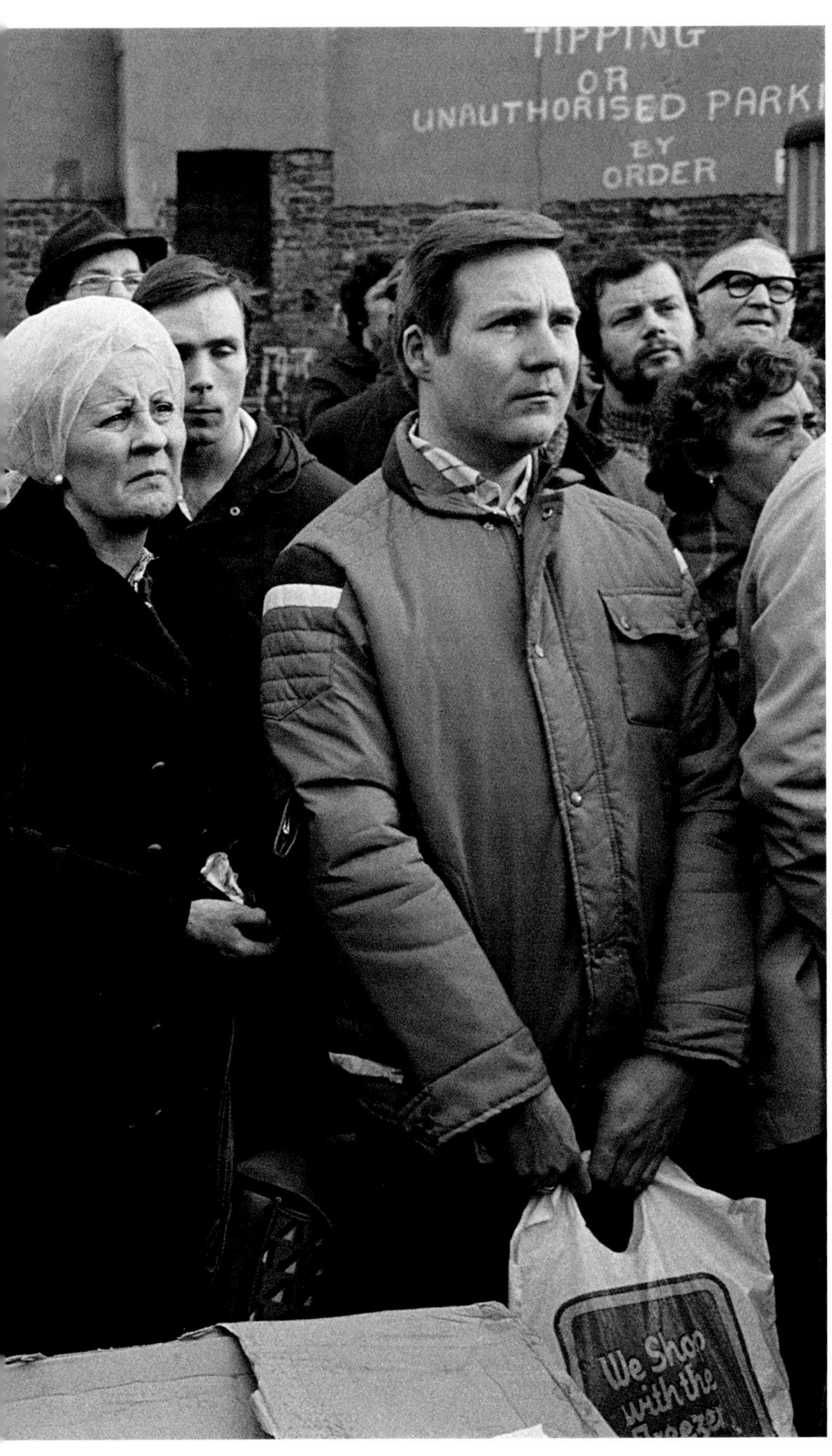

Cygnet Street, London E1, 1980

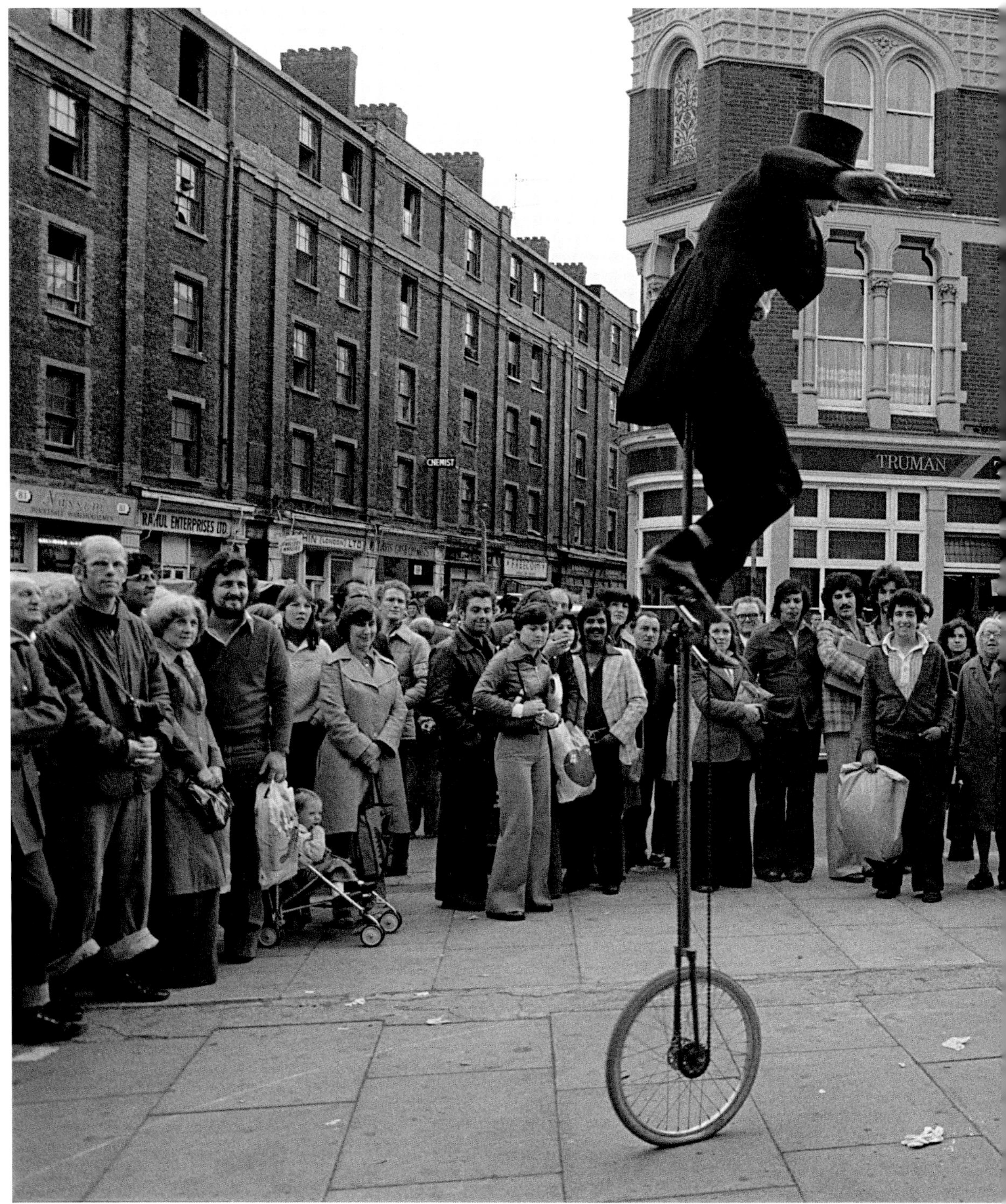

CHEMIST
TRUMAN
Nasseri
RAHUL ENTERPRISES LTD.

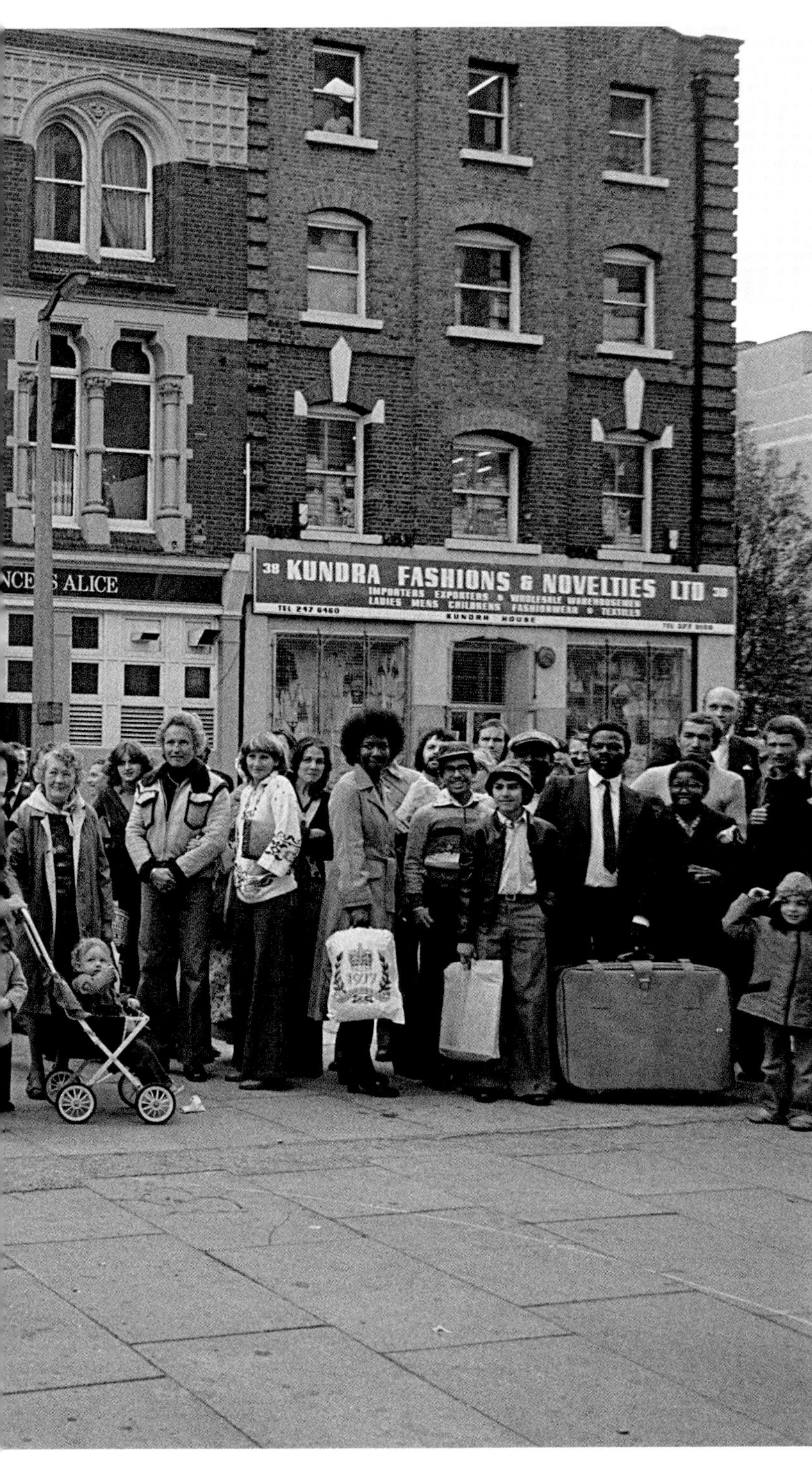

Commercial Street,
London E1, 1977

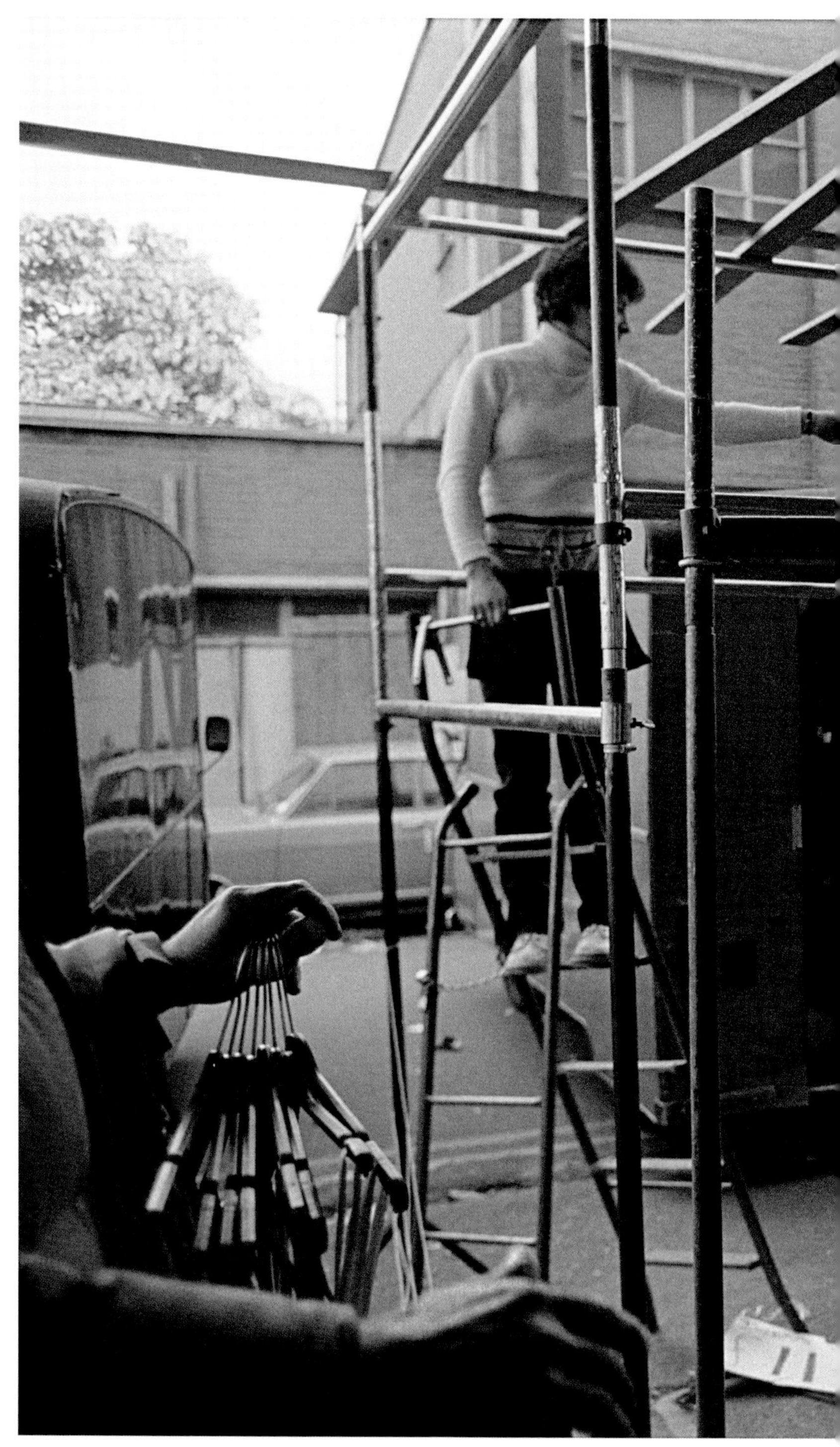

Goulston Street, London E1, 1980

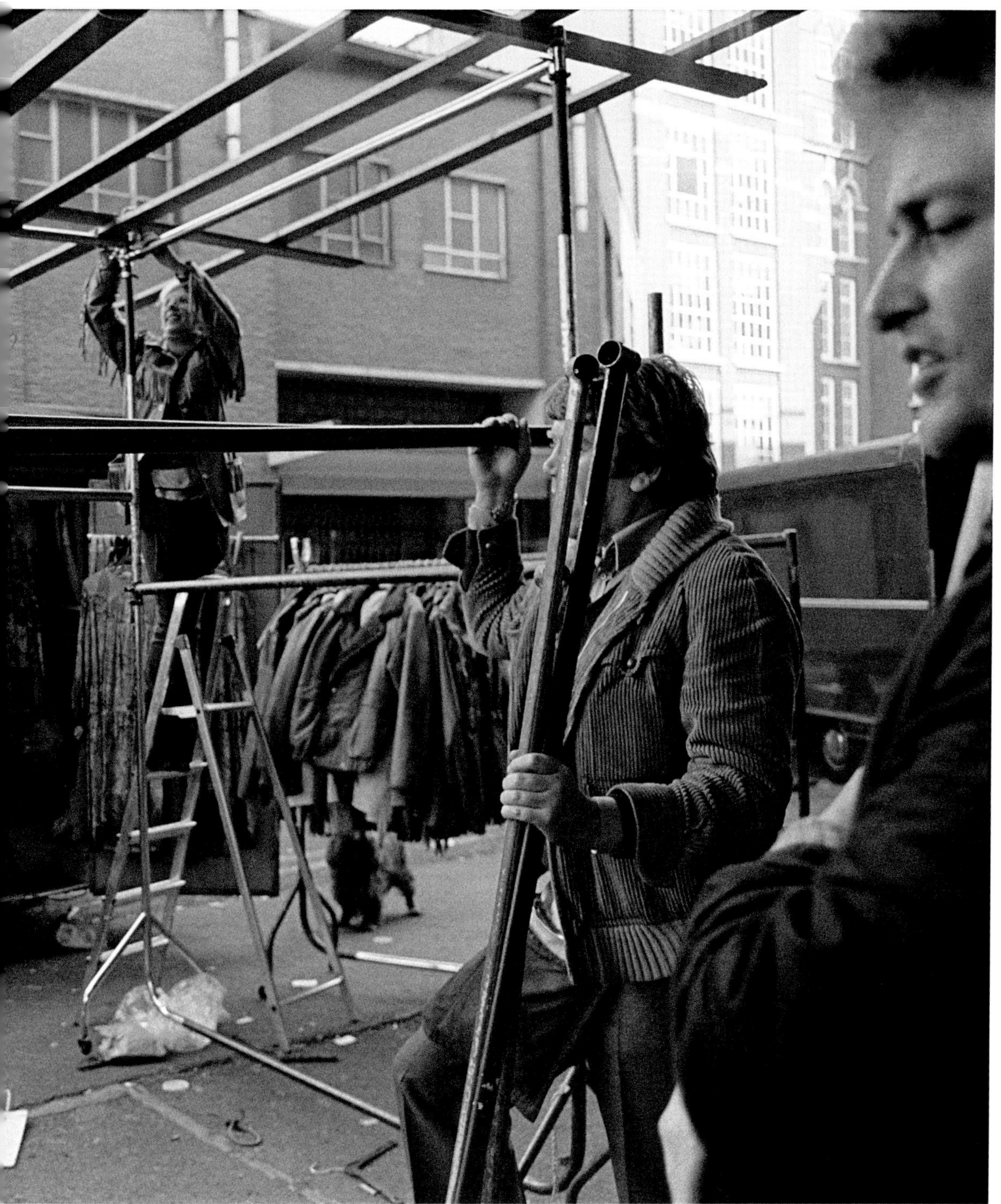

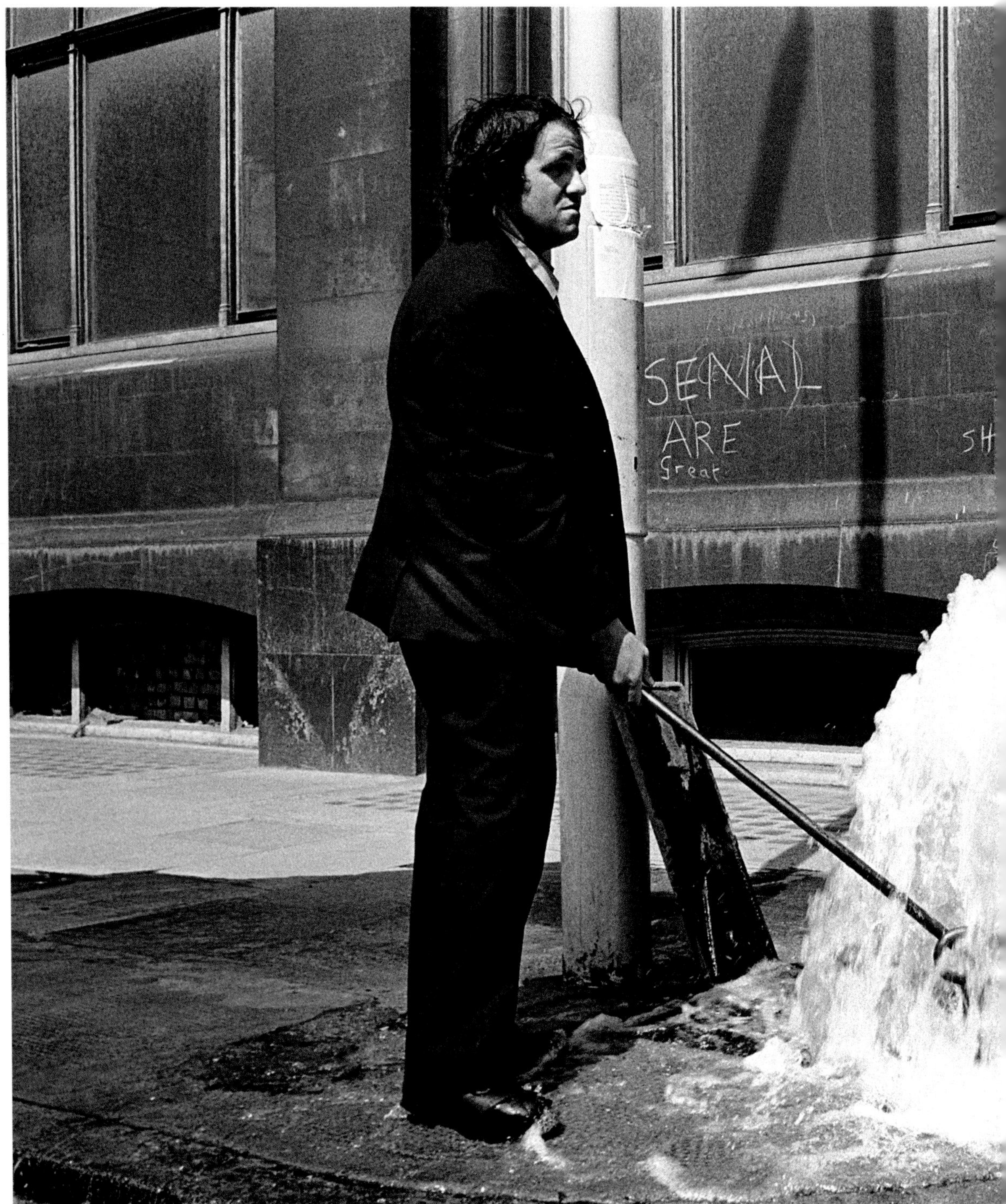
SENAL
ARE
Great
SH

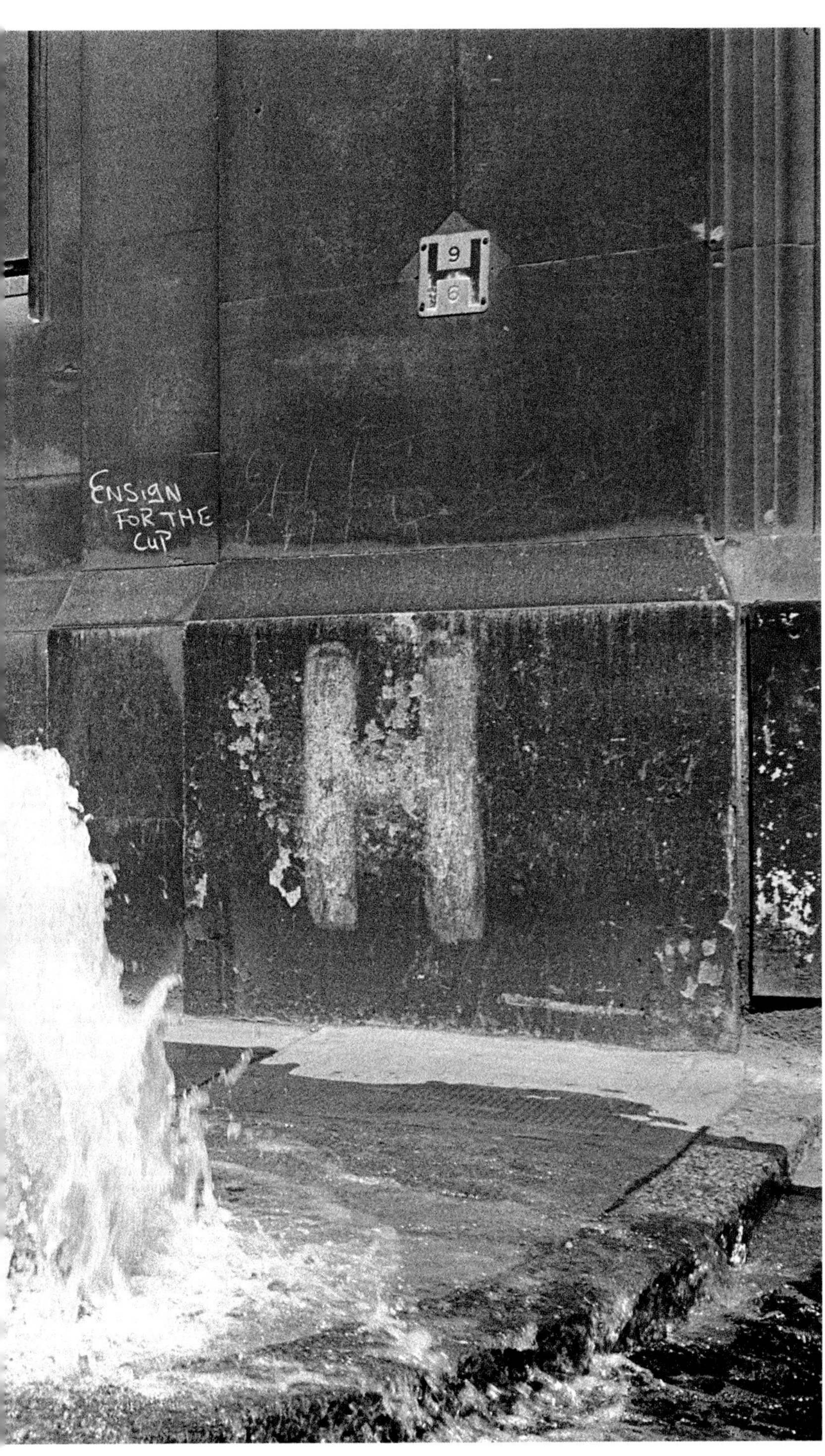

Leman Street, London E1, 1975

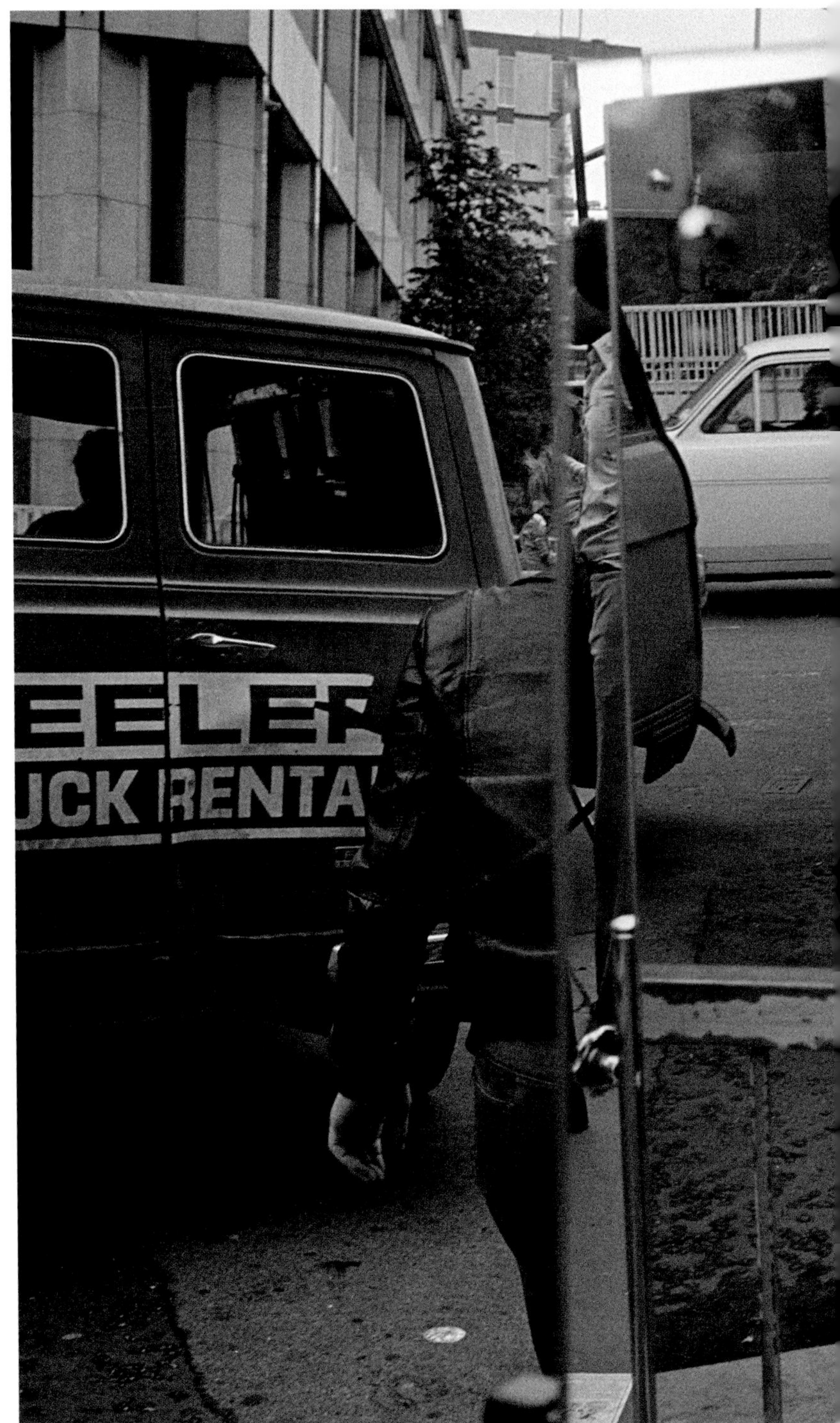

Middlesex Street and
St Botolph Street, London E1, 1977

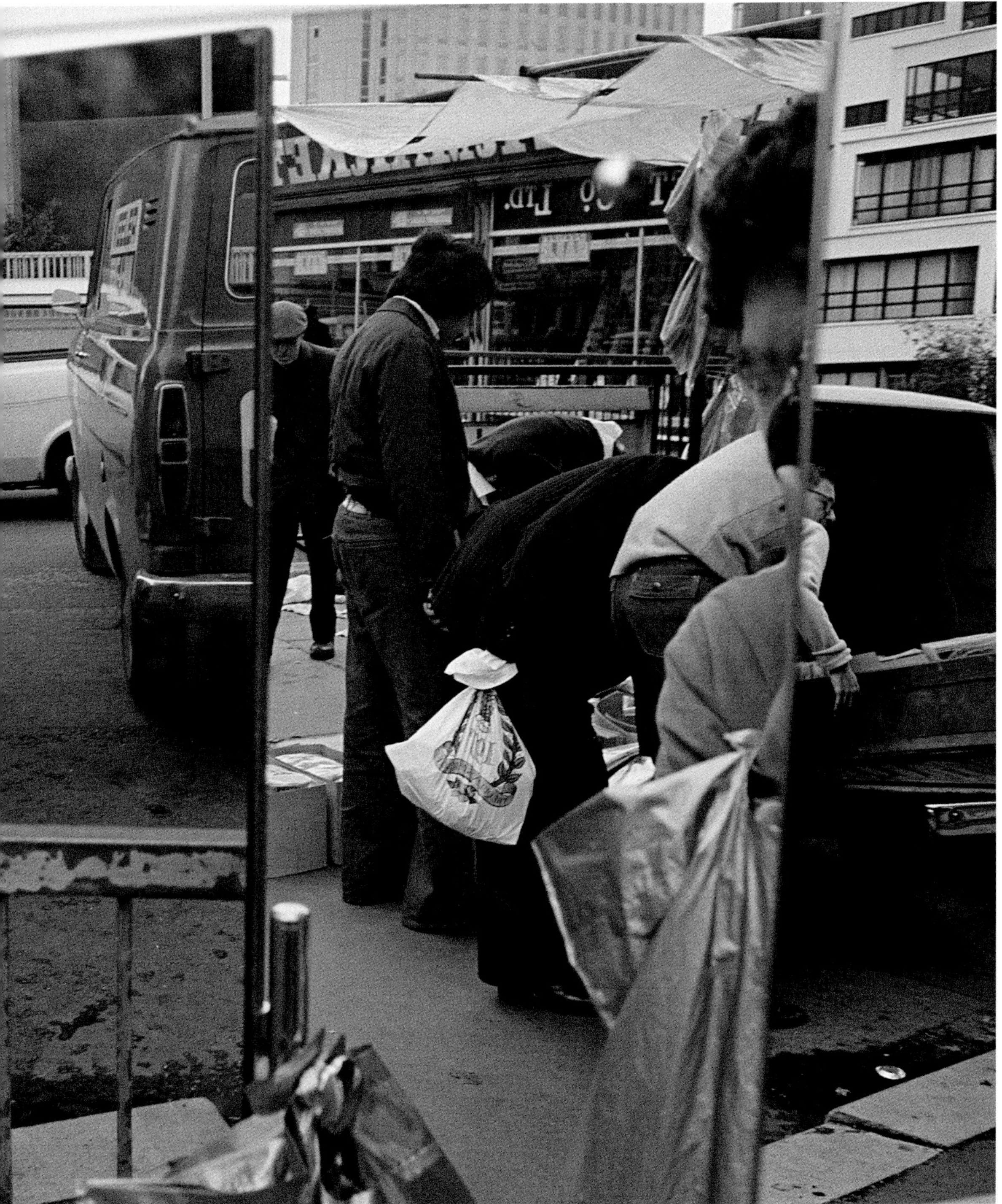

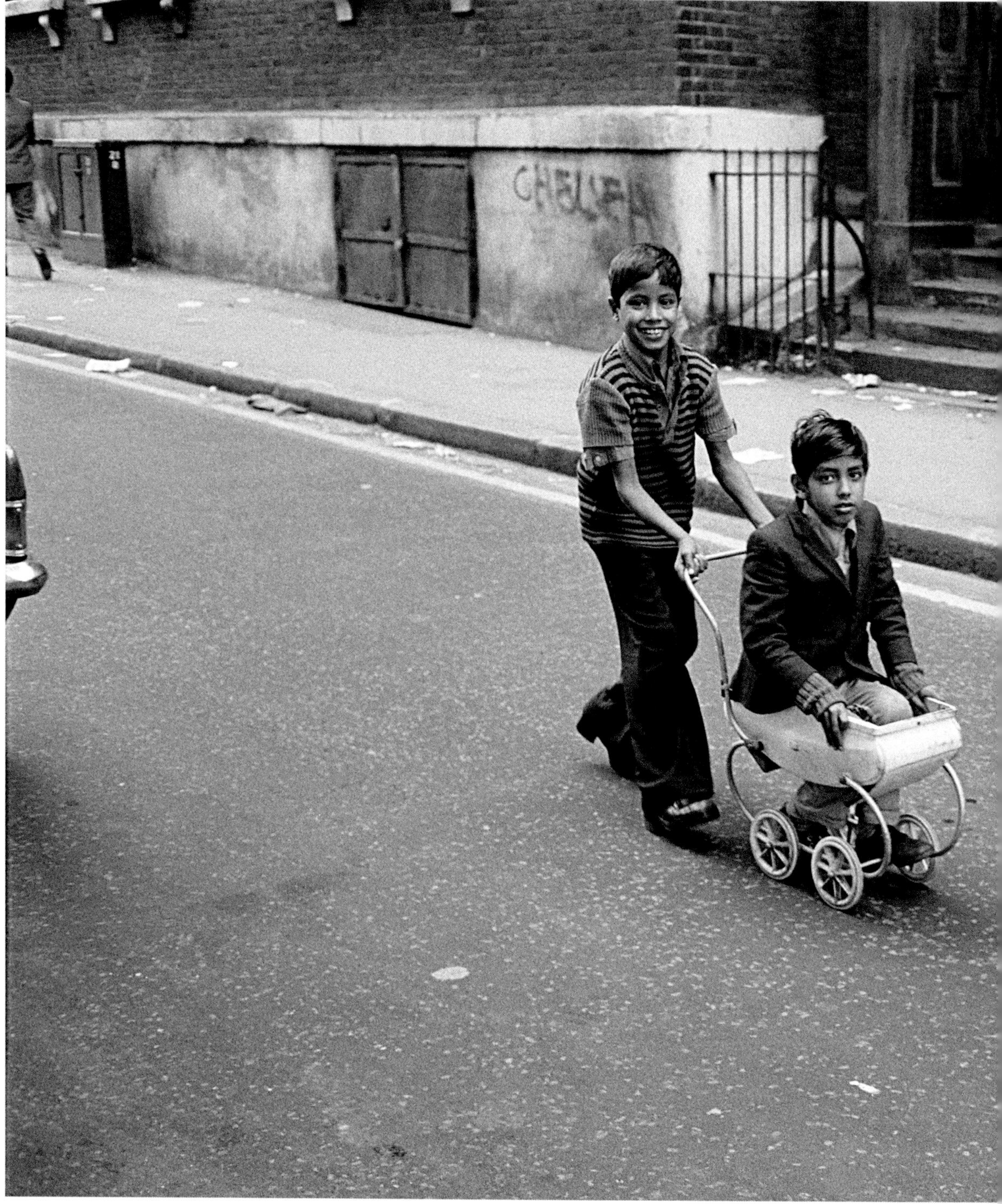

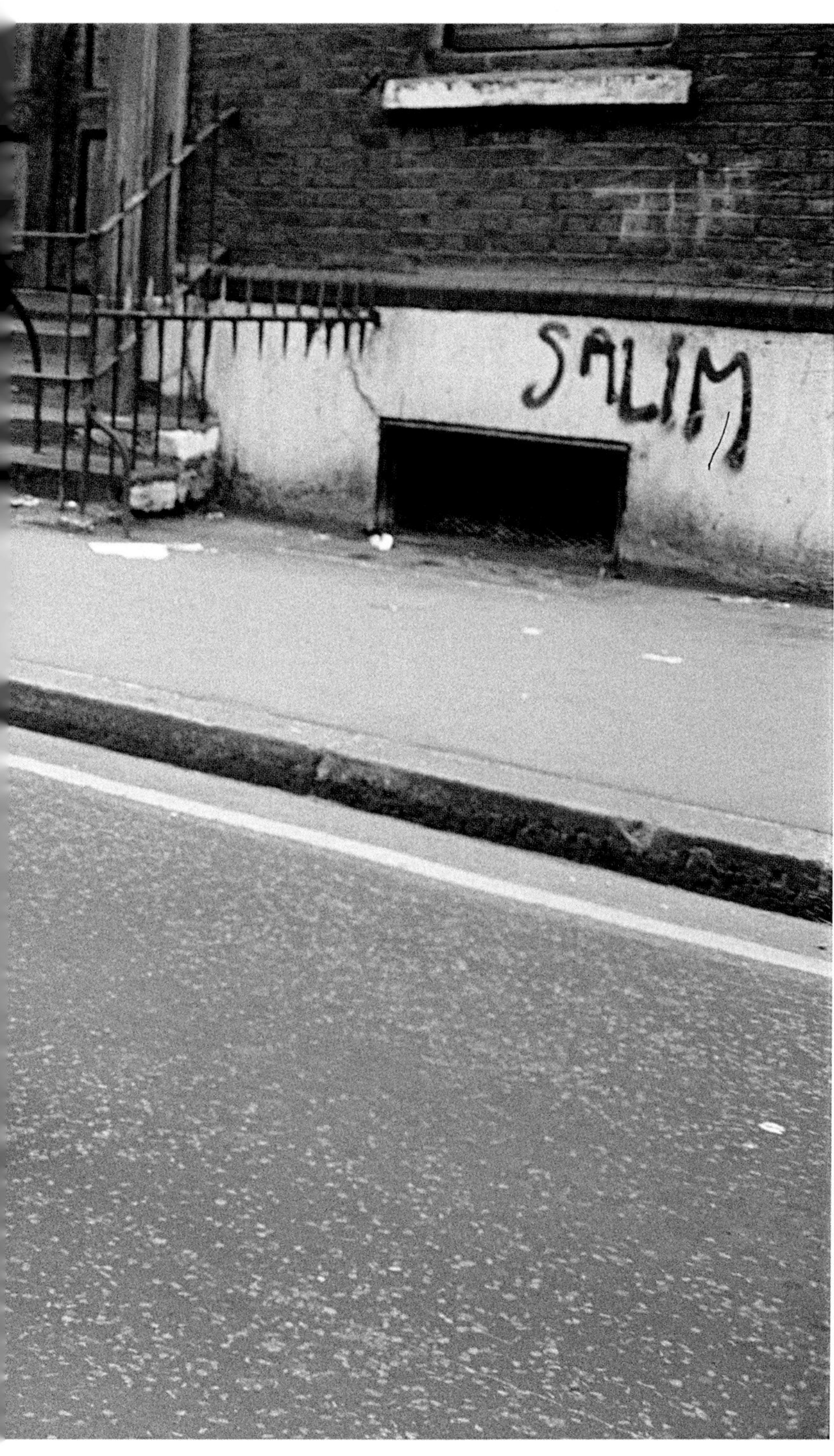

Brick Lane, London E1, 1975

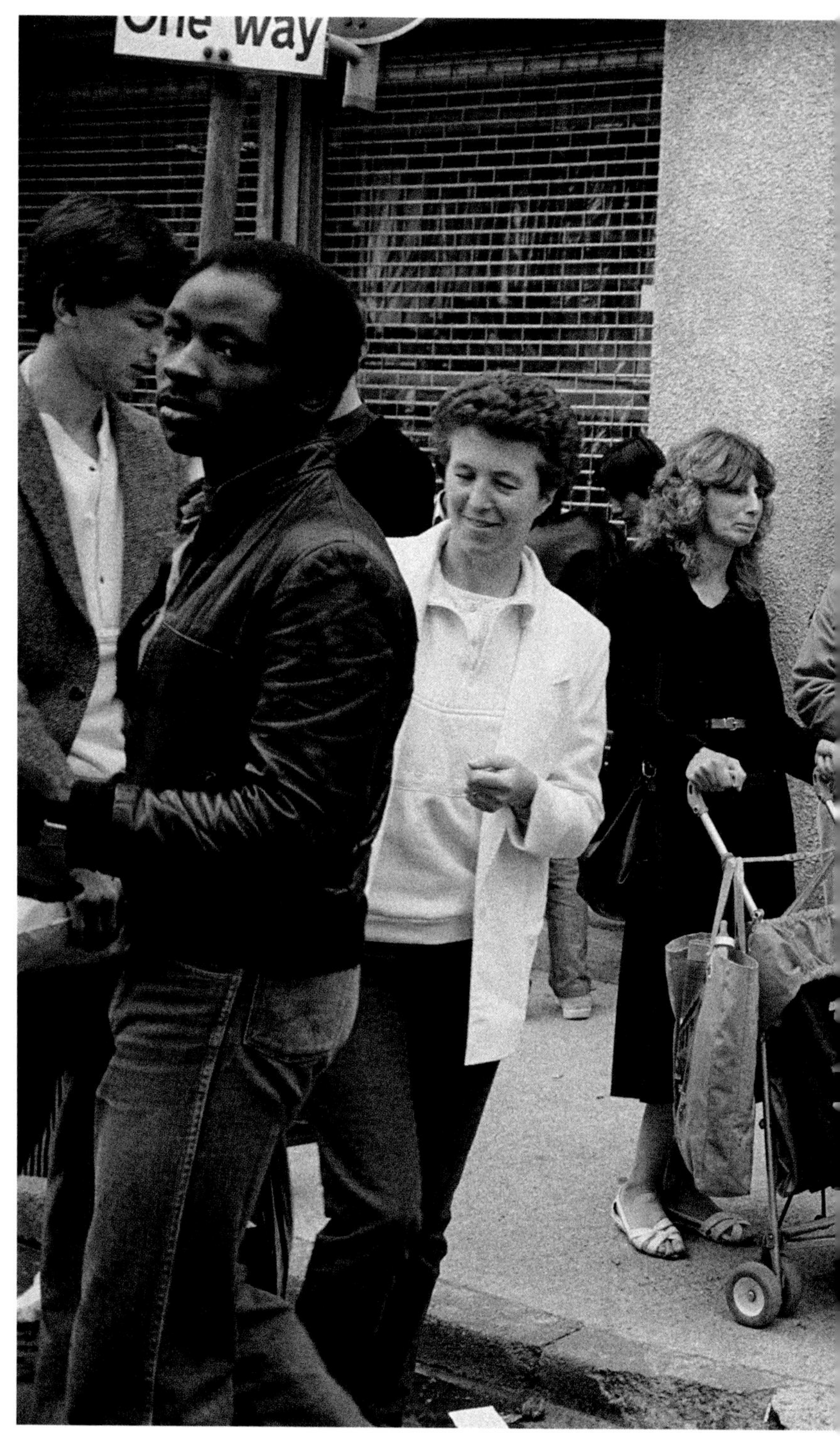

Brick Lane, London E1, 1985

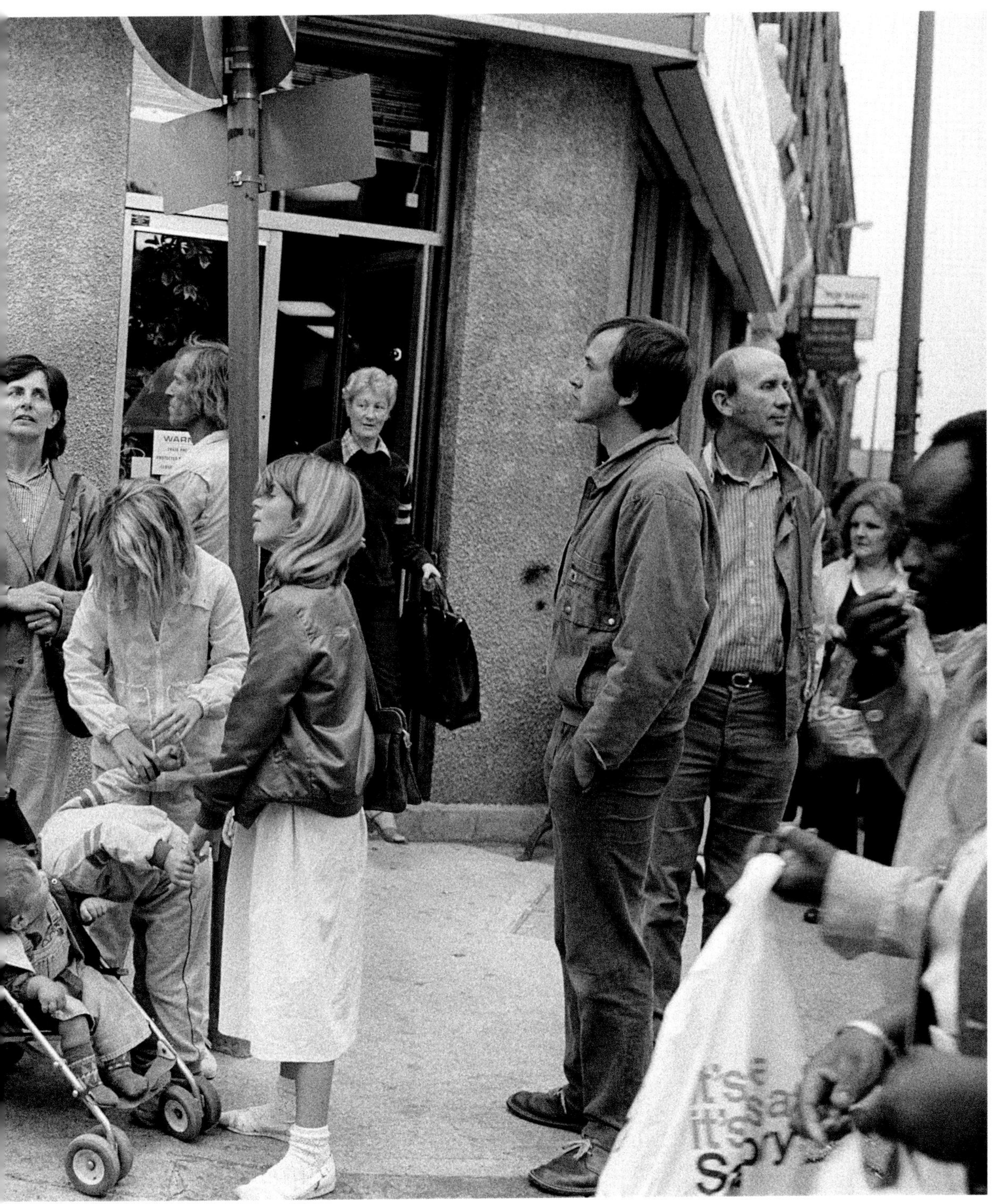

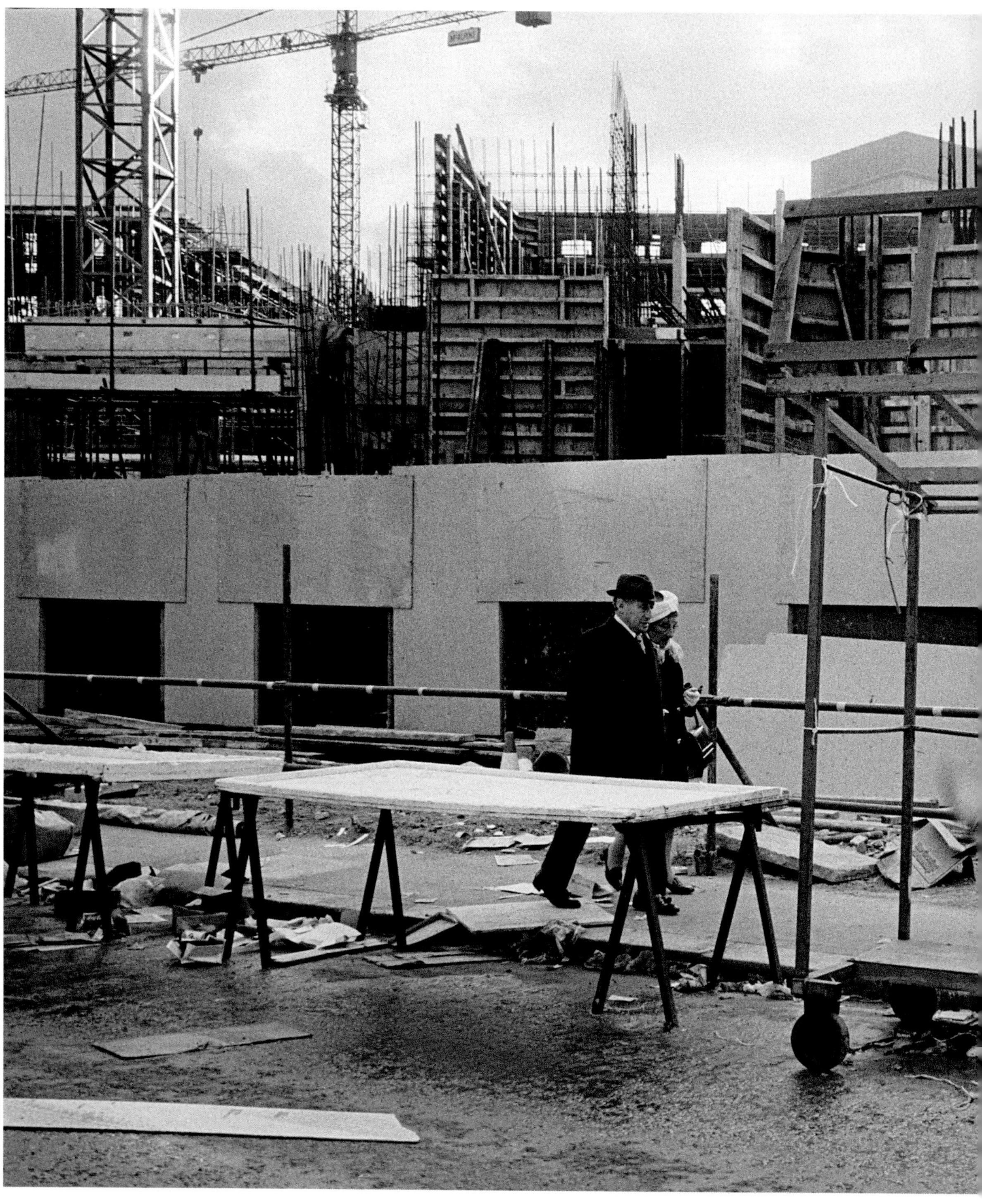

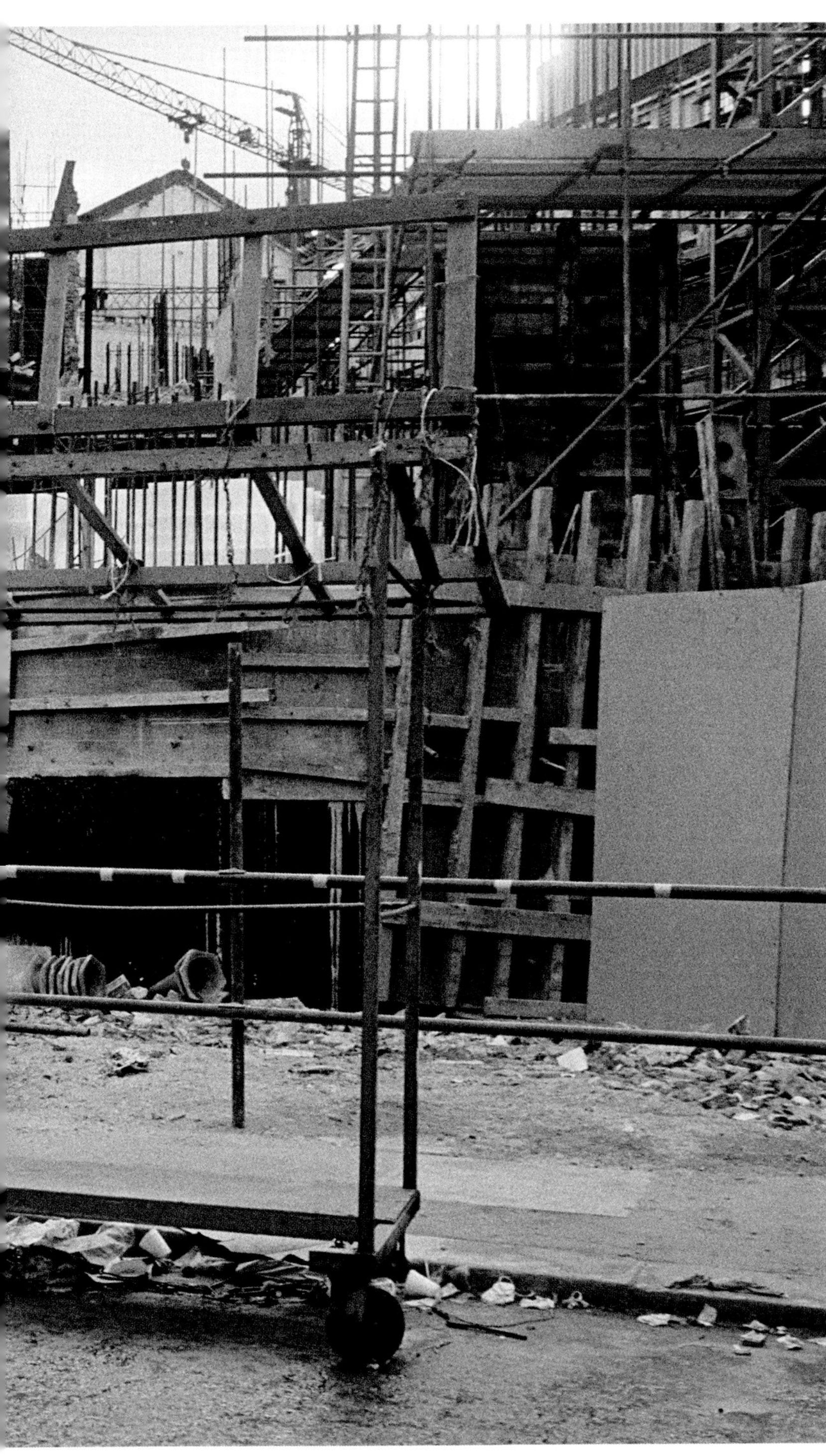

Middlesex Street, London E1, 1980

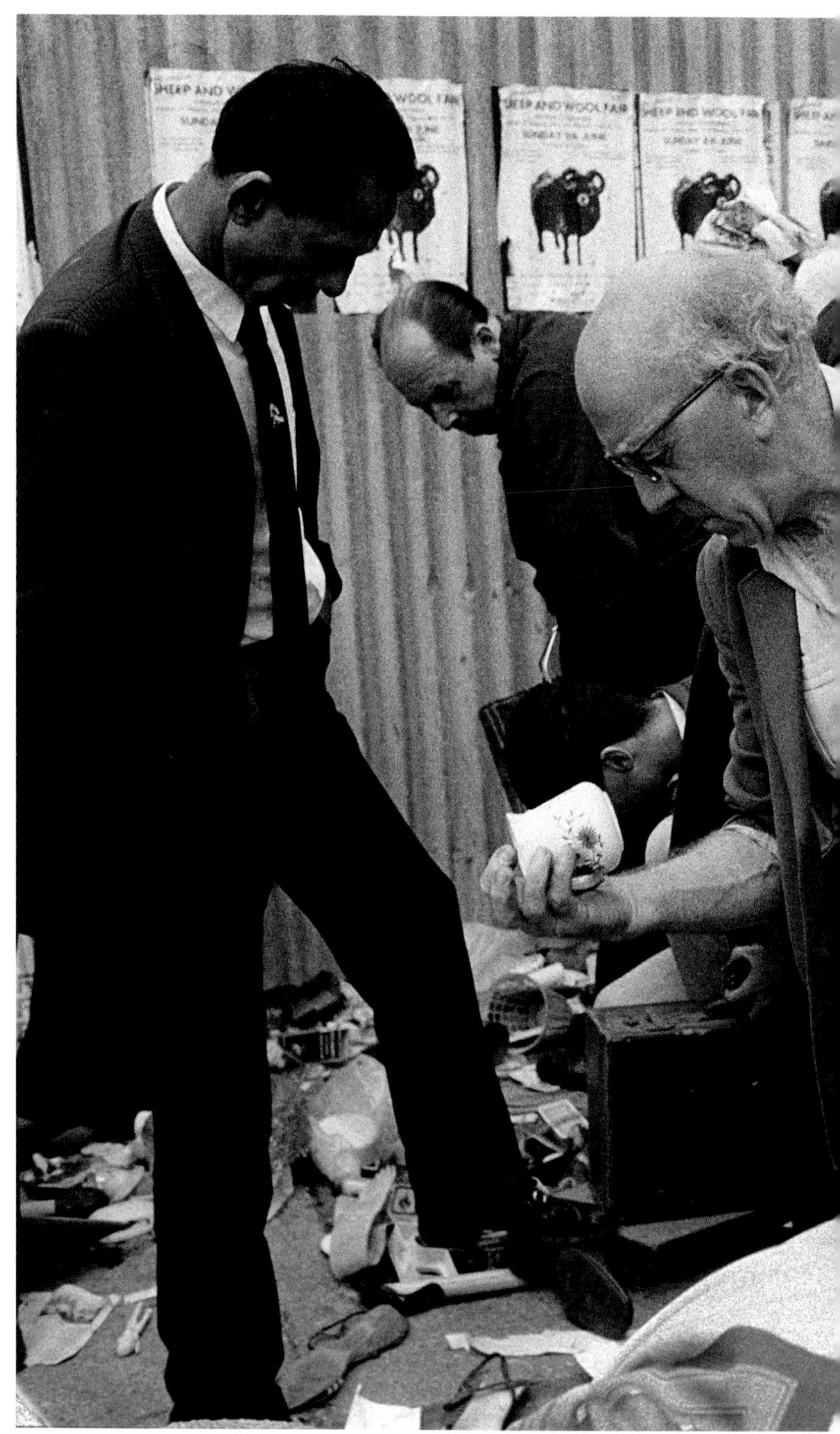

Cheshire Street, London E2, 1986

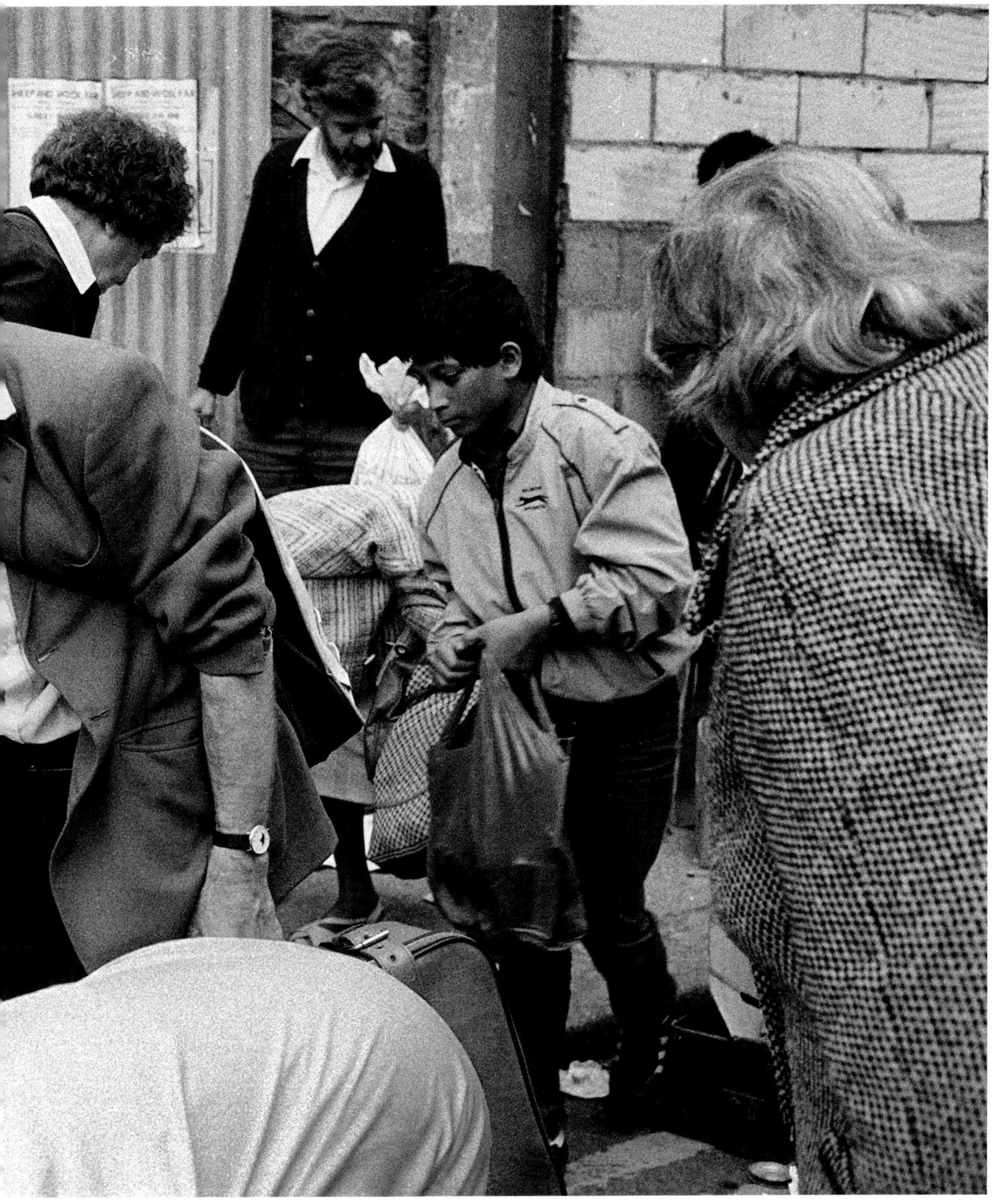

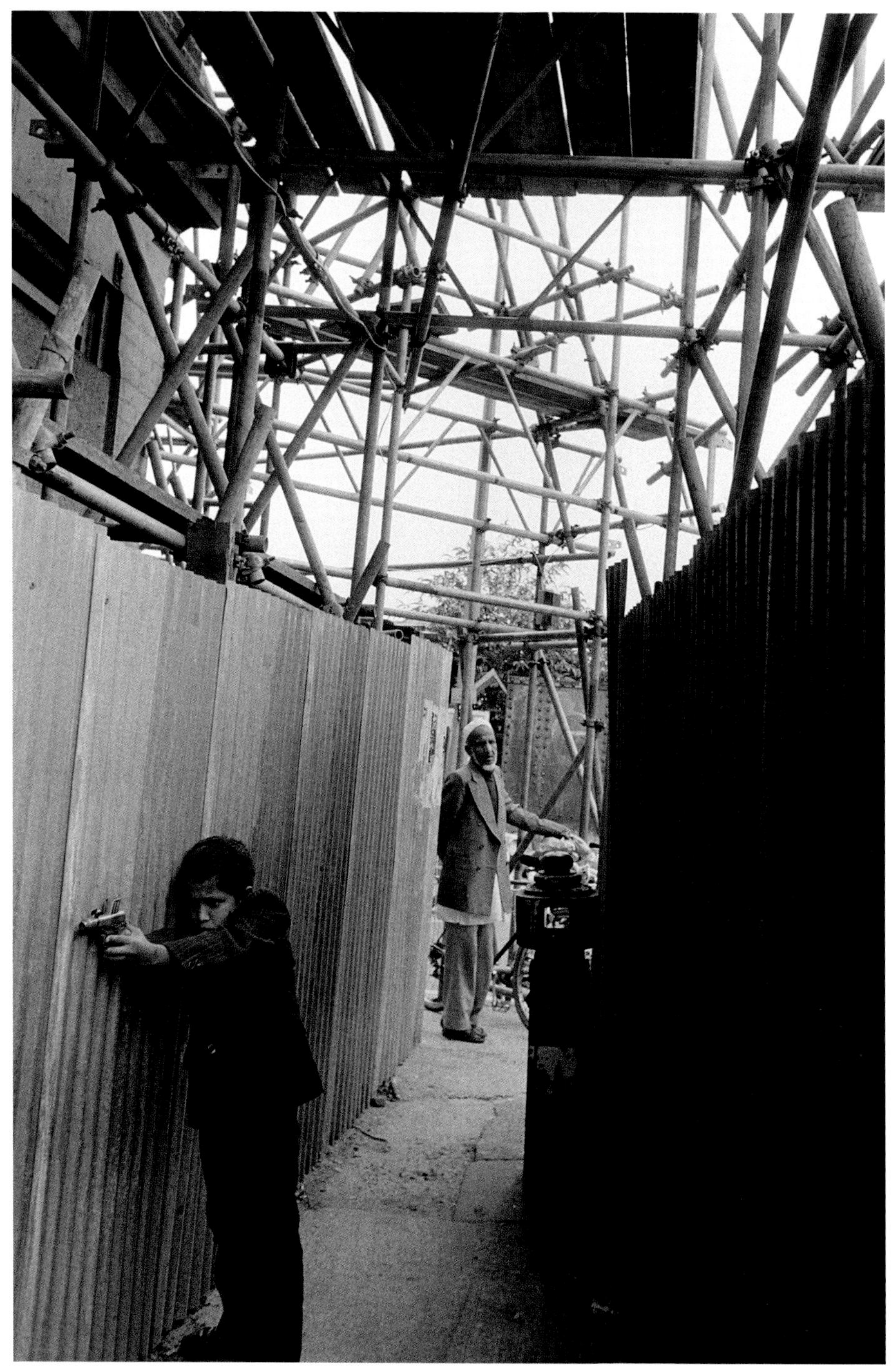

Pedley Street, London E1, 1985

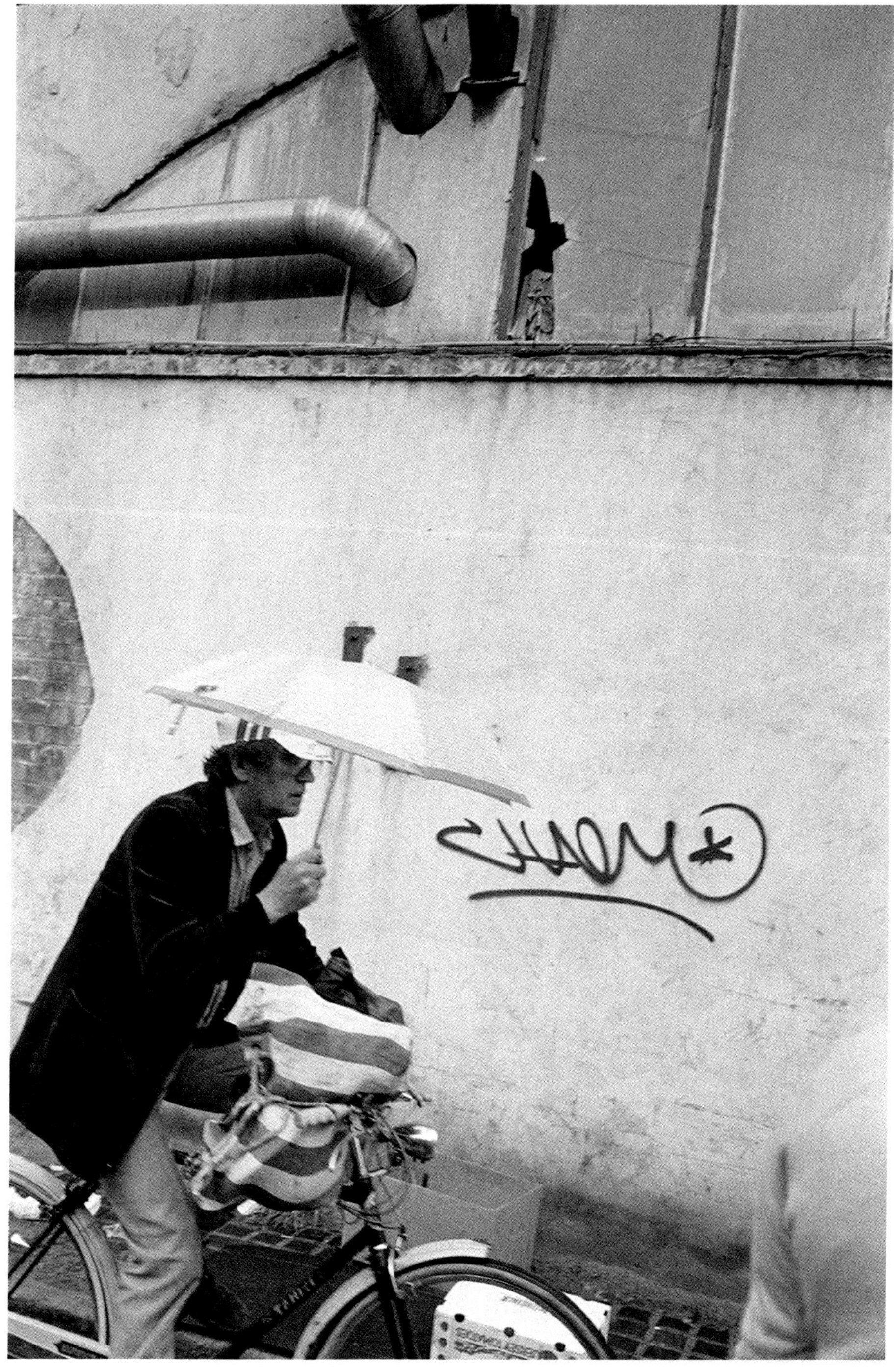

Grimsby Street, London E2, 1988

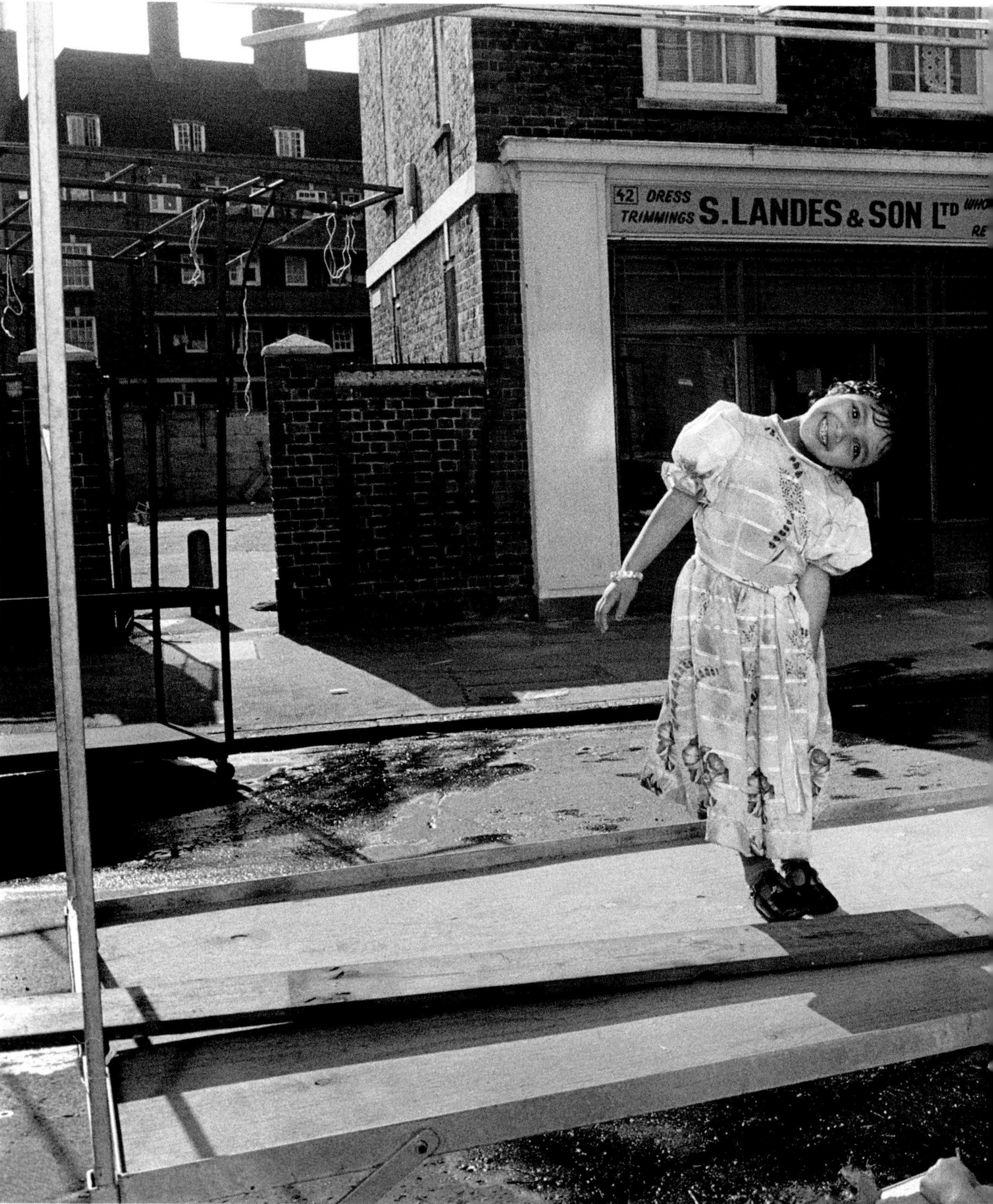

42 DRESS TRIMMINGS S.LANDES & SON LTD WHO
RE

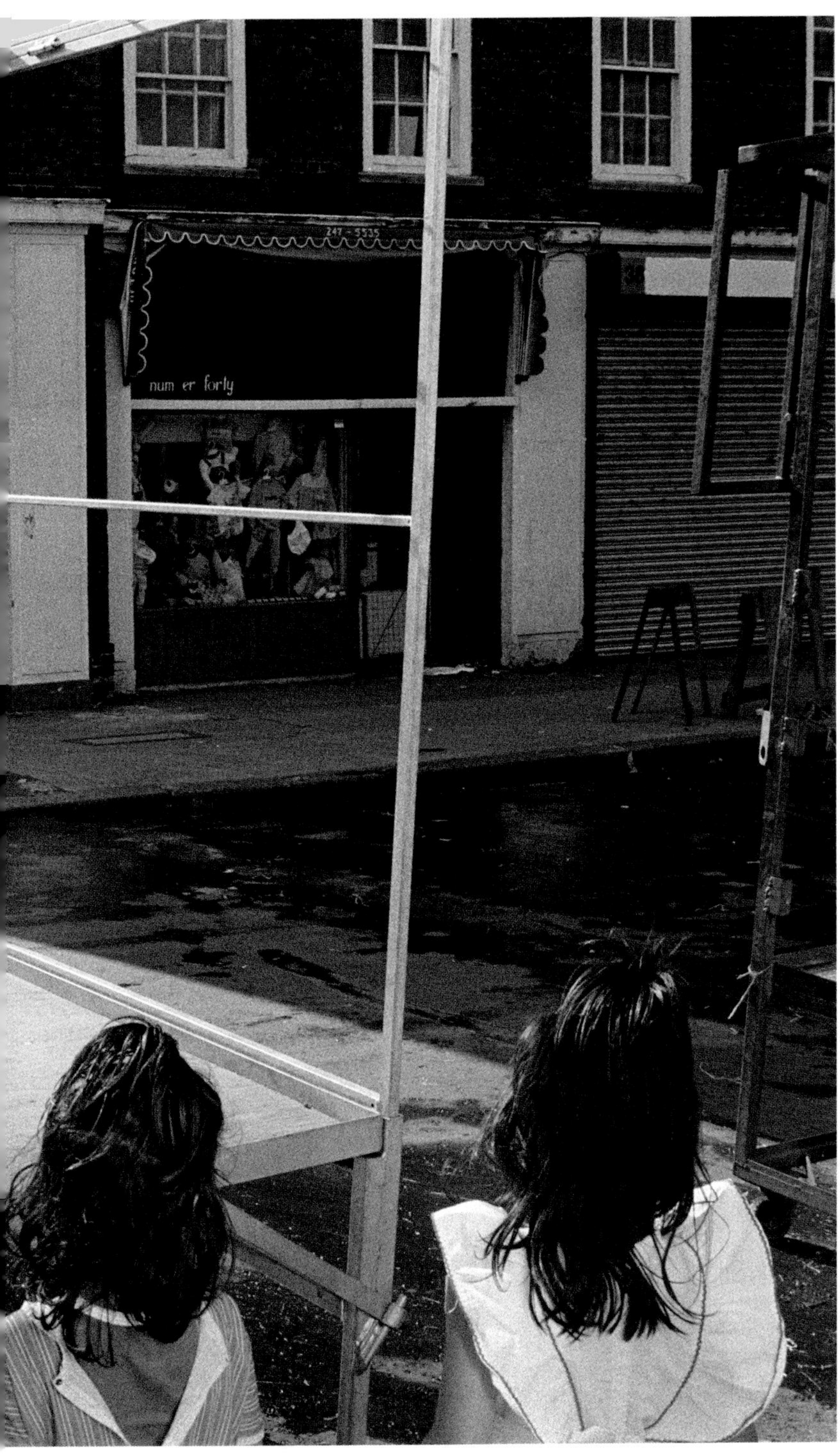

Toynbee Street, London E1, 1988

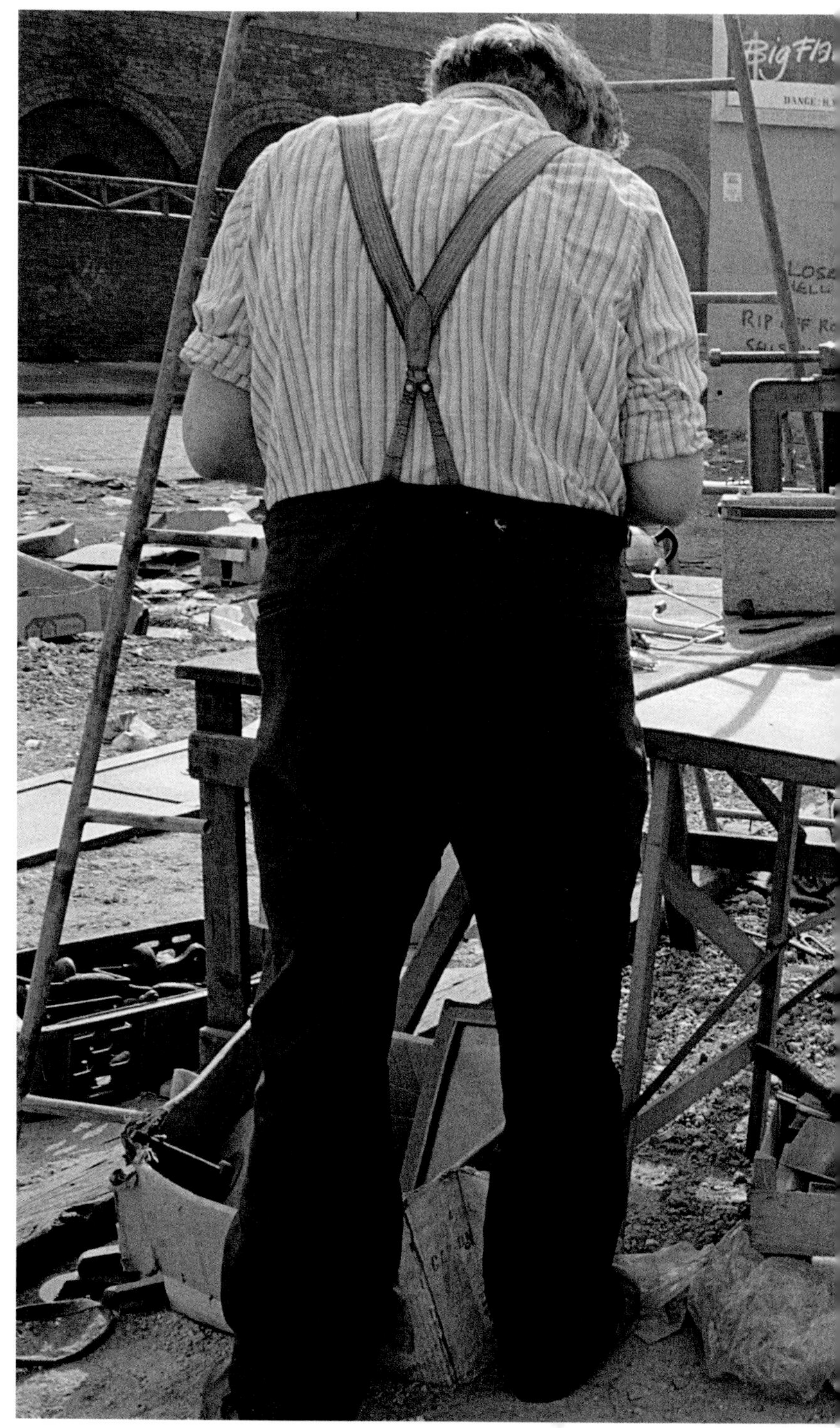

Sclater Street, London E1, 1981

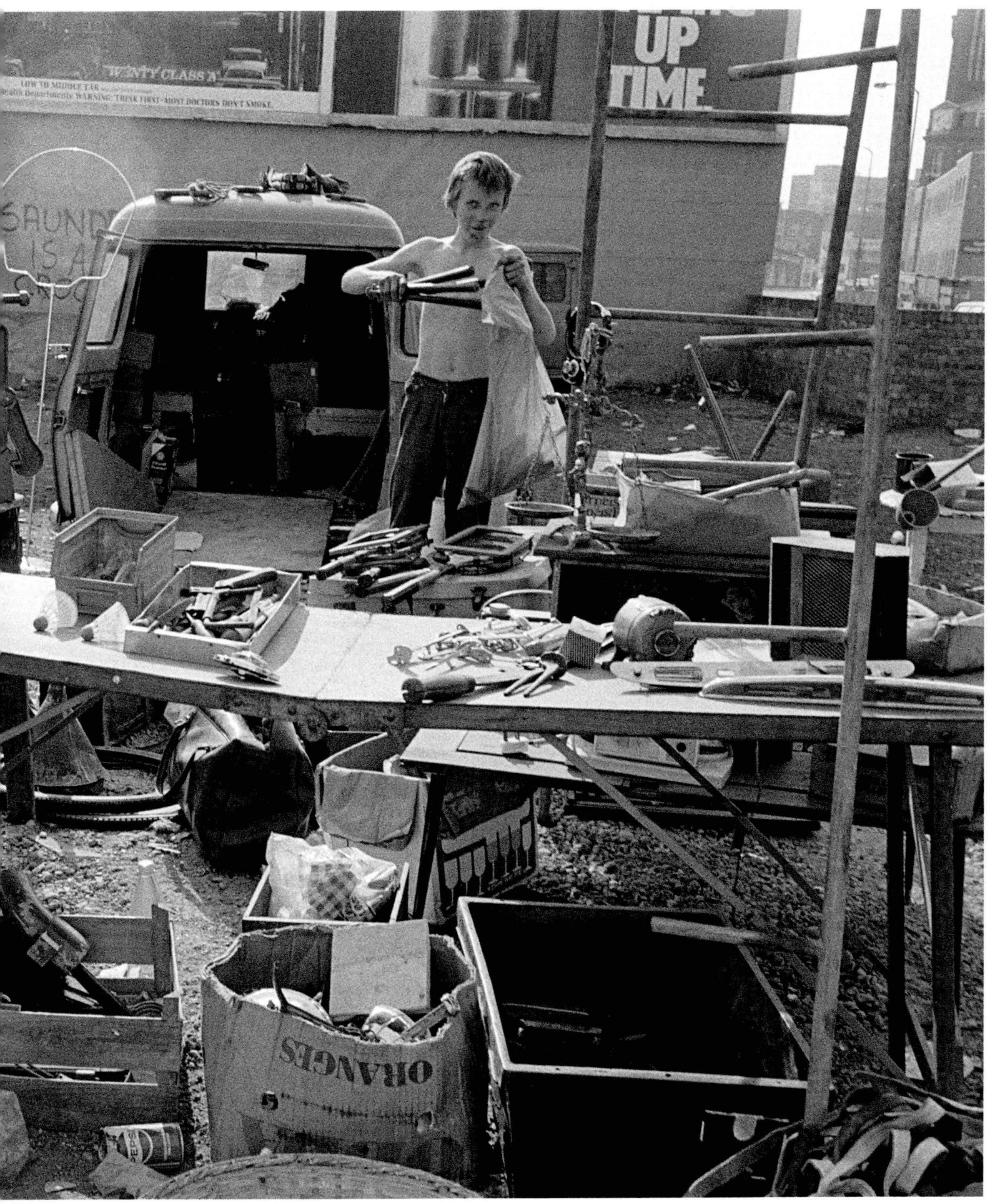

UP
TIME
TWENTY CLASS A
LOW TO MIDDLE TAR
Health Departments' WARNING: THINK FIRST—MOST DOCTORS DON'T SMOKE
SAUND
IS A
SHOO
ORANGES

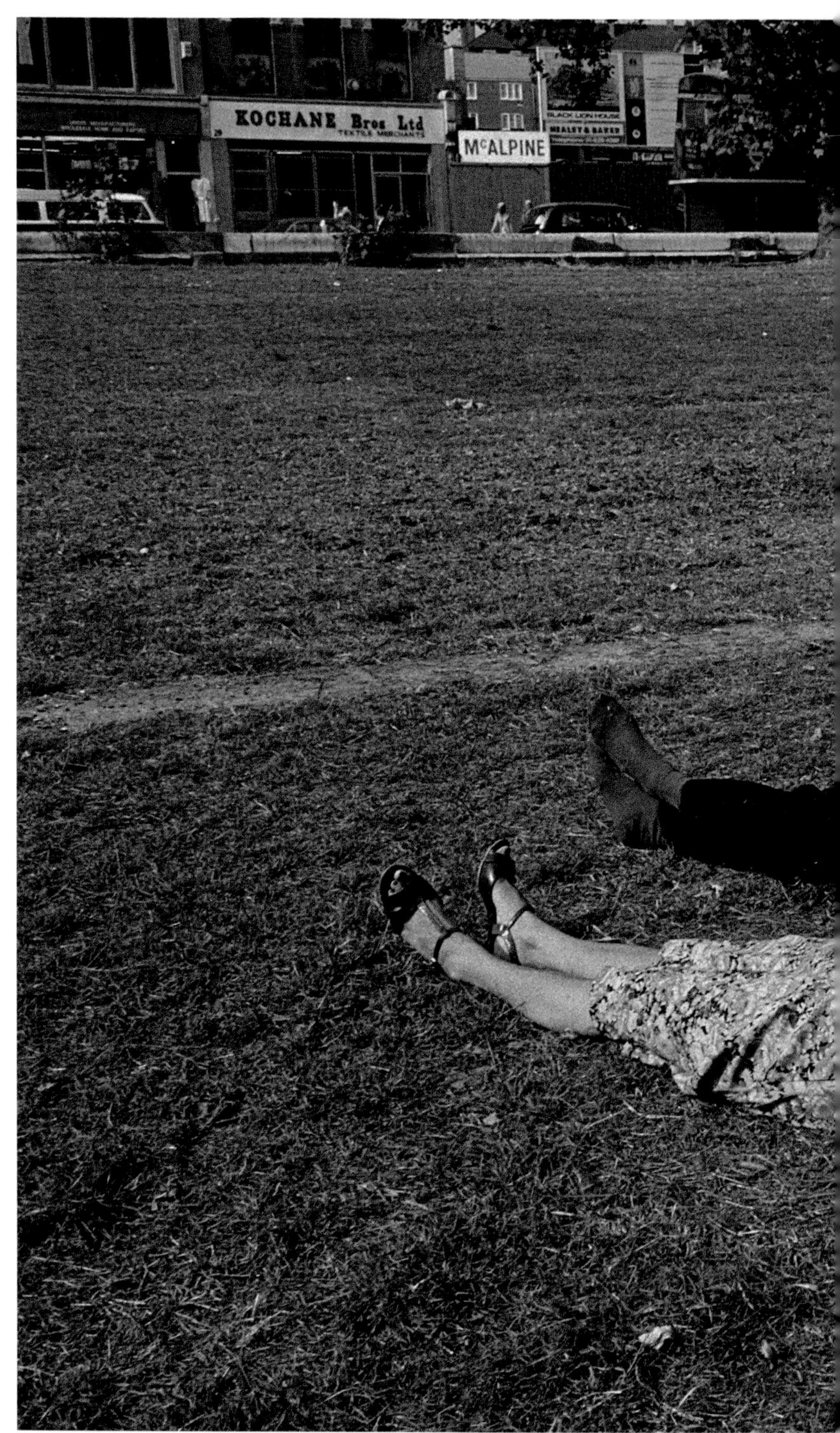

St Mary's Park (now Altab Ali Park),
Whitechapel Road, London E1, 1981

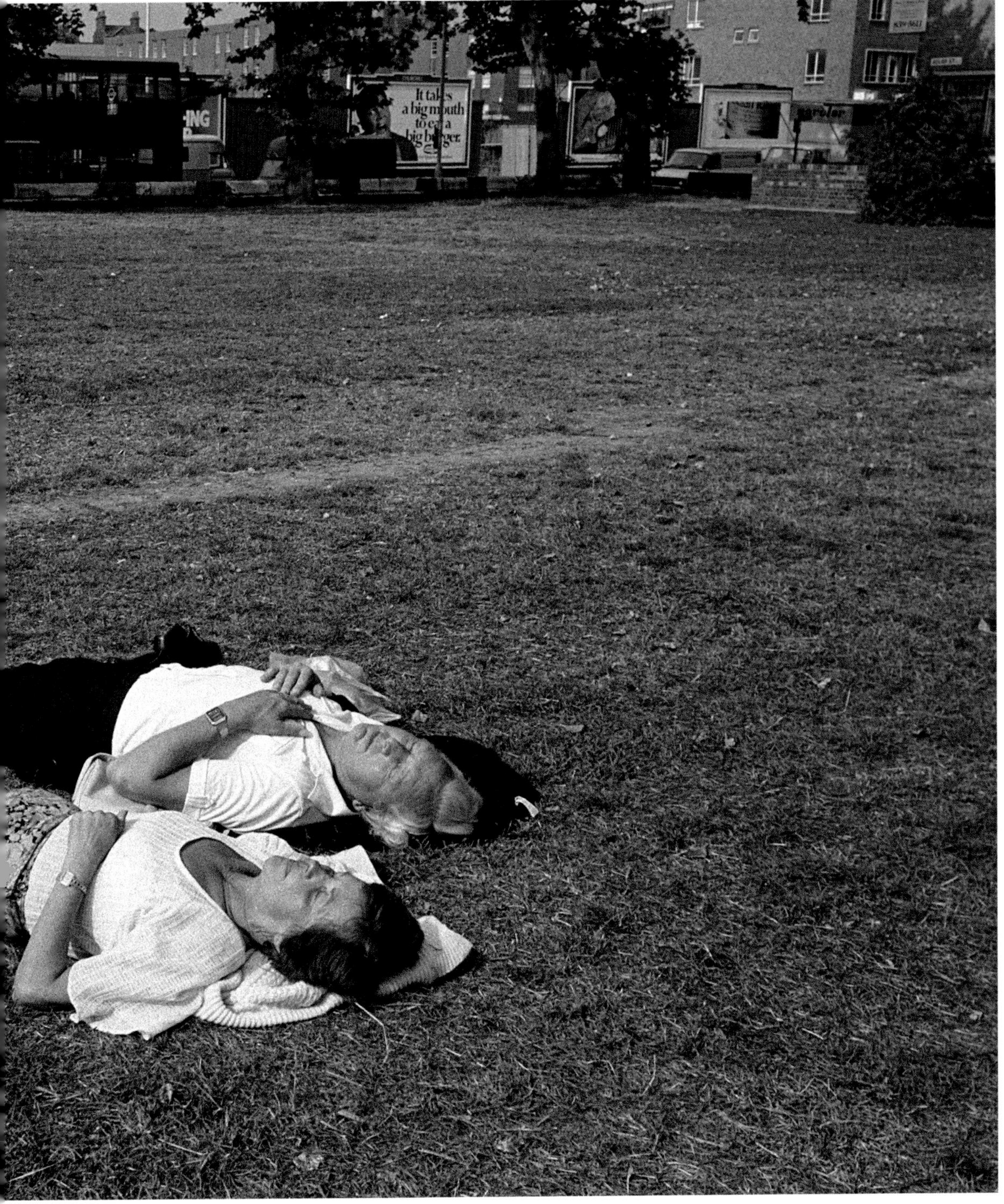
It takes
a big mouth
to eat a
big burger.

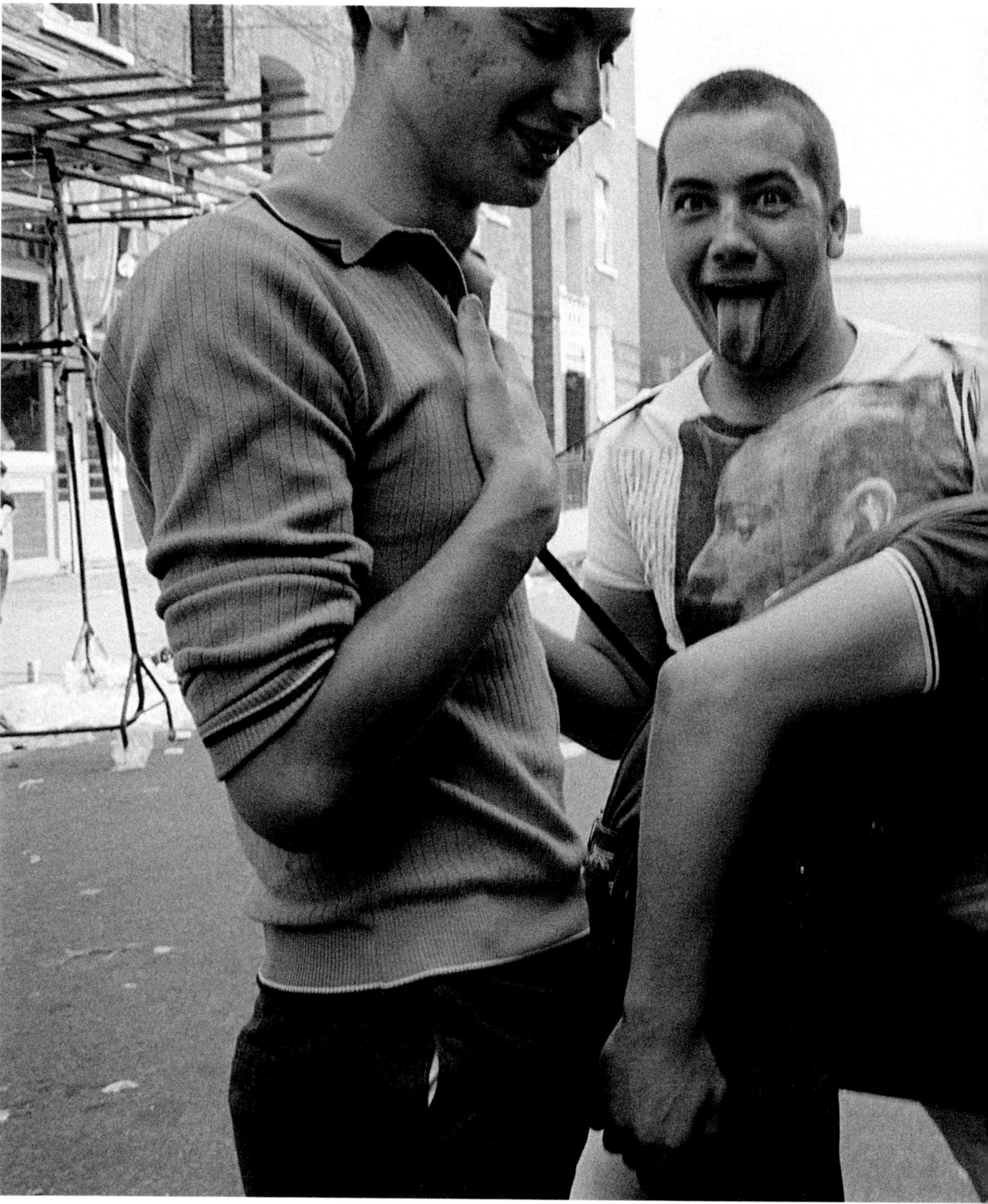

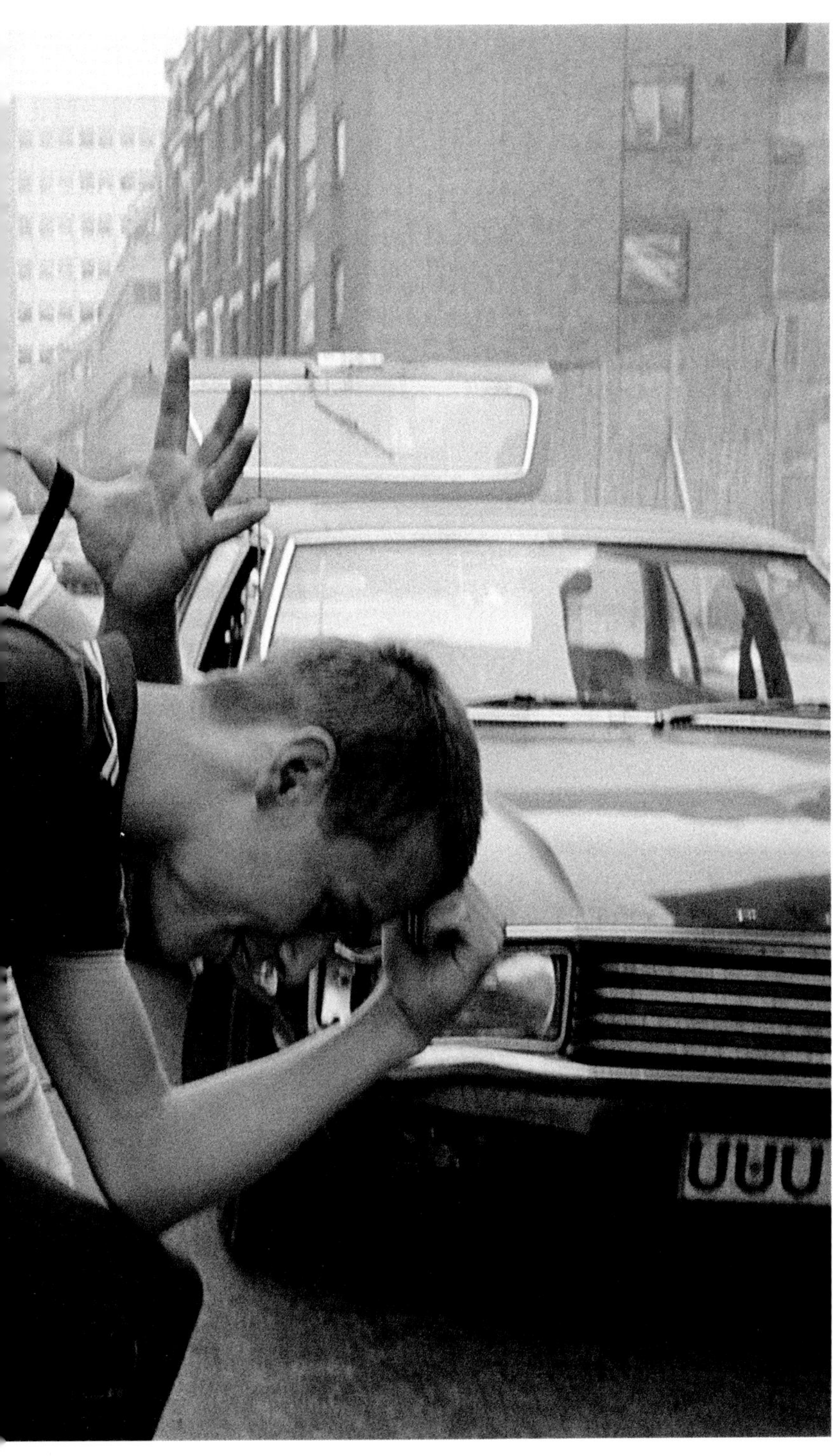

Wentworth Street, London E1, 1980

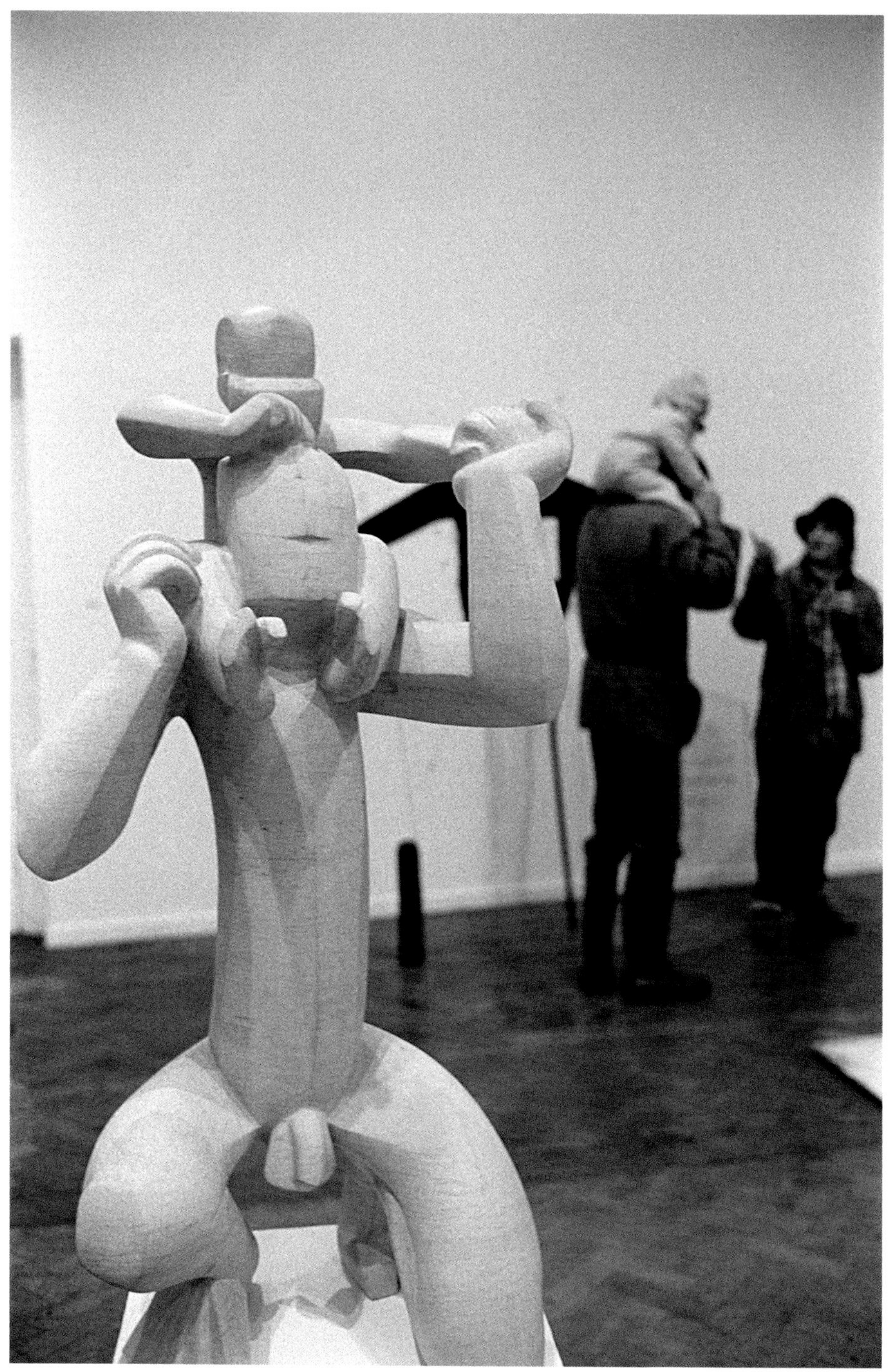

Whitechapel Gallery, Whitechapel High Street, London E1, 1981

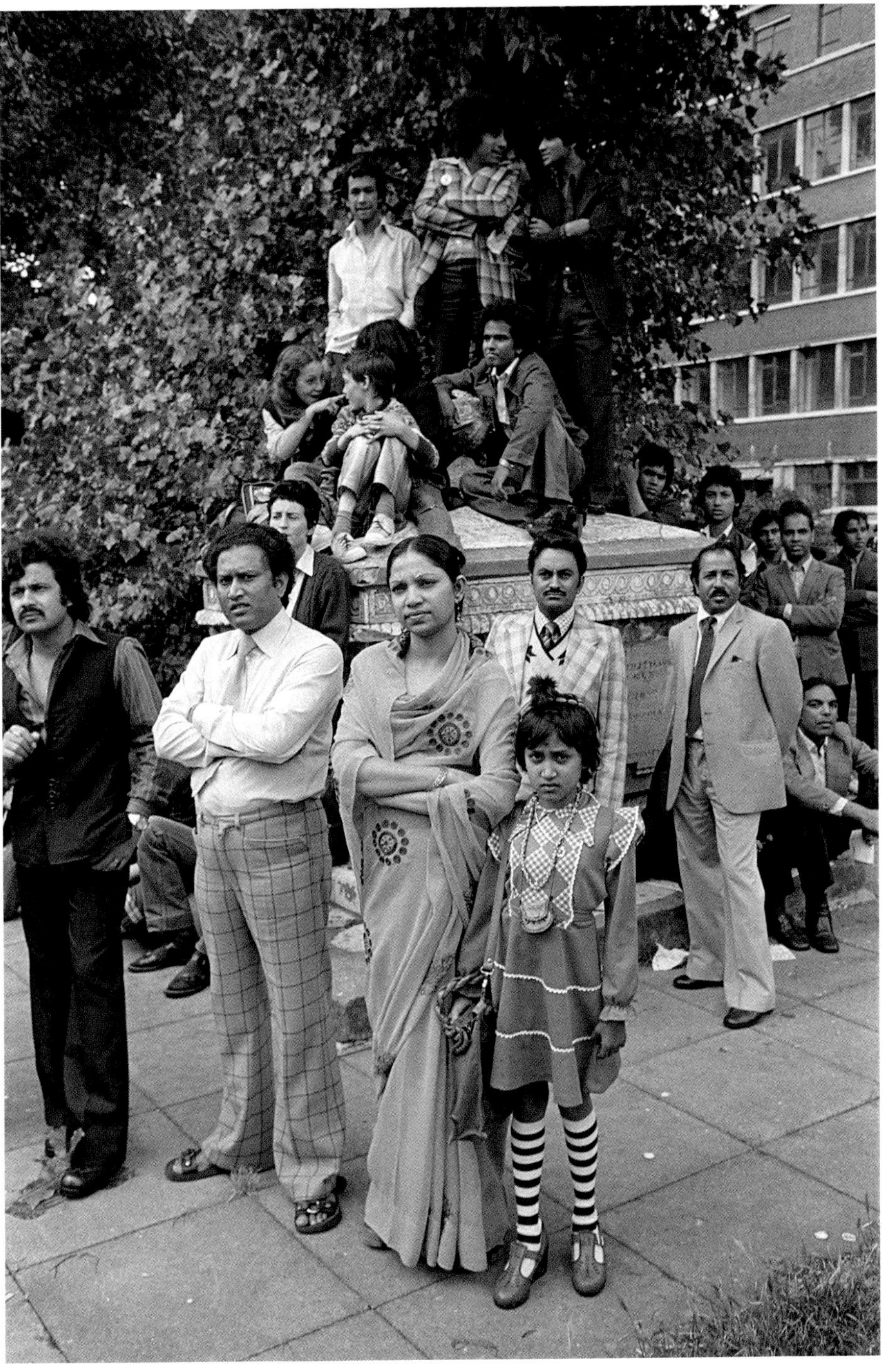

St Mary's Park (now Altab Ali Park), Whitechapel Road, London E1, 1978

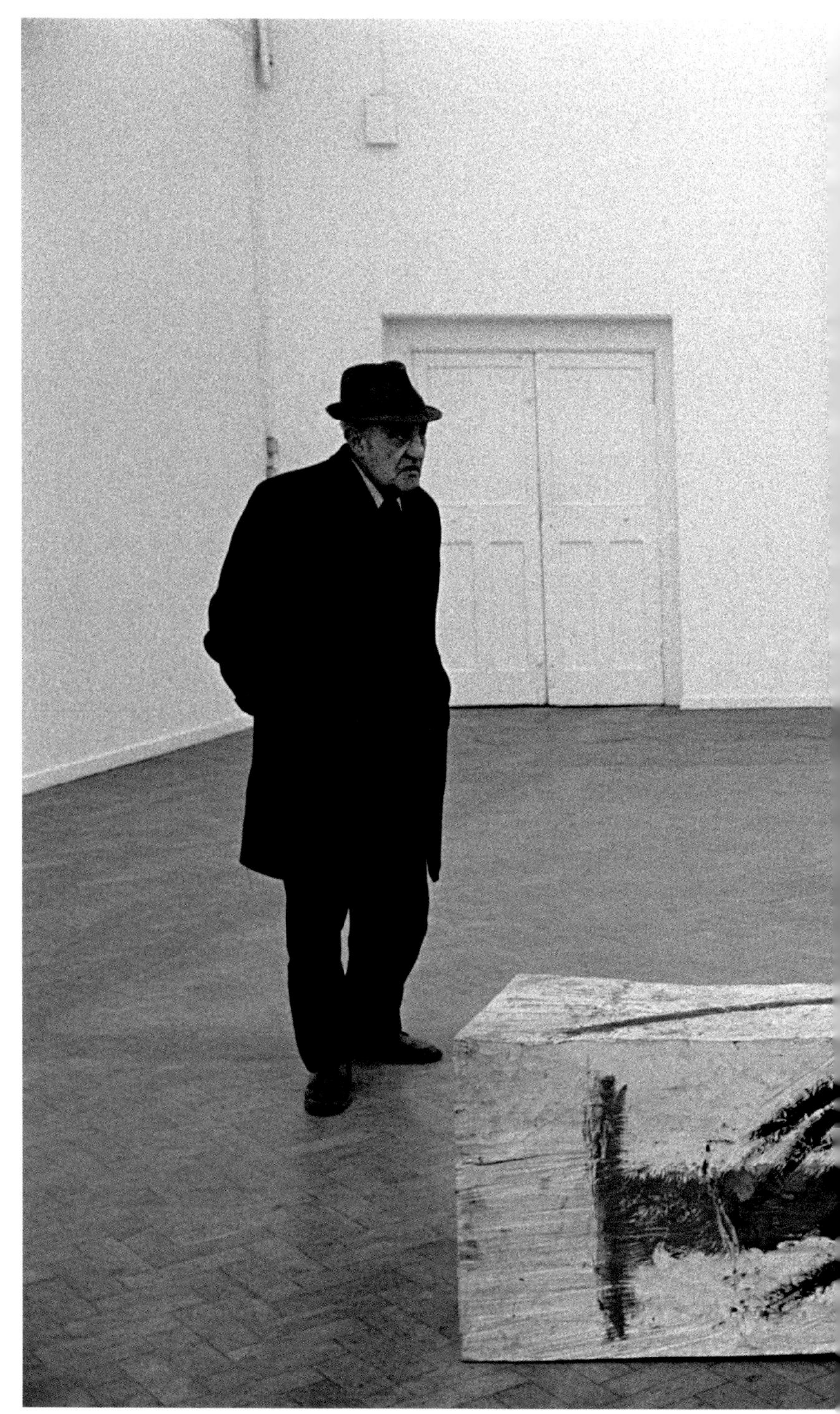

Whitechapel Gallery, Whitechapel
High Street, London E1, 1981

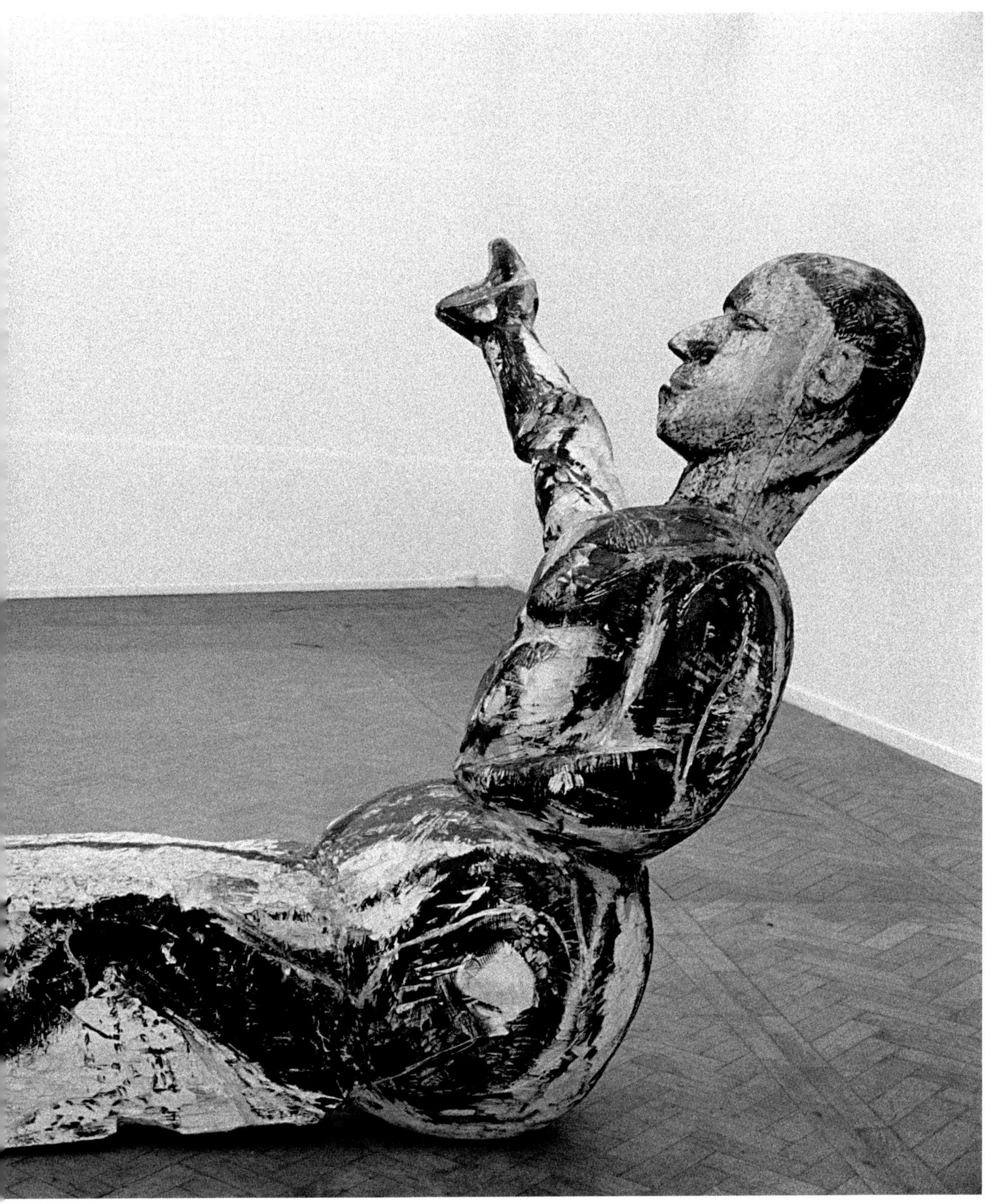

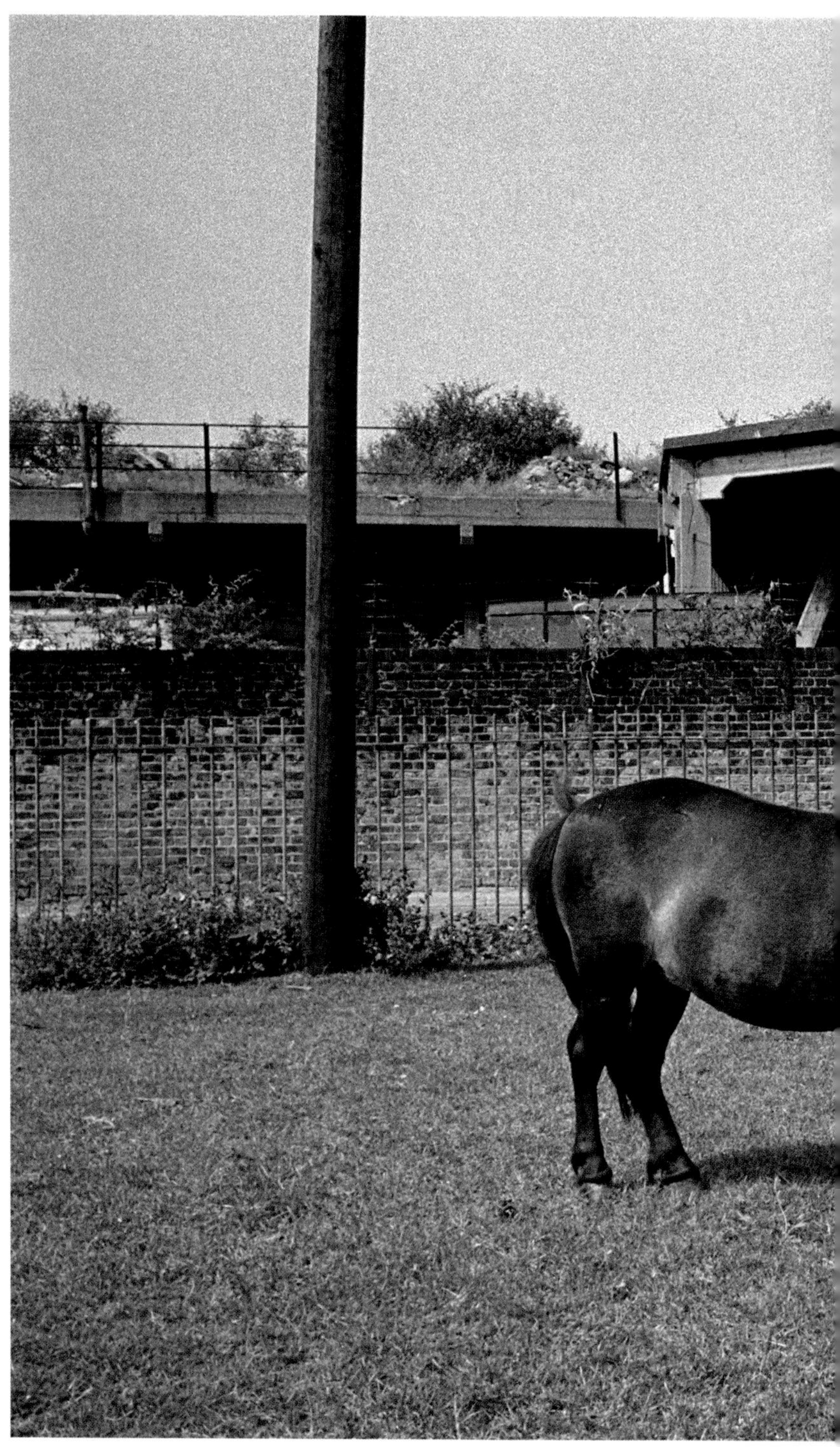

Allen Gardens, Buxton
Street, London E1, 1992

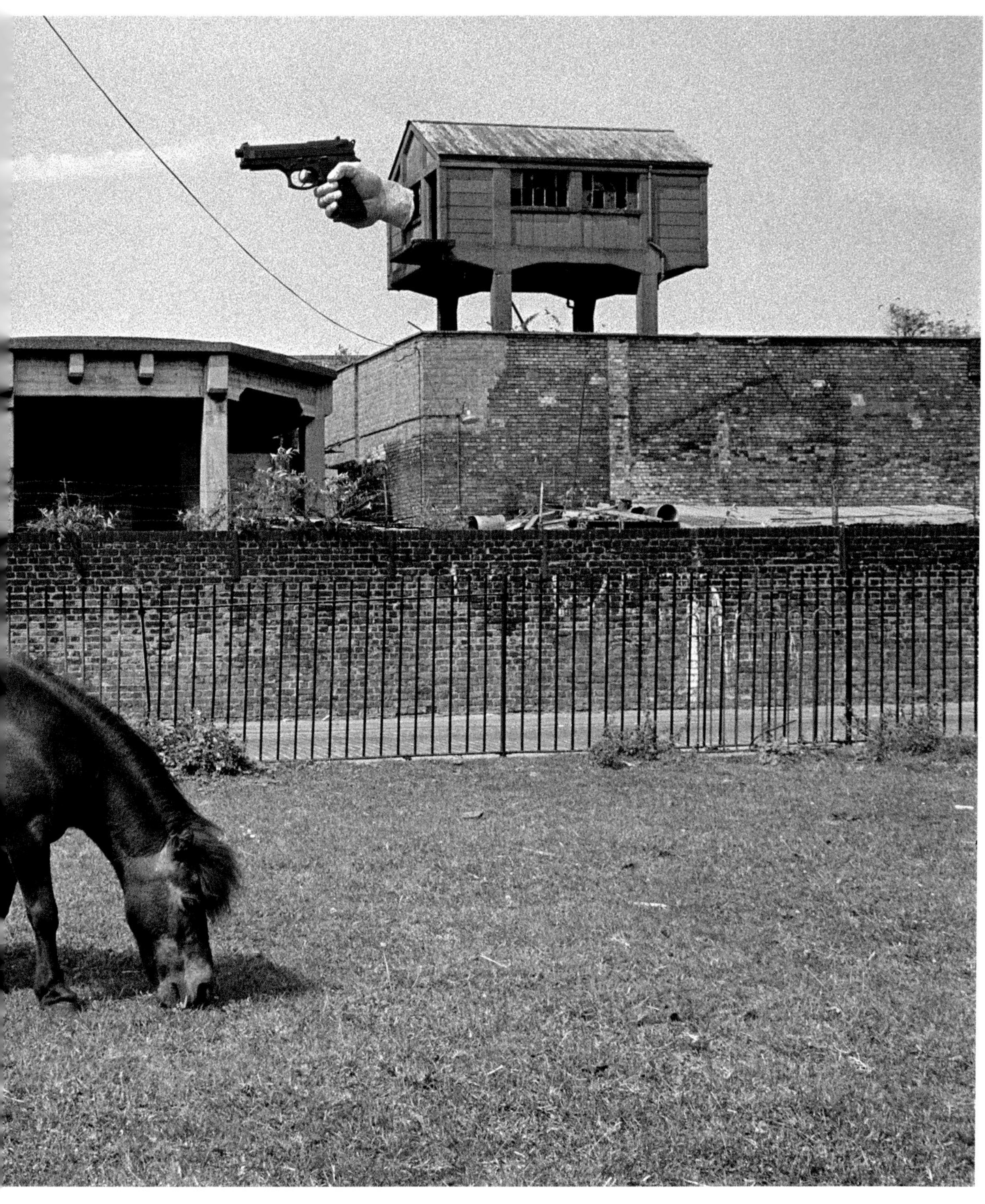

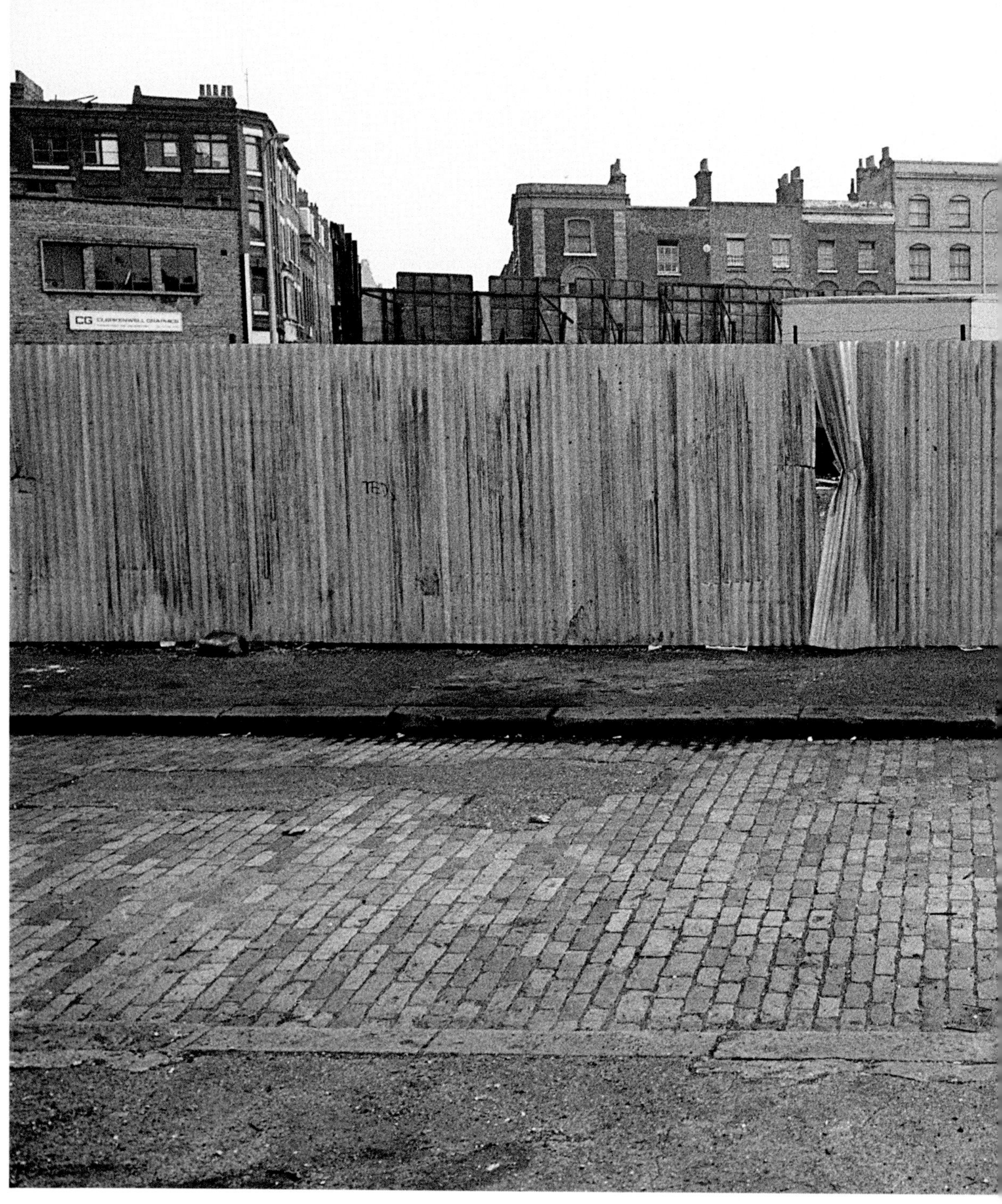

CG CLERKENWELL GRAPHICS

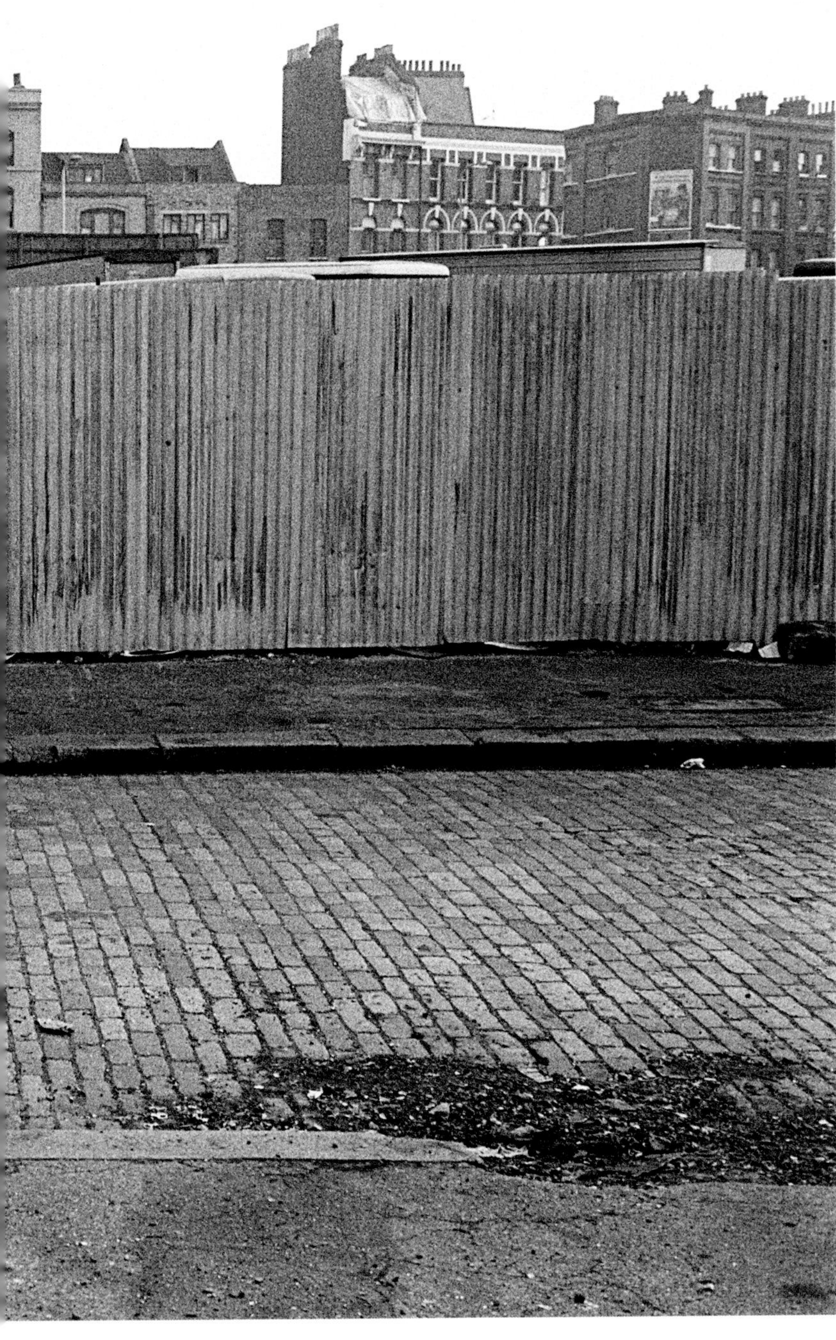

Bacon Street, London E1, 1978

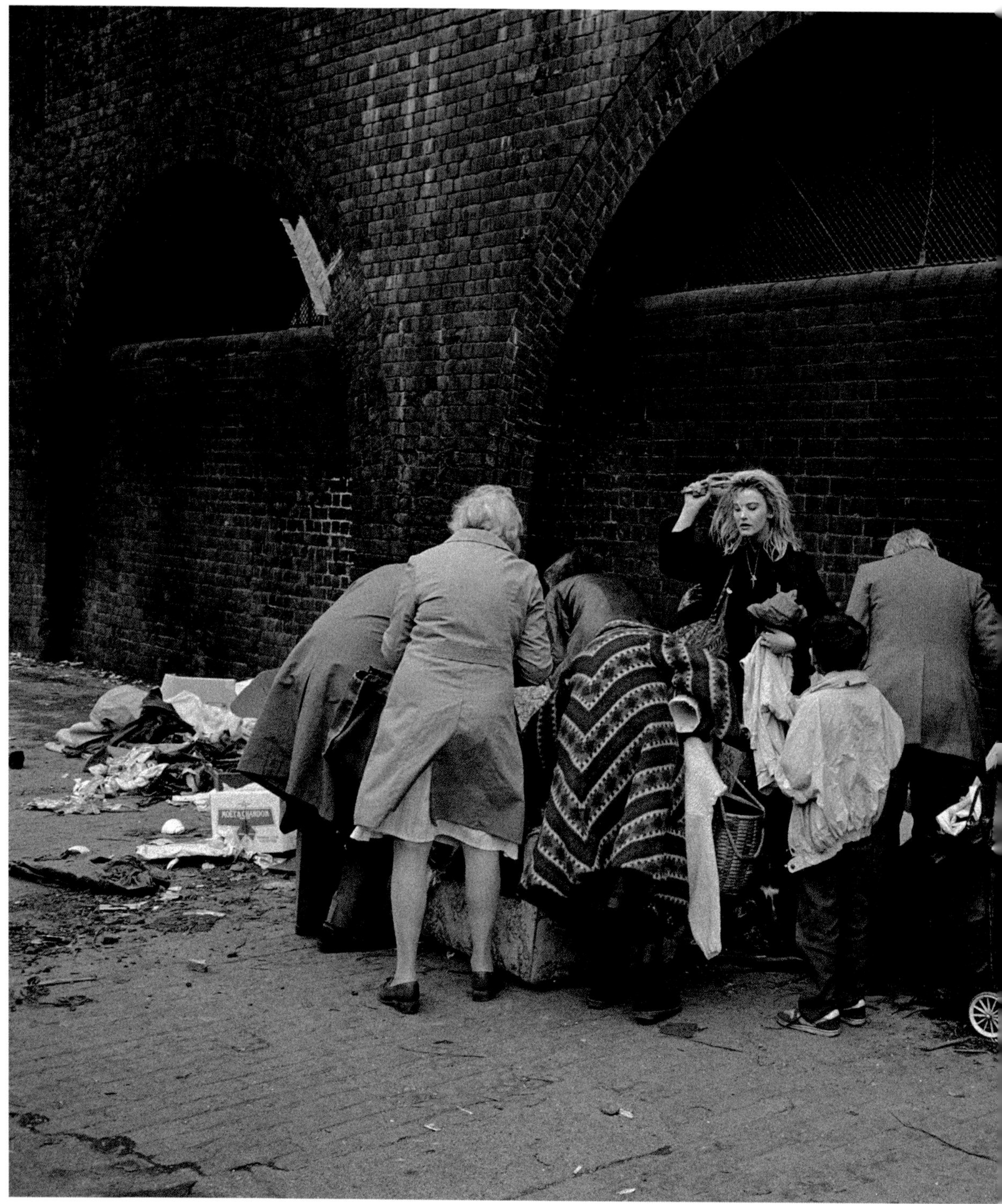

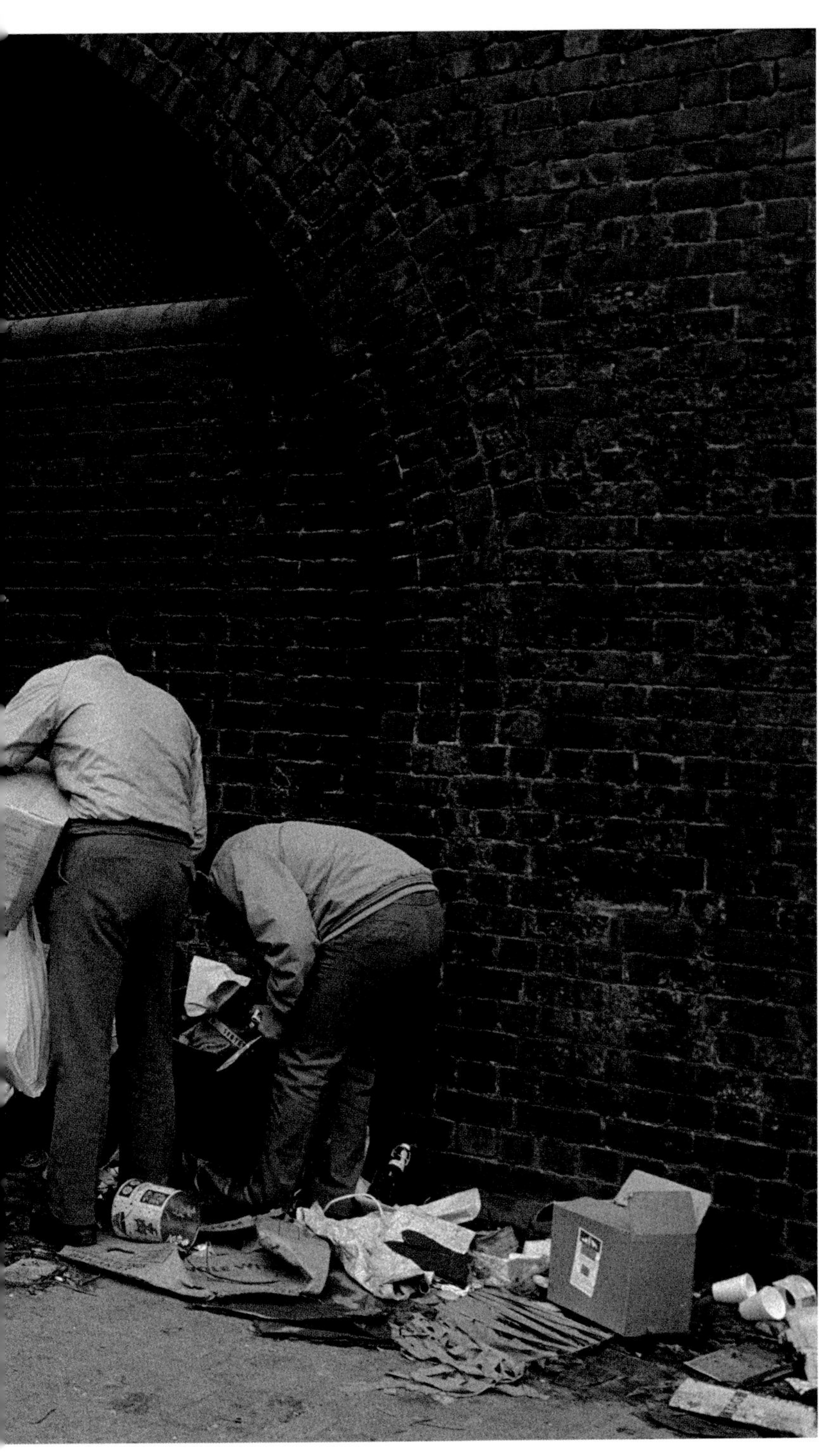

Grimsby Street, London E2, 1988

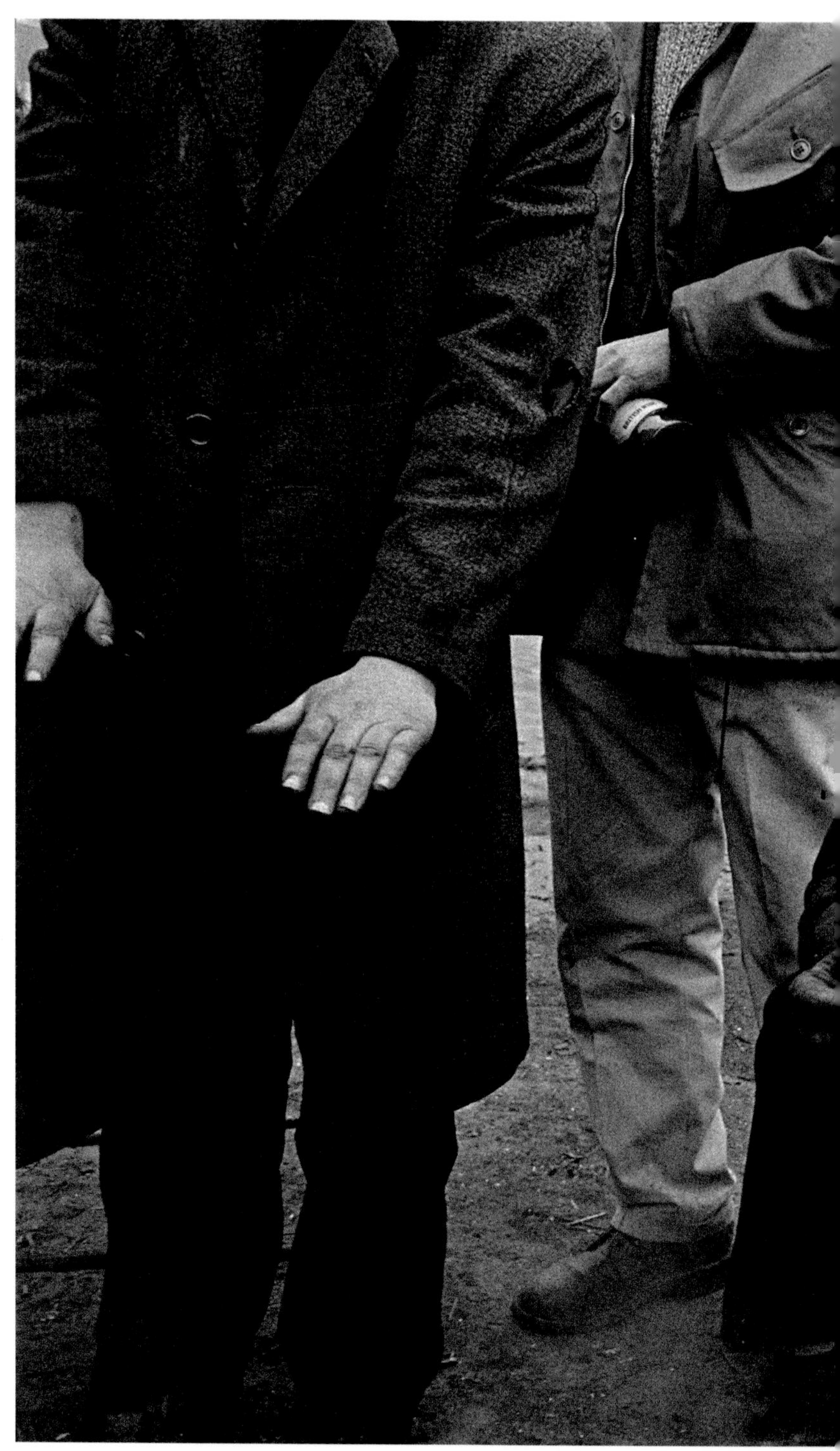

Brushfield Street, London E1, 1976

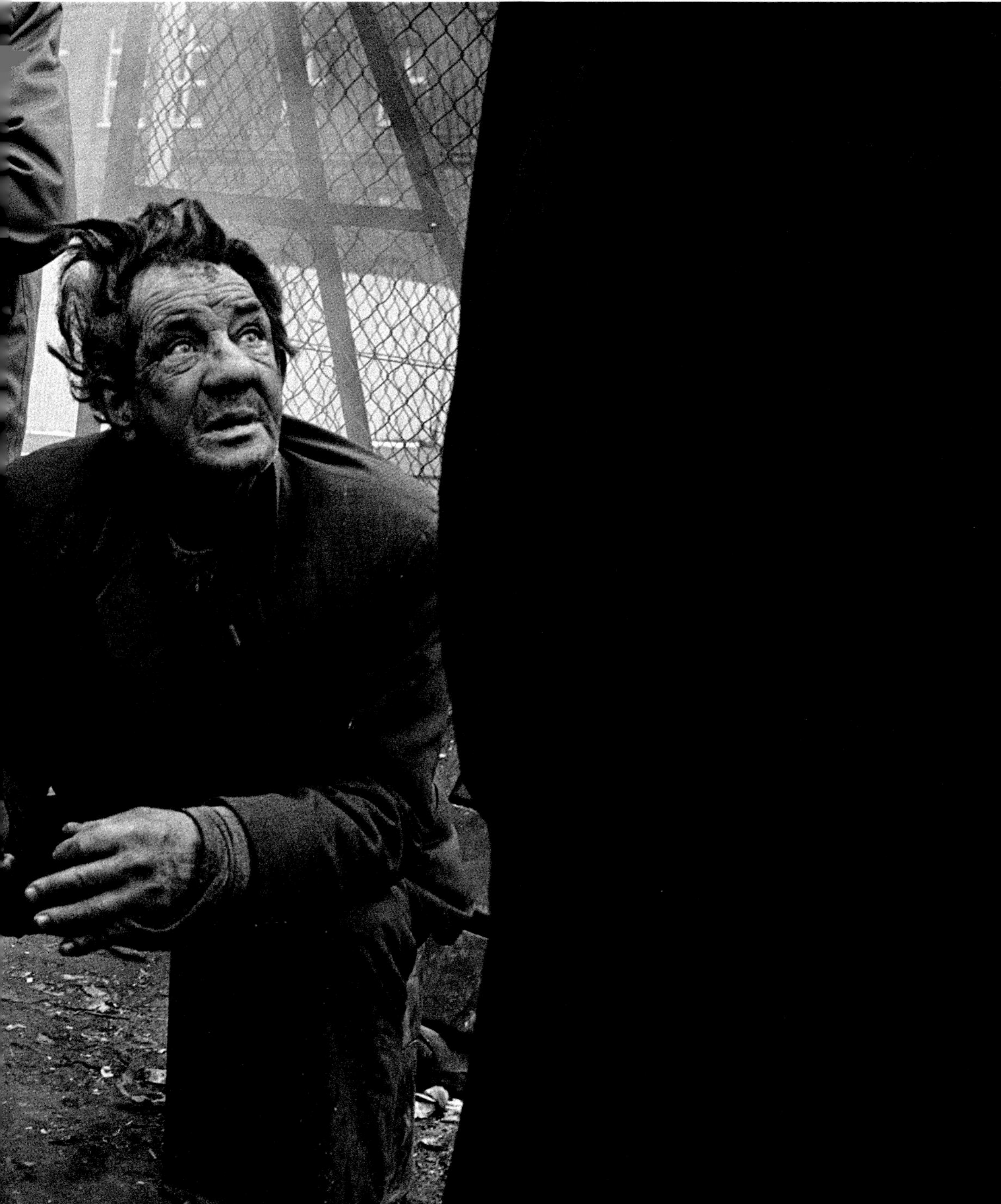

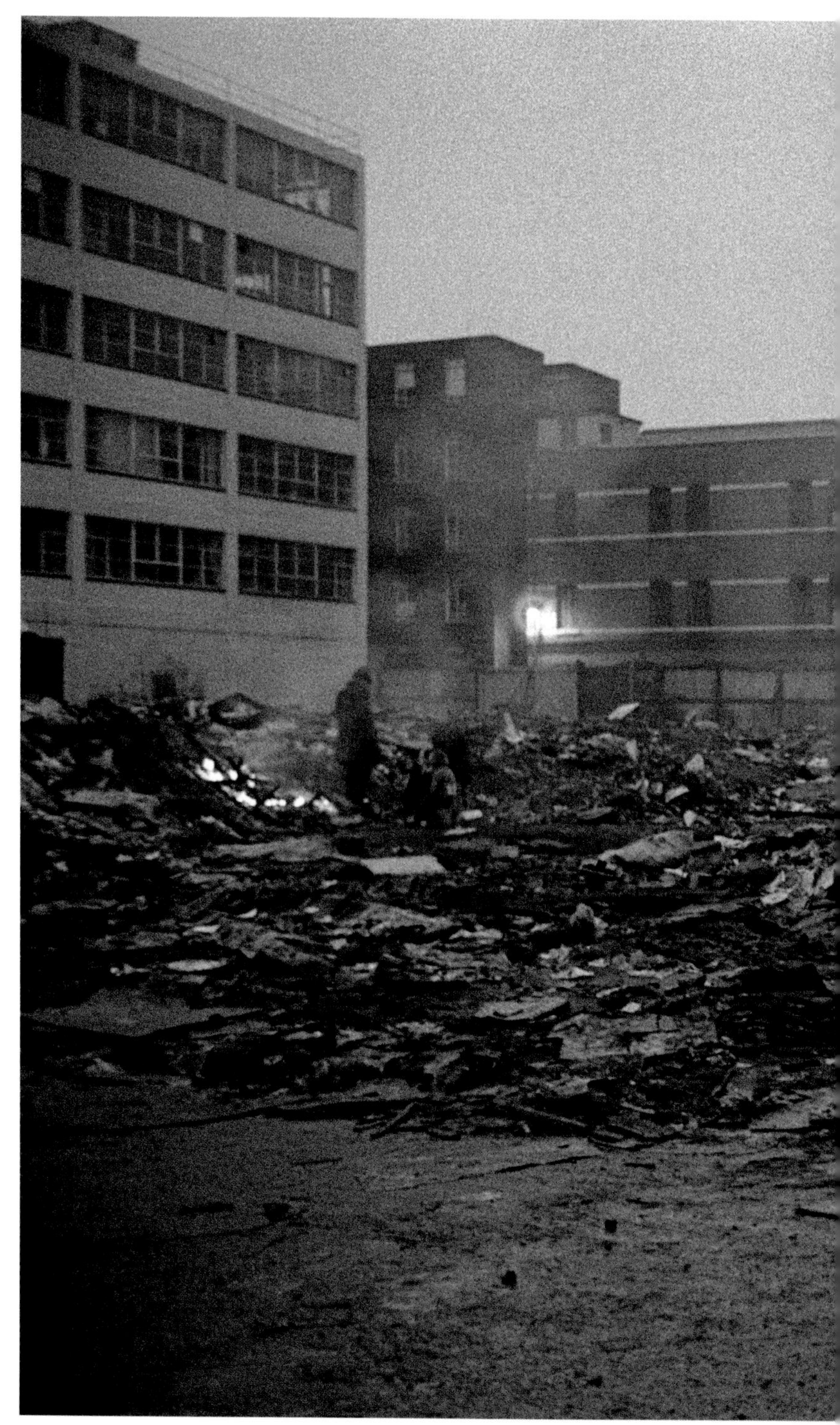

Lolesworth Street, London E1, 1980

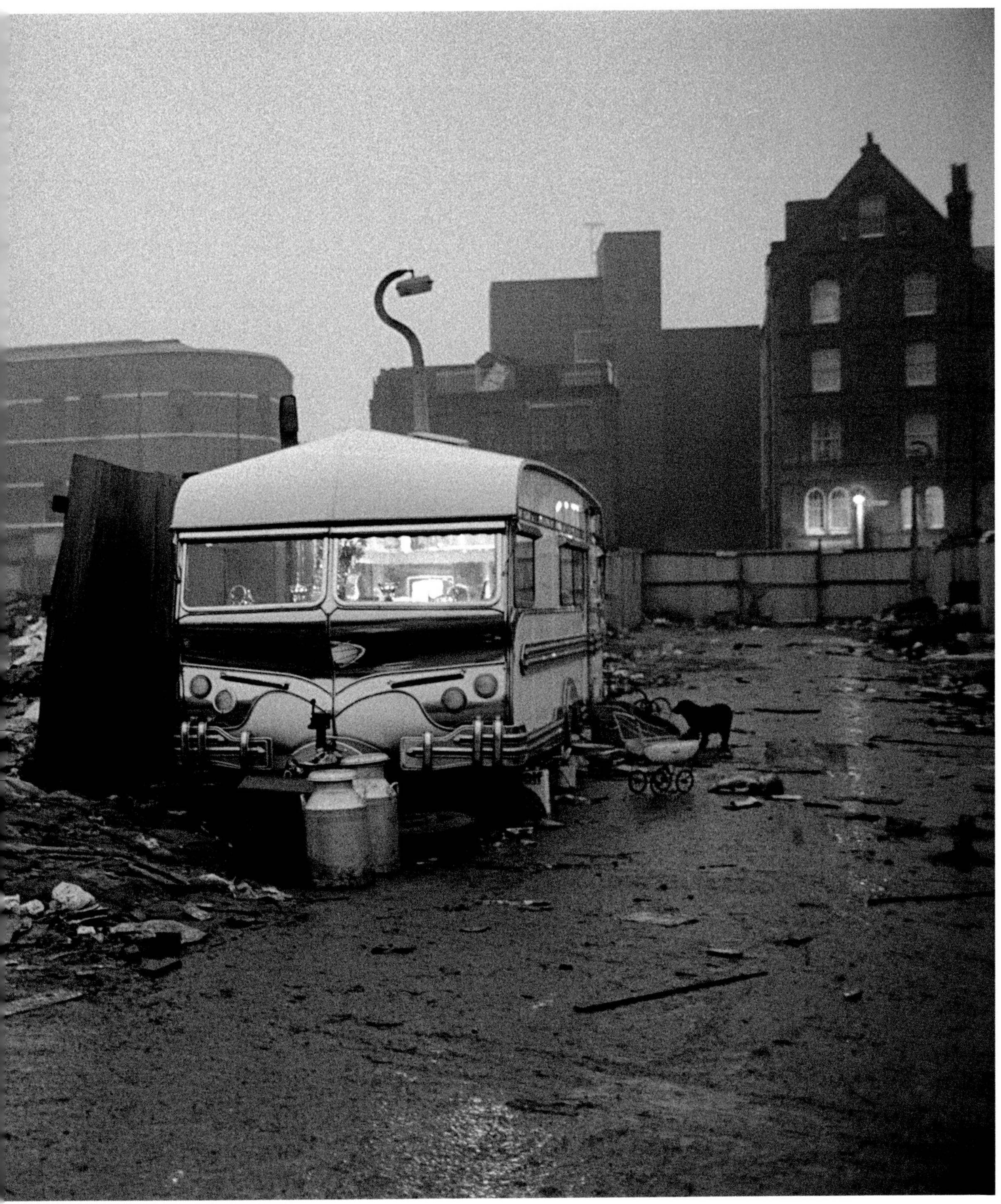

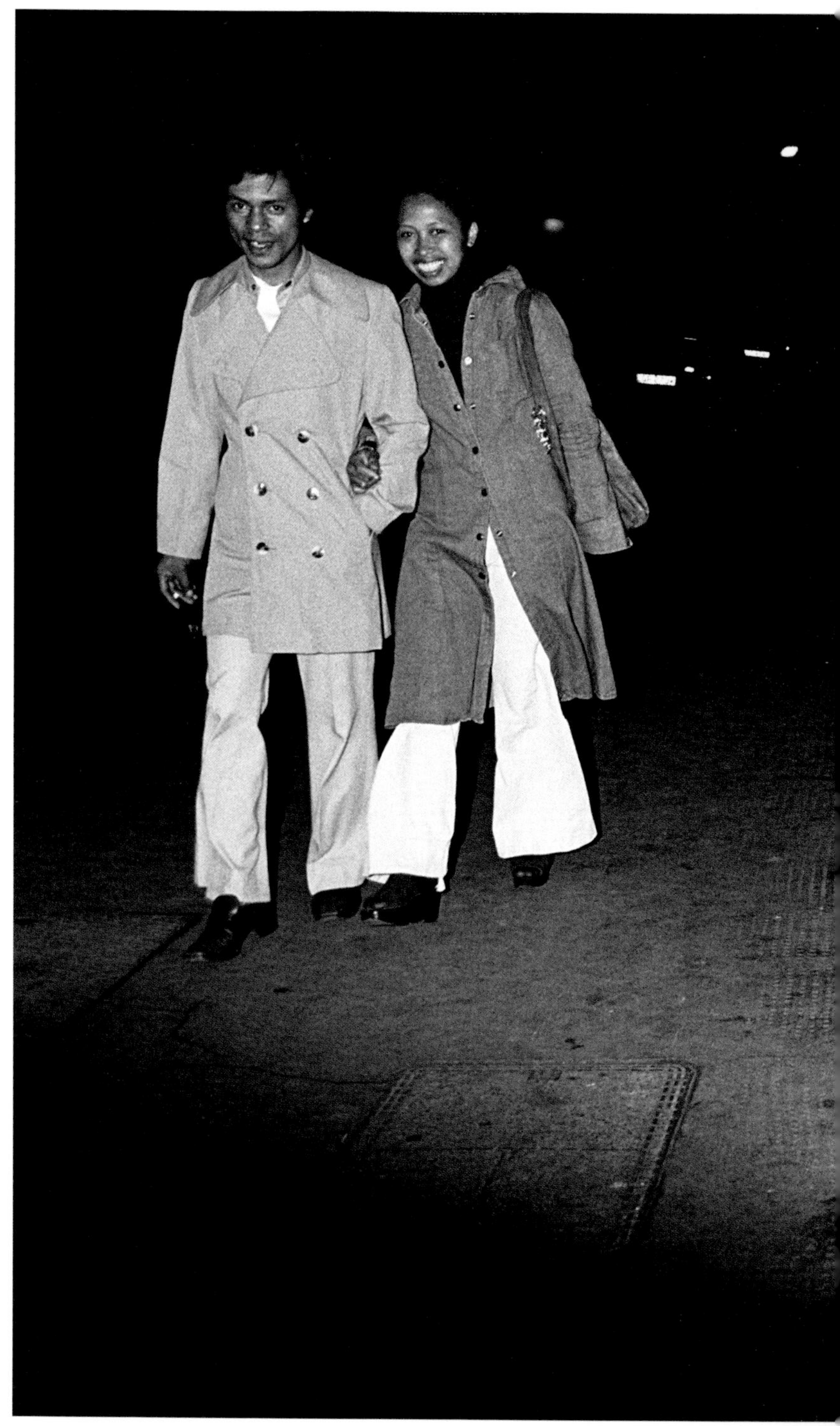

Brick Lane, London E1, 1975

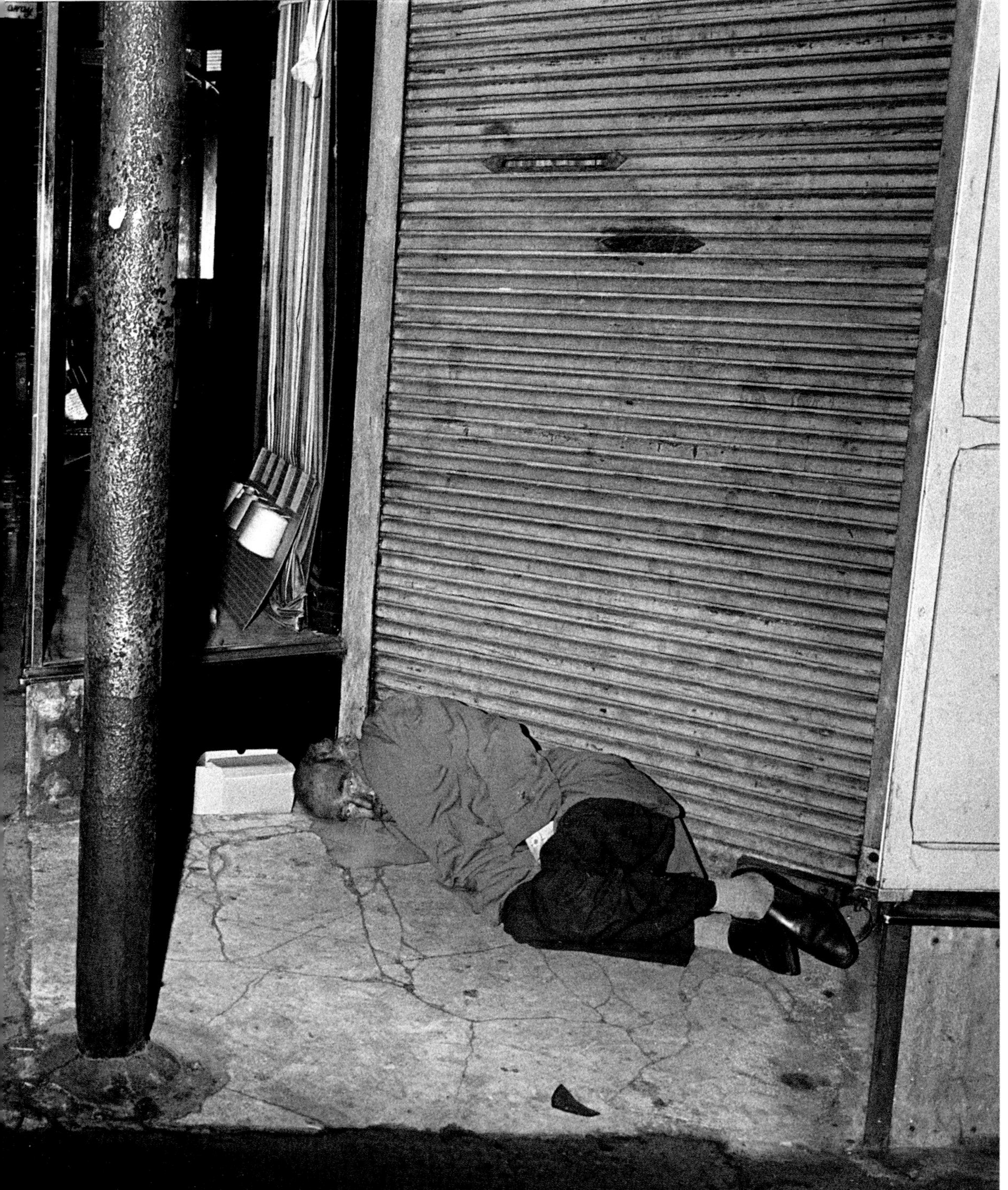

Soundtrack

The photographs in this book were made between 1974 and 1992. They capture the hustle and bustle of people at two east London markets and, in so doing, something of the character of London itself.

Here is the accompanying soundtrack to the images – some notable events that happened during the period in which these people were queueing for fruit and veg, rummaging through secondhand clothes, discussing politics and haggling over pirated tapes of music and movies.

1974
- *The Godfather Part II*, Francis Ford Coppola
- 'Waterloo', Abba
- Harold Wilson becomes UK Prime Minister
- Muhammad Ali beats George Foreman in the 'Rumble in the Jungle'
- Richard Nixon resigns after Watergate scandal

1975
- 'Bohemian Rhapsody', Queen
- 'No Woman, No Cry', Bob Marley and the Wailers (live recording)
- *Jaws*, Steven Spielberg
- *The Rocky Horror Picture Show*, Jim Sharman
- Vietnam War ends
- Microsoft is founded by Bill Gates and Paul Allen

1976
- 'Anarchy in the U.K.', Sex Pistols
- *Taxi Driver*, Martin Scorsese
- Nadia Comăneci scores a 10 at Olympic Summer Games in Montreal
- James Callaghan becomes UK Prime Minister
- VHS is invented
- Betty Williams and Mairead Corrigan win the Nobel Peace Prize

1977
- *Annie Hall*, Woody Allen
- *Saturday Night Fever*, John Badham
- *Star Wars*, George Lucas
- Jimmy Carter becomes USA President
- Death of Joan Crawford, Elvis Presley, Groucho Marx and Charlie Chaplin

1978
- 'Wuthering Heights', Kate Bush
- First successful birth of a test tube baby (Louise Brown)
- Space Invaders video game released
- Pope John Paul II elected

1979
- *Monty Python's Life of Brian*, Terry Jones
- *The Hitchhiker's Guide to the Galaxy*, Douglas Adams
- 'I Wanna Be Your Lover', Prince
- Margaret Thatcher becomes UK Prime Minister
- Troops from the Soviet Union invade Afghanistan
- Mother Teresa wins the Nobel Peace Prize

1980
- '9 to 5', Dolly Parton
- World Health Organisation declares that smallpox has been eradicated
- John Lennon assassinated
- Pac-Man video game released
- Start of Iran-Iraq War, lasts until 1988

1981
- 'Just Can't Get Enough', Depeche Mode
- 'Every Grain of Sand', Bob Dylan
- MTV goes on the air
- Ronald Reagan becomes USA President
- First Women's Peace Camp protest against US Cruise Missiles at RAF Greenham Common
- Royal wedding of Prince Charles and Lady Diana Spencer

1982
- 'Billie Jean', Michael Jackson
- *The Colour Purple*, Alice Walker
- First artificial human heart created
- CD player is released
- London's Thames Barrier comes into operation
- Argentine Navy cruiser, General Belgrano, is sunk during the Falklands War by the Royal Navy submarine Conqueror with the loss of 323 lives

1983
- 'Girls Just Want to Have Fun', Cyndi Lauper
- 'Every Breath You Take', The Police
- The Internet, created to support communication
  between scientists, launches
- The first episode of *Blackadder* is released
- The camcorder is released

1984
- 'Heaven Knows I'm Miserable Now', The Smiths
- 'Glory Days', Bruce Springsteen
- *Paris Texas*, Wim Wenders
- The virus that causes AIDS,
  later named HIV, is discovered
- The Apple MacIntosh is created
- Miners' Strike starts in Britain, lasts a year

1985
- 'Material Girl', Madonna
- *The Handmaid's Tale*, Margaret Atwood
- *Brazil*, Terry Gilliam
- Super Mario Bros video game
- Live Aid benefit concert held simultaneously
  in London and Philadelphia
- Mikhail Gorbachev becomes Soviet leader,
  leading to 'glasnost' and 'perestroika' policies
- Wreckage of the RMS Titanic is discovered

1986
- 'The Miracle of Love', Eurythmics
- 'West End Girls', Pet Shop Boys
- *Castle In The Sky*, Hayao Miyazaki
- Nuclear power plant at Chernobyl, Ukraine explodes
- Space shuttle Challenger explodes after liftoff

1987
- *The Princess Bride*, Rob Reiner
- 'Fairytale Of New York', The Pogues
- Start of first Palestinian Intifada
- Arms control Intermediate-Range Nuclear Forces
  Treaty signed by United States and the Soviet Union
- The peaceful 'People Power Revolution' ends
  dictatorship and restores democracy in the Philippines

1988
- 'Express Yourself', NWA
- 'Everybody Knows', Leonard Cohen
- Soviet Union starts withdrawal of
  troops from Afghanistan
- Massive strikes throughout Poland in
  support of the Solidarity trade union

1989
- *When Harry Met Sally*, Rob Reiner
- *Remains of the Day*, Kazuo Ishiguro
- 'Fight the Power', Public Enemy
- Tiananmen Square protests and massacre, Beijing
- *The Simpsons* starts airing
- George Bush becomes USA President
- Berlin Wall falls
- Scientists at CERN, Switzerland, begin
  work on the World Wide Web

1990
- *Pretty Woman*, Garry Marshall
- *Edward Scissorhands*, Tim Burton
- Nelson Mandela released unconditionally
  after 27 years in prison
- John Major becomes UK Prime Minister
- Germany unifies
- The Human Genome Project begins

1991
- 'Nevermind', Nirvana
- 'Unfinished Sympathy', Massive Attack
- *Thelma & Louise*, Ridley Scott
- *Riff-Raff*, Ken Loach
- USSR dissolves

1992
- *Reservoir Dogs*, Quentin Tarantino
- 'Friday I'm in Love', The Cure
- 'I Will Always Love You', Whitney Houston cover
- *Malcom X*, Spike Lee
- Establishment of Bosnia and Herzegovina
- Olympic Summer Games in Barcelona

Acknowledgements

My thanks to:

Ben Morris for his help in researching the Soundtrack.

Gordon Haslett, Philip Magee and
Konstantin Sergeyev for their feedback.

Hoxton Mini Press for continuing to support
my Eastender series, and for another
highly enjoyable collaboration.

Paul Trevor
August, 2024

(overleaf) Commercial Street and Toynbee Street, London E1, 1979

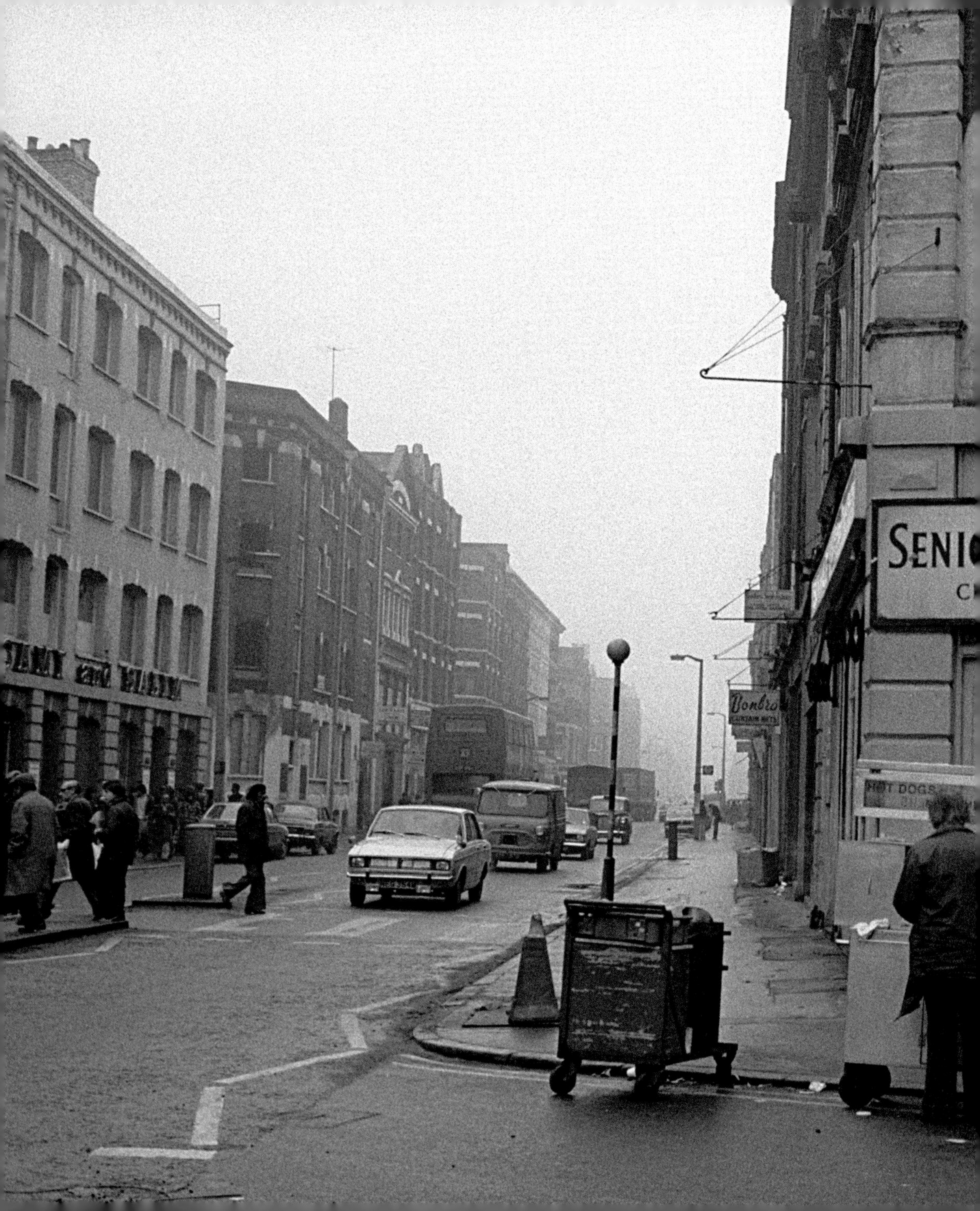

SENIO
HOT DOGS

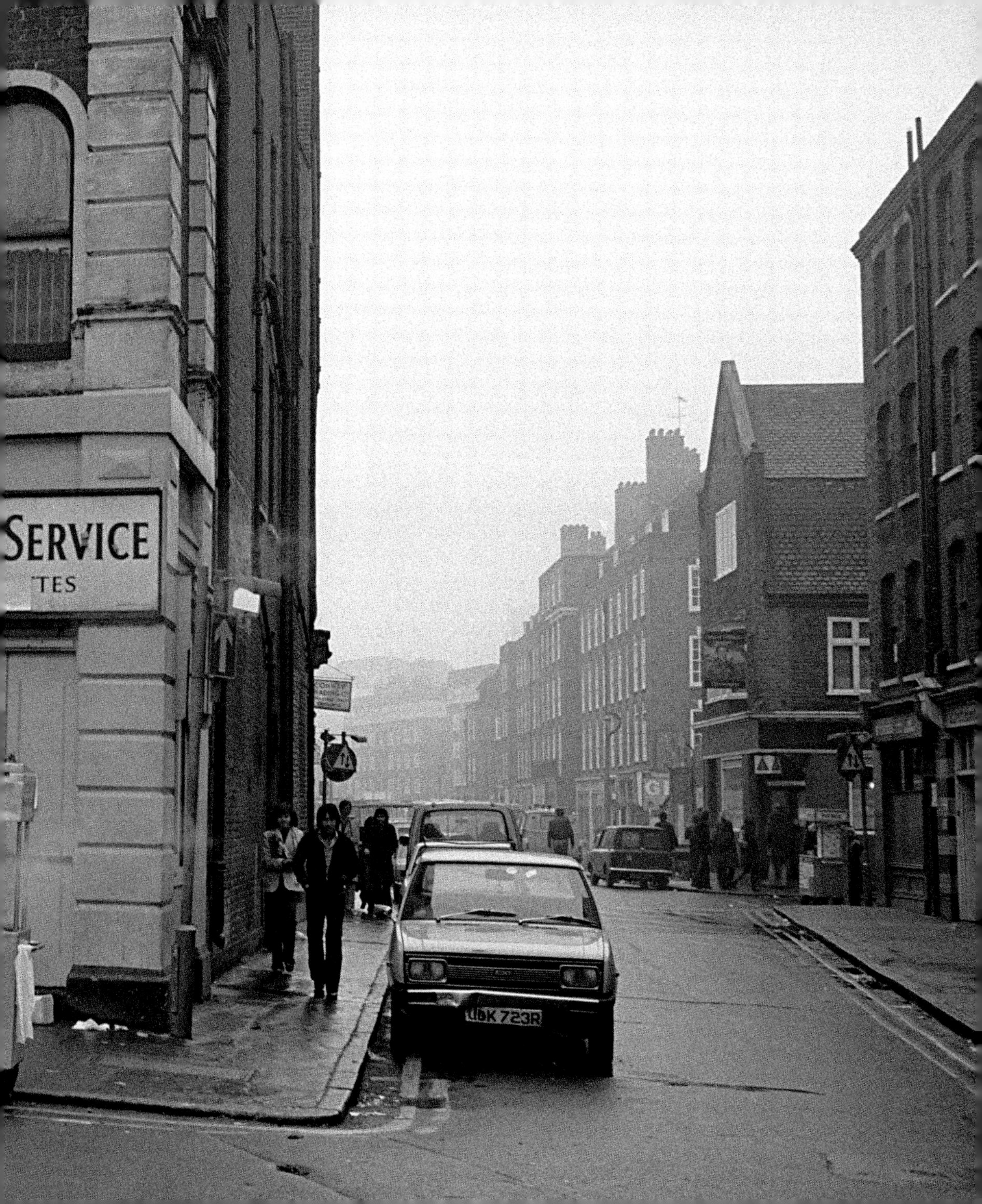
SERVICE
TES
DK 723R

Market Day
First edition, first printing

Market Day is the third book of Paul Trevor's Eastender series.
Hoxton Mini Press published *Once Upon a Time in Brick Lane*
in 2019 and *In Your Face* in 2020

Published in 2024 by Hoxton Mini Press, London
Copyright Hoxton Mini Press 2024.
All rights reserved.

Photographs and Soundtrack: © Paul Trevor
Editing: Florence Ward
Production design: Richard Mason
Proofreading: Leona Crawford

A CIP catalogue record for this book is
available from the British Library.

The right of Paul Trevor to be identified as the creator of this Work has
been asserted under the Copyright, Designs and Patents Act 1988.

No part of this publication may be reproduced, stored in a
retrieval system, or transmitted in any form or by any means,
electronic, mechanical, photocopying, recording or otherwise,
without the prior written permission of the copyright owner.

ISBN: 978-1-914314-82-7
Printed and bound by Livonia Print, Latvia.

Hoxton Mini Press is an environmentally conscious publisher,
committed to offsetting our carbon footprint. This book is
100 per cent carbon neutral, with offset purchased from with
offset purchased from the printer's offsetting scheme.

Every time you order from our website, we plant a tree.
www.hoxtonminipress.com